RENEWALS: 69 **DATE DUE**

INTERNATIONAL POLITICAL ECONOMY SERIES
General Editor: Timothy M. Shaw, Professor of Political Science and Director of International Development Studies, Dalhousie University, Nova Scotia.

The global political economy is in profound crisis at the levels of both production and policy. This series provides overviews and case studies of states and sectors, classes and companies in the new international division of labour. These embrace political economy as both focus and mode of analysis; they advance radical scholarship and scenarios.

The series treats polity–economy dialectics at global, regional and national levels and examines novel contradictions and coalitions between and within each. There is a special emphasis on national bourgeoisies and capitalisms, on newly industrial or influential countries, and on novel strategies and technologies. The concentration throughout is on uneven patterns of power and production, authority and distribution, hegemony and reaction. Attention will be paid to redefinitions of class and security, basic needs and self-reliance and the range of critical analyses will include gender, population, resources, environment, militarisation, food and finance. This series constitutes a timely and distinctive response to the continuing intellectual and existential world crisis.

Robert Boardman
PESTICIDES IN WORLD AGRICULTURE

Inga Brandell (*editor*)
WORKERS IN THIRD-WORLD INDUSTRIALIZATION

Bonnie K. Campbell (*editor*)
POLITICAL DIMENSIONS OF THE INTERNATIONAL DEBT CRISIS

Bonnie K. Campbell and John Loxley (*editors*)
STRUCTURAL ADJUSTMENT IN AFRICA

Jerker Carlsson and Timothy M. Shaw (*editors*)
NEWLY INDUSTRIALIZING COUNTRIES AND THE POLITICAL ECONOMY OF SOUTH–SOUTH RELATIONS

David P. Forsythe (*editor*)
HUMAN RIGHTS AND DEVELOPMENT
THE UNITED NATIONS IN THE WORLD POLITICAL ECONOMY

David Glover and Ken Kusterer
SMALL FARMERS, BIG BUSINESS

William D. Graf (*editor*)
THE INTERNATIONALIZATION OF THE GERMAN POLITICAL ECONOMY

Steven Kendall Holloway
THE ALUMINIUM MULTINATIONALS AND THE BAUXITE CARTEL

Matthew Martin
THE CRUMBLING FAÇADE OF AFRICAN DEBT NEGOTIATIONS

James H. Mittelman
OUT FROM UNDERDEVELOPMENT

Dennis C. Pirages and Christine Sylvester (*editors*)
TRANSFORMATIONS IN THE GLOBAL POLITICAL ECONOMY

Garry Rodan
THE POLITICAL ECONOMY OF SINGAPORE'S INDUSTRIALIZATION

Ennio Rodríguez and Stephany Griffith-Jones (*editors*)
CROSS-CONDITIONALITY, BANKING REGULATION AND THIRD-WORLD DEBT

Jorge Rodríguez Beruff, J. Peter Figueroa and J. Edward Greene (*editors*)
CONFLICT, PEACE AND DEVELOPMENT IN THE CARIBBEAN

Patricia Ruffin
CAPITALISM AND SOCIALISM IN CUBA

Roger Southall (*editor*)
LABOUR AND UNIONS IN ASIA AND AFRICA

Arno Tausch
TOWARDS A SOCIO-LIBERAL THEORY OF WORLD DEVELOPMENT

Fiona Wilson
SWEATERS: GENDER, CLASS AND WORKSHOP-BASED INDUSTRY IN MEXICO

David Wurfel and Bruce Burton (*editors*)
THE POLITICAL ECONOMY OF FOREIGN POLICY IN SOUTHEAST ASIA

Sweaters

Gender, class and workshop-based industry in Mexico

Fiona Wilson
Lecturer in Development Studies
Roskilde University Centre, Denmark

St. Martin's Press   New York

© Fiona Wilson 1991

All rights reserved. For information, write:
Scholarly and Reference Division,
St. Martin's Press, Inc., 175 Fifth Avenue,
New York, N.Y. 10010

First published in the United States of America in 1991

Printed in Hong Kong

ISBN 0-312-06110-2

Library of Congress Cataloging-in-Publication Data
Wilson, Fiona.
Sweaters: gender, class, and workshop-based industry in Mexico /
Fiona Wilson.
p. cm.—(International political economy series)
Includes bibliographical references and index.
ISBN 0-312-06110-2
1. Women clothing workers—Mexico—Santiago Tangamandapio.
2. Clothing trade—Social aspects—Mexico—Santiago Tangamandapio.
3. Santiago Tangamandapio (Mexico)—Industries, Rural. I. Title.
II. series.
HD6073.C62M69   1991
331.4'87146'097237—dc20   90-25829
                                                              CIP

Contents

List of Maps and Tables vii
Preface viii

1 Industrial Restructuring and Regional Growth 1
  The regional setting 1
  Mexico's garment industry 5
  The national context 7
  Sub-contracting hierarchies and informalisation 10
  Gender and social reproduction 16
  The investigation's analytic framework 18

2 The Region and its History 23
  The town of Santiago Tangamandapio 23
  Historical precedents 25
  The industrial history of an 'informal' capital 28

3 Economic and Social Relations before 1960 34
  Questions of origins 34
  Forces leading to migration 35
  Family and gender relations in historical perspective 51
  Household relations in the ranchos 51
  Household relations after settlement in the town 53
  Women as a potential labour supply 73

4 The Rise of a Rural Industry 76
  Industrial expansion and workshop ownership 76
  Production, labour process and technological change 89
  Markets, profits and workshop differentiation 97
  Strategies of accumulation 107
  Relations among workshops 119

5 Labour Relations and Workers' Strategies 122
  Labour relations in the workshops 122
  Workers' struggles 140
  The place of labour struggle in workshop transformation 154

6	**Relations of Gender and Class Outside the Workshops**	**157**
	Changing contexts	157
	Social origins of workshop workers	159
	Domestic industry: women's industry	161
	Family and gender relations of workshop workers	167
7	**A Tentative Model of Workshop-based Production**	**191**
	Origins of capitalised workshop production	191
	Dynamics and directions of change	196
	Implications of gendered production	200

Appendices
I Discussion of the Fieldwork Methodology 207
II Dollar–Peso Exchange Rate: 1985–88 212

Glossary 213

References 214

Person Index 217
Subject Index ••

List of Maps and Tables

Maps

1.1 The western-central regions of Mexico — xii
2.1 Santiago Tangamandapio, Michoacán — 24
2.2 Nineteenth-century textile centres in Michoacán — 27
4.1 Long-distance markets of Santiago workshops — 99

Tables

4.1 Characteristics of selected workshops in mid-1986 — 106
5.1 Wages of women workers in the Hernández workshop, early 1986 — 134
6.1 Changes in numbers of very large families: 1950s to 1980 — 184
6.2 Changes in family size: 1950s to 1980 — 184

Preface

I have long been suspicious of 'impact' studies in development research. What I have in mind are the studies which attribute sweeping powers to external forces of change (sometimes named as 'capitalism') and which depict local people as passive non-entities thrown around by processes over which they have no control. This is not to deny the violence or the irrevocability of the socio-economic changes wrought on societies of the Third World. Instead, I question the underlying assumptions of those theories in social science on which impact studies are based in that they privilege economic tendencies at a macro level and give them an overwhelmingly determining role.

As I have argued elsewhere (1985), the central problematic often formulated in studies of impact is how particular developments or capitalist interventions (such as agricultural modernisation, the rise of new export industries, the growth of informal manufacturing) affect the lives of particular social groups (such as peasants or women). The forces of capital are usually treated as representing an independent variable on which everything else depends. Some people become local agents or beneficiaries; the vast majority lose out; none are able to remain as they were before. The relationship of the economic realm with the social realm is seen as one way; externally induced economic change or intervention of capital affects peasants/women, but peasants/women do not affect capitalism or, for that matter, the course of history. Thus the impact model presumes that pre-existing socio-economic relations, institutions and arenas of struggle in a locality are largely irrelevant in either accounting for or in obstructing processes of change.

This narrow one-sided view of processes of change has not gone unchallenged, and the critiques have come from various quarters. I have been most influenced by the arguments of feminist researchers especially concerning the way women in different periods and places have been incorporated into industrial labour forces. These studies demonstrate not only how pre-existing inequalities in local societies rooted in gender, class and ethnic relations are capable of moulding the form taken by capitalist intervention but also how they can determine whether or not capital intervenes at all (see, for example,

Elson and Pearson, 1981; Arizpe and Aranda, 1981; Roldán, 1982; Stolcke, 1988).

A critique of impact studies and dissatisfaction with the underlying postulates of certain theories of social change were the mainsprings which led to the research on which this book is based. I wanted to understand a widespread phenomenon of recent years: the expansion of small-scale, modern, manufacturing industries which employ a predominantly female labour force in rural areas of countries labelled as being relatively industrialised and as occupying a position on the semi-periphery of the global economy.

I wanted to explore rural industrialisation not only from the perspective of what was good or profitable for capital, I also wanted to examine the processes and transformations at work in the context of a particular locality (in Mexico) and see these through the eyes of the people most actively involved. This double objective demanded that I pay attention to local manifestations of gender and class relations both in the past and present and focus on the actions of particular groups in local society; those investing in new industries in the Mexican countryside over the last thirty years as well as those labouring in them and negotiating the terms of their employment. Since it was primarily women who constituted the labour force, a sub-theme has been to explore local social and economic changes as seen through women's eyes comparing the worlds of contemporary workshop workers, their mothers and grandmothers.

The analysis presented in this book is tentative and exploratory. I have tried to avoid making inferences that lead to simple explanations of cause and effect. Instead, I try to suggest on the one hand the interplay between prevailing relations of social inequality and the form taken by small-scale industry and, on the other, the way new forms of production can serve to open up potentials and present spaces in which people can act.

I have tried to interweave different types of information in the text. Material on the histories, actions and opinions of people from a small town in Mexico is set together with an interpretation of the structures in which their lives are set. To do this, I adopt different writing styles. I have included passages which refer to the way individuals speak about their experiences. These passages (indented in the text) are not direct quotations; they are written in an anecdotal form to summarise points, terms and ideas coming through in the way people recount their life stories. These passages act as both exemplification and a counterpoint to my analysis. In the last chapter the writing style alters once again; here, my aim is to mark the move from analysis of a specific case to a more abstract discussion underlining important general points and drawing conclusions from the Mexican example. These conclusions are presented so as to facilitate comparisons with findings from other case studies.

All research endeavours build on a ferment of ideas contributed by others; this investigation has been no exception. I was especially fortunate to be included in a series of workshops (organised by the Social Science Research Council, New York, in the early 1980s) that focused on gender relations and the family in Latin America. Much of the inspiration behind this book flowed from these debates, and in particular from the explorations of Martha Roldán, Lourdes Benería and Verena Stolcke into the lives of working women in Latin America. In Mexico, my research investigation benefited greatly from the support and advice of Patricia Arias and Jorge Durand, at that time working at El Colegio de Michoacán, Zamora, whose work on the growth of rural industry in western central Mexico was so enlightening. And I also appreciated the help of Pedro Luna, University of Nayarit, who had begun earlier to explore the history of Santiago Tangamandapio.

To the people of Santiago Tangamandapio, Michoacán, I owe a deep debt of gratitude. So many assisted me and my family and made us feel welcome right from the start. A very special thanks goes to Rosa García who became my guide, principal field assistant and friend during my stay as well as to her mother, Doña Josefina Lua, and Teresa Torres who also assisted me with the investigation. Don Luis Ochoa very kindly made his own material on Santiago's history available to me and Don Samuel Navarro was an invaluable source of information on the rise of the workshop industry and on a host of other topics. Countless discussions with friends helped put me in touch with life in Santiago; my particular thanks goes to Lucila Cuevas, Aurelio García, Don Jesús García, Edilmira González, Guadalupe Manzo, Rafael Rios and Serafín Rios.

The principal actors in this narrative are the owners and workers of small manufacturing workshops; throughout my time in the town I was treated with great kindness and tolerance by both groups and thanks to them I have been able to grasp something of the past and present of the workshop industry. I have tried to reproduce events and dates as accurately as possible but all persons in the narrative have been given pseudonyms.

The initial research in 1986 was made possible through a year's grant from the Danish Council for Development Research and this was supplemented by funding from the Centre for Development Research, Copenhagen. These funds permitted me to return for short visits to Santiago in 1987 and 1989 and financed the translation of the manuscript into Spanish.

In the course of writing and reviewing the text, I have been enormously grateful to friends and colleagues in Mexico and Scandinavia for their help and enthusiasm, especially at times when my energy was flagging. Colleagues at International Development Studies, Roskilde University Centre, and at the Centre for Development Research, Copenhagen, have greatly assisted me in clarifying my arguments and in better communicating what I wanted to say. I am particularly grateful to Signe Arnfred, Roskilde University Centre, for her detailed comments on the manuscript and to Pastora Rodríguez Aviñoá, University of Guadalajara, who not only produced a very fine Spanish version but also gave invaluable editorial suggestions for the text as a whole. I thank Ane Toubro and Aase Hansen, Centre for Development Research, for battling patiently with my ever changing drafts and Ingrid Hastrup Jensen, Roskilde University Centre, for drawing the maps.

Finally I want to thank Roger Leys and Peter Wilson Leys for sharing the Mexican adventures and for being such supportive, lively and caring companions.

FIONA WILSON

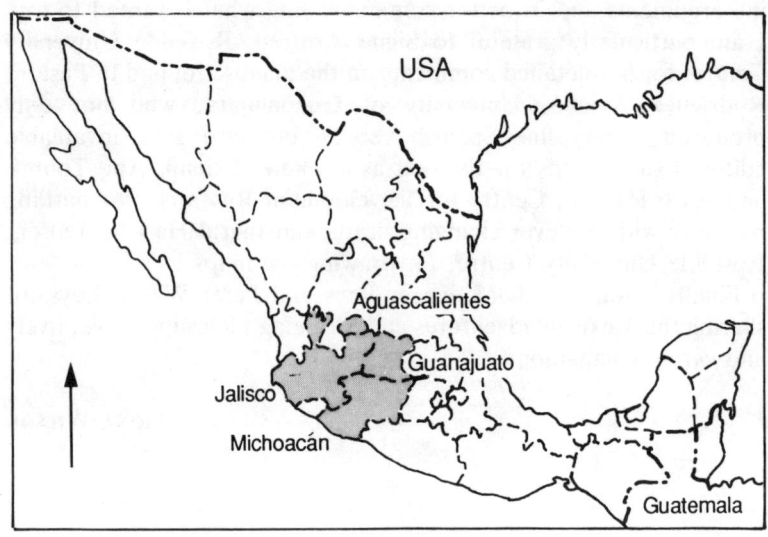

Map 1 The western-central regions of Mexico

1 Industrial Restructuring and Regional Growth

THE REGIONAL SETTING

The focus of this research investigation is on the spread of manufacturing industry to an extensive rural region in Mexico during the last twenty-five years. It is a theme that I came across almost by accident. A chance visit to Mexico in 1984 brought me in contact with researchers and students at El Colegio de Michoacán who were discovering and asking questions about the growth of sub-contracting and various types of industry in small towns in the state of Michoacán. Their findings were intriguing. They hinted at major changes in the organisation of production and a diffusion of 'non-traditional' types of industry. Though the situation was far from clear there was evidence to suggest that processes were at work which contradicted many of the assumptions often made about the Mexican countryside. These new phenomena and processes demanded attention and exploration in many places and at various levels of analysis.

Industry is expanding in a large region of western-central Mexico comprising most of the states of Jalisco, Aguascalientes, Michoacán and Guanajuato (see Map 1.1). In this region there is a marked division between the irrigated areas where agri-business and export agriculture have flourished (including the major zones of 'strawberry imperialism')[1] and the poor uplands of rain-fed farming. Though the specific histories of these zones have differed, nevertheless peasants in both have suffered impoverishment and dispossession as a result of capitalist accumulation in agriculture. There, the old stereotype of the self-sufficient peasantry has been dead a long time. The vast majority of rural families have been unable to produce even half of their subsistence needs of maize and beans; former peasants have been pushed into wage labouring for local agri-business or into migration.

The region has been subject to massive male out-migration; men have sought wage work in the Mexican cities or in the USA since the time of the Revolution. Yet even from the barren uplands, migration has not necessarily led to the permanent abandonment of the home region. Much of the migratory movement has been temporary or seasonal. Even when men work in the cities or US for most of their working lives, wives and children might remain in the rural locality. People in the region did not conform to the popular image of the urban migrant who permanently left the countryside for life in the city. The long period in which temporary migration was prevalent and men straddled two contrasting worlds has strongly influenced the social and political characteristics of regional society. But the doubleness of the migrants' lives and work experiences have not been easy to understand or capture. Where the enduring nature of temporary migration has been recognised, men have generally been classed in the ambiguous social category of semi-proletarians.[2]

The phenomena and processes this investigation wishes to address have arisen as a result of developments affecting some more privileged groups from the class of semi-proletarians. At particular points in time, former migrants managed to gain access to trades and capital and have chosen to return home to small towns with new economic activities. Returning migrants have often been depicted in a favourable light locally as pioneers who have struggled to introduce new forms of production in order to aid the depressed home region. The activities have given the pioneers apparent wealth and independence and by employing a wage labour force, incomes and benefits have been distributed more widely.

In western-central Mexico, new forms of industrial production seem to have appeared first in the more depressed upland zones where only limited modernisation of agriculture had previously taken place. Later, industrialisation spread; new specialisations developed in some rapidly expanding towns in the zones of agri-business, while elsewhere agricultural activities have been transformed into 'industrial' farming. It can be argued that these trends towards industrialisation demonstrate that regional populations, though impoverished and dislocated are not passive in the face of the externally induced changes that have jeopardised their former livelihoods and undermined their ways of life. Under particular circumstances they act and usher in new phases of regional economic change.

At first only scattered individuals returned home with industrial and commercial expertise they had acquired in the large towns. But during the last twenty-five years the movement has gathered force; from slow beginnings in the 1960s, investment in industrial activities appears to have grown markedly in the 1970s and has continued to expand until the mid-1980s. There has been considerable variation according to industrial branch; but according to some commentators, certain activities in the region have continued to thrive even in the 1980s, notwithstanding the country's economic recession and harsh austerity programmes.

No overall survey of industrial enterprise in the region has yet been compiled. At a rough guess there are at least fifty small upland towns in the western-central region which have now developed industrial specialisations occupying a significant proportion of the local population. They are linked not only to major cities like Guadalajara, León, Aguascalientes but also to smaller, less generally recognized commercial and wholesaling centres which supply national and regional markets.

The branches of industrial activity predominating in the region involve products and labour processes that have long been linked with women's work as defined in local gender divisions of labour. Overwhelmingly these activities fall under the heading of garment and shoe manufacture. But they are easily recognised as 'new' from their form of organisation, technology, type of workforce and markets. The new industries do not appear to have grown directly out of artisanal activity. This does not mean to say that history is irrelevant rather that it is more appropriate to look for historical precedents in the more distant past.

Taking a longer time perspective one discovers that the region excelled in textile and garment production during much of the colonial period and in short sharp bursts in the nineteenth century. In its latter phase, production was organised in factories, workshops and domestic enterprises most of which were swept away at the time of the Revolution. The present diffusion of industry to western-central Mexico may therefore be seen as part of a more fluid cyclical pattern of regional change and may well build on 'hidden' traditions and skills that go far back in time.

Among the different industrial specialisations now found in the region are the following. Small towns around León (Guanajuato) produce 'fashion' shoes, the region now ranking as a major production zone in the country. Sweaters and other garments of knitted cloth are made in many centres in Michoacán often linked with the towns Moroleón and Guadalajara. Cheap 'fashion' clothing sewn from factory-produced cotton cloth comes from a mass of centres in Los Altos de Jalisco; some towns specialise in men's trousers, others in women's and children's clothing. Blue jean manufacture is centred on Irapuato, Guanajuato; cotton sheet production in San Miguel de los Altos. Other small centres specialise in glass blowing, especially glass spheres that are painted and used as Christmas decorations. The range of products is widening; newer activities include the forging of metal parts for Guadalajara's machine tool industry and the production of plastic bags (Arias, 1988).

Production in the small towns is organised in a variety of ways. Factory production may predominate (as with blue jeans manufacture); or production is divided between workshops and industrial home workers (as in shoe and sweater manufacture where the adornment phase in both has generally been put out to home workers); or production is undertaken by domestic enterprises which may also put out work to industrial home workers (as with some types of 'fashion' and knitted clothing).

The different types of industrial activities have given rise to different expressions of gendered production. In some industrial branches, women constitute the entire labour force. In the workshops producing cotton clothing in Los Altos de Jalisco, workers and labour supervisors are all women; owners living in Guadalajara visit the workshop once a week to deliver the garment pieces and take back the sewn product and leave a female relative in charge of production (Arias, 1988). In the blue jean factories of Irapuato, young women constitute the labour force while labour supervisors are male (Steenbeek, 1988). Other industrial branches are characterised by gender segregated production as in workshop-based knitwear manufacture where male loom operators knit the cloth while women cut, sew, adorn and finish the garments.

Why have the new industries spread to the western central region of Mexico? Understanding the choice of specialisation, forms of production and commercial organisation demand that studies are made of the characteristics and tendencies within those branches of the industry now predominating. The garment industry can be taken as an example.

MEXICO'S GARMENT INDUSTRY

The Mexican garment industry is enormously varied and has a number of distinctive features, as Arias (1986) has pointed out. In recent years, enterprise specialisation has become increasingly marked in terms of raw materials used, type and quality of product. Specialisation has lain behind the heterogeneity of production forms now found and the predominantly small size of production unit. The industry has the following characteristics. In 1975, some 75 per cent of registered firms in the national garment industry employed less than five workers while the sector is thought to have occupied around 15 per cent of the total labour force. About half of the activity is located in Mexico City, but this is a lower level of concentration than for other industries. Some garment manufacture has grown up in every state but the proliferation (outside the capital) is most marked in the western-central region. In comparison with other industrial sectors, garment manufacture is less technologically advanced. This means that as a proportion of total production costs, labour ranks high (on average 20.8 per cent) compared with manufacturing industry as a whole (16.6 per cent). Sub-contracting has long been common.

These characteristics do not denote a backward, unchanging form of production. On the contrary, one of the most salient features of recent years has been the garment industry's creation of and response to a highly volatile market. Increasingly, the Mexican industry produces 'fashion' clothing in which styles, materials, colours, decorations and trims change at specific times of the year (the 'autumn' and 'spring' collections). Women's clothing has been particularly prone to fashion change, but so now to an ever greater extent is men's clothing. Furthermore, the market for fashion clothing has been rapidly expanding; no longer does demand originate only from the urban middle and upper classes but 'fashion' has become part of mass consumption in various regions of the country. While different markets exist, distinguished as much by quality as by product type, all are subject to rapid change.

Fashion changes affect the branches of the garment industry in different ways. In sweater manufacture, for example, the raw material (acrylan) stays the same but colour, style and adornment alter, with a major change in production lines being made once a year. This branch is subject to major seasonal fluctuations in demand as sales virtually come to a stop during the hottest months of January to June. Style changes may be relatively less marked in sweater manufacture; nevertheless 'last' year's stock cannot be stored for sale in the following season.

Women's clothing made of factory-produced cloth is the most responsive to fashion change; it is also the branch where quality and price differentials are the most obvious. But while being the most volatile, this branch is also potentially the most profitable. It has been calculated that on average women's 'fashion' clothing can earn 2 pesos for every peso invested, whereas the national industrial average is only 1.3 pesos per peso invested.[3]

The manufacture of both fashion clothing and clothing subject to seasonal fluctuations of demand requires highly *flexible production* conditions. Producing firms need to respond quickly to orders: labour is hired or laid off at short notice; intensive work over long hours alternates with periods of little work. This means that though more capital intensive techniques are replacing labour, there are obstacles stopping the introduction of more fully automated production processes.

In this context, the manufacture of fashion clothing may easily lead to sub-contracting at various levels. A division of management may appear in which large city enterprises take decisions relating to style changes, secure the inputs needed and sub-contract production out to myriad small enterprises with 'flexible' production. In this industry, commercial interests may play a dominating role. As Arias (1986) has commented: 'In practice, though in ways that are difficult to discern, dealers have become the real owners and main beneficiaries of the small-scale clothing industry that we see proliferating.' In the new production regions, other levels of sub-contracting may emerge such as where workshops or domestic enterprises in small towns put work out to surrounding Indian communities.

Flexible production has become associated with *clandestinity*. With the growth of sub-contracting, the clothing industry has been pushed out to poor urban peripheries and to towns and communities of the country's interior, where production has been much easier to hide. This has had repercussions on the work of inspectors and other officials seeking compliance with the law and it has also obscured the nature of the changes taking place for academic and political analysts.

In a minority of the industrial centres, production and commercial activities are readily apparent. In booming clothing towns such as

Zapotlanejo (close to Guadalajara) or Moroleón, a mass of front room shops are selling what back room workers produce. Classified as 'family based' enterprise, these producers have little to fear from the authorities. In contrast, industrial production is concealed in the vast majority of centres; workshops and factories are purposely hidden from public view. A casual observer is quite unaware of the activity behind the closed doors and boarded windows. Nevertheless some telling signs are difficult to conceal: the hum and clank of machinery, the festoons of electric power cables, the numbers of vans in the streets and the throngs of young women going to and from work. Physical concealment is associated with clandestinity. The workshops and small factories (unlike 'family based' enterprise) are subject to many laws governing taxation, minimum wage, provision of social security and other workers' benefits. Yet the industries' relation with the law varies and many local people, proud of the industrial development, reject the rights assumed by the state to interfere in local affairs.

This introductory description of the garment industry has suggested the superimposition of different analytical models. One model is consistent with the kind of industrialisation associated with the term 'post-Fordism': modern flexible production in relatively developed economies geared to meet highly differentiated and rapidly changing consumer tastes in situations where costs of 'distance' no longer lead to the concentration of activities in large urban regions. The other model points to processes of 'informalisation', the maintenance of backward forms of production and the retreat from urban to rural locations. These two perspectives are not contradictory; the point is that more detailed analysis must attempt to discuss both in the light of empirical findings. Before beginning with the Mexican case study, however, it is necessary to say more about the arguments and evidence put forward for informalisation. This demands adopting a more macro approach in order to outline broader processes discernible in Mexico.

THE NATIONAL CONTEXT

Mexico is one of the most quoted examples of a Newly Industrialising Country. Patterns of transnational investment and industrial growth in Mexico (and South East Asia) led to hypotheses in the late 1970s that a new world capitalist era was dawning characterised by some as a new international division of labour and by others as a globalisation of production. According to the former view, a massive movement of capital was taking place from the developed market economies to low cost production sites in the Third World. According to the latter, the increasingly centralised control and co-ordination by transnational corporations created increasing international interdependence and gave the corporations greater leverage over national governments (as Gordon, 1988, argues). In Mexico, the expansion of international sub-contracting and the growth of export industries along the border with the USA was seen as evidence for both these tendencies.

Recently, however, doubt has been cast on the extent and global significance of the two internationalisation theses as well as on the real nature of Mexico's involvement in the world system.[4] Mexico can be said to exhibit two different economic patterns. Due to accident of location ('so far from God and so close to the USA'), the US economy has penetrated much of northern Mexico and has easily been able to utilise Mexican labour. But seen from a Latin American perspective, Mexico is therefore something of a special case. Neither Mexican nor Latin American labour is especially 'cheap' when compared with other regions; owing to the long history of working-class struggle in the larger Latin American countries, states have been forced to offer certain concessions to labour and these have found expression in progressive labour legislation. Apart from northern Mexico, export oriented industrialisation has never been more than a marginal feature in the majority of Latin American economies. According to Gordon (1988), in total, Latin America's share in exports of manufactures rose only slightly in the 1970s (in marked contrast to Hong Kong, South Korea, Taiwan and Singapore).

The other industrial pattern found in Mexico brings the country into line with the rest of Latin America. Characteristically, industrial growth and the involvement of the transnational corporations have been driven by growth within domestic and regional markets rather than by an expansion of manufactured exports. Despite the growing international problems in the 1970s, Mexico did not yet suffer unduly and the economy was less disrupted by declining demand for exports in the developed market economies. The rate of industrial growth declined but not seriously partly because Mexico took steps to insulate the economy against balance of payment pressures by introducing tighter controls on imports. However, this policy only brought temporary relief. By the 1980s the country was endeavouring to sustain growth by borrowing heavily thus greatly increasing the level of foreign debt. With the eruption of the debt crisis in the early 1980s, Mexico was obliged by the IMF and World Bank to introduce austerity programmes which had the effect of reducing wages and effective domestic demand. Industrial growth rates plummeted: in the early 1980s they were only 20 per cent of their 1966–73 levels.

From a general overview of national industrial growth several *periods* can be distinguished. The 1960s and early 1970s saw rapid industrial expansion; this was checked in the 1970s with some slowing down in growth rates; economic crisis struck hard in the early 1980s when the country was suddenly exposed to the full force of the global economy. Mexico now found itself part of a changing international system. By the early 1980s greater ideological and political legitimacy was being given to supply-side economics where market mechanisms and cost competitiveness were being given overwhelming emphasis. This crystallised in a global strategy of structural adjustment and stabilisation and a 'rolling back of the state' so that poverty alleviation and universal social security were no longer priority issues in development planning.

The changing fortunes of Mexican industry seen at the national level does not mean that all branches or sectors have followed the same trajectory. In particular, there have been complex responses in terms of internal industrial 'restructuring' where capital has sought to lower production costs as a way of offsetting declining profits. With the limited industrial decline of the 1970s, a certain degree of restructuring took place. Pressures mounted with the deepening recession in the early 1980s and three related aspects of industrial restructuring have come to the fore. One is the greater emphasis placed on systems of sub-contracting by the transnationals and other large businesses which 'put out' parts of production processes to enterprises with cheaper production costs. A second is the greater use made of forms of production labelled 'backward', 'clandestine' and 'informal'. And a third is the increasing employment of a young female labour force, primarily in 'backward' clandestine production, but also in certain branches of 'formal' factory-based production. Relations among these tendencies will be explored in greater detail.

SUB-CONTRACTING HIERARCHIES AND INFORMALISATION

Relations between current directions of technological change and industrial reconstruction have recently been taken up by Castells (1986). He suggests a broad framework in which to view possible tendencies relevant to Mexico. The more industrialised countries (including Mexico), Castells argues face a prospect of

> the increasing disarticulation of the national economy . . . between a highly dynamic sector incorporated into the world economy both as a producer and a market and a series of destructured segments that will mix their roles as sub-contracting sweatshops for the internationalised sector, as caterers of goods and services for specific sub-markets and as daily inventors of survival strategies (pp. 36–7).

In the 'destructured segments' processes of informalisation are at work which are defined as 'processes related to production and distribution activities characterised by differential profitability based on the absence of compliance with institutional rules that each society has defined as legitimate, in a constantly changing process of demand and negotiation'.

Informalisation is seen as a fundamental political-economic process representing a new form of control by the dominant classes and characterised by the disenfranchisement of a large sector of economic practices often with the open or semi-covert support of the state. The absence of institutional regulations may concern the work process (status of labour, conditions of work), forms of management (systematic fiscal fraud) or the activities themselves (considered criminal, such as smuggling). Among the consequences of the informalisation process are: reduction in the cost of labour, increasing profitability of capital, heterogeneous work and class situations, the undermining of the power of organised labour and serious shocks to the fiscal equilibrium of the state (Roldán, 1987).

The future scenarios depicted by Castells of increasing disarticulation of national economies, processes of informalisation and the disenfranchisement of economic practice are both provocative and depressing. As visions of future trends, such projections are not suitable to be 'tested' by empirical evidence. Nevertheless, we can still ask about the manifestations of these processes in the case of Mexico as a way of elaborating the line of thought.

Sub-contracting hierarchies in Mexico City have recently received attention in the book by Benería and Roldán (1987). They base their study on a view from 'below', tracing the intermediate and final destinations of products produced by the bottom rung in the hierarchy, the industrial home workers. These are women employed on piece-rates to perform isolated parts of labour processes for a wide range of industries including those manufacturing plastics, electronics, and cosmetics as well as in garment, textile and food production. From this starting point Benería and Roldán reconstruct sub-contracting hierarchies so as to include levels of illegal or clandestine enterprises usually ignored in other studies. One example they give from the electronics industry presented the following structure. Industrial home workers were employed irregularly by an unregistered workshop (with six workers) to produce electric coils using simple equipment. The small workshop worked under contract to a nationally-owned firm employing 350 workers to make antennas which in turn worked under contract to a transnational firm, employing 3000 workers to make electrical appliances. This firm sub-contracted some 70 per cent of its production.

At the lower end of the hierarchy, sub-contracting has crossed the boundary between 'legality' and 'clandestinity'. The workshops and industrial home workers form a central part of the underground economy where workers are neither recognised nor protected by labour legislation or trade unions. Furthermore, crossing this boundary is associated with a sharp difference in the way *production is 'gendered'*. Women cluster in the most exploited forms of production and types of work; under present processes of capital restructuring, these most exploited forms are probably expanding.

While multi-level sub-contracting hierarchies like that described above may be found increasingly in modern industries in Latin America (Scott, 1979), different organisational forms are associated with industrial sectors long characterised by small units of production. For example in garment and shoe manufacture the vast majority of workers are employed in unregistered, unprotected places of work. In Mexico since the late 1970s, a number of detailed case studies have focused on these industries and have revealed the complexity of sub-contracting links and the concealment of much women's waged employment. Among the first wave of studies were those by Creel (1977), Padilla (1978), Arias (1980), Lailson (1980), Alonso (1982, 1984) and Calleja (1984). Discussion has continued and important collections have recently appeared on the industrial structure of Guadalajara (Arias, 1985) women's work in western Mexico (Gabayet *et al.*, 1988) and on the effects of recession (Arias and Durand, 1985; and Alonso, 1988).

The general situation for small-scale producers in garment and shoe production can be sketched out in the following way. National economic growth has been associated with the expansion of complex systems of credit financing operating at different levels and amongst different networks of interests. Starting capital to enter production may be raised from several sources: wage work in the US or large cities, from private or intra-family loans, or more occasionally from bank loans. But the sum needed is usually relatively small if a producer can find a niche within the largely informal systems of credit advancing and restitution whereby barriers of entrance are lowered and producers can pay back outstanding debts with goods once in production. In this system, commercial relations must be distinguished both in terms of price and credit – the length of time before payment is demanded. And it is through credit, rather than through price per se, that differential relations of power and control can be observed.

One prime instigator of the proliferation of small-scale production in Mexico in the last twenty-five years has been the efforts on the part of large (often transnational) firms to extend the market for (usually imported) capital goods, part of the sales policy being the extension of favourable credit terms. In this situation larger producers are keen to buy new machinery from distributors and off-load obsolete machinery on to newcomers and may agree to repayment in product over a period of many months. Thus from the perspective of an individual producer access to machinery has often taken place in two stages: an earlier investment in second-hand goods (paid for in kind, in instalments) and a later investment in new machines made available through hire-purchase schemes run by the distributing firms. Acquisition of inputs also involves credit: workshops purchasing products of the chemical industry (acrylic thread, plastics), leather or cotton cloth, try to enter agreements so as to delay payment until after the goods have been produced and sold.

The marketing of products takes place in a parallel system of credit advances and restitutions, with different types of customer distinguishable by the deals arranged. Workshops and small factories may have regular sub-contracting links with large businesses controlling input supply or marketing outlets, or they may work under periodic contracts of 'forward buying' where goods are partly paid for before they are produced. Such sub-contracting deals may be relatively beneficial (due to lower risks) or relatively prejudicial (due to lower profits) to the production enterprises. But there is another large group of small-scale producers who retain greater commercial autonomy. They accumulate not only on the basis of relations of production but also through commercial profits. By taking charge of sales these enterprises try to produce 'cheap' and sell 'dear'. In the situation outlined by Castells where there is an increasing disarticulation of national economic systems, the possibilities may increase for small independent 'merchant' producers to find commercial profits within the trading system.

To take the garment industry again as an example, recession and industrial restructuring are seen in the literature as having two faces. The first is a vertical shifting of production 'down the scale': from registered to unregistered enterprises and from small to 'micro' units of production. There have been several indications of this, though statistically it is virtually impossible to demonstrate. One telling figure is the decline recorded in the registered production of textiles and garments; the Mexican press stated that production had fallen some 20 per cent in the period from March 1985 to March 1986.[5] While a proportion of this decline was attributable to the austerity programmes and lower consumer demand, nevertheless one can also infer that the decline was indicative of some movement of production underground to unregistered enterprises proliferating in poor urban areas as well as in rural hinterlands.

Guadalajara has long been famous as a centre of garment production and estimates have been given periodically as to the size of the respective registered and unregistered sectors. For example, in the early 1980s there were reputed to be some ten 'illegal' clothing workshops and thirty 'illegal' knitwear workshops for every registered enterprise (Lailson, 1985). More recently, the President of the National Council for the Garment Industry reported that in the city there were some 1200 registered workshops, but in addition there were at least 2000 unregistered workshops in the urban area and 'thousands more' in the surrounding small towns.[6]

Unregistered garment enterprises have not necessarily all remained small. The size, extent, and degree of 'illegality' of garment factories in central Mexico City were brought to the public's notice as a result of the earthquake destruction in September 1985. More than 500 illegal factories were closed due to earthquake damage, and more than 1600 women workers were killed in the 200 factories which collapsed burying the labour force (Alonso, 1988). Public attention dwelt on the extreme callousness of owners who chose to rescue machinery rather than workers, and the tragedy served to reveal the appalling working conditions of the unprotected workers. The public outcry and the garment workers' subsequent attempts at unionisation seem to have pressed owners of capital to relocate their activities outside Mexico City and/or to re-organise production so as to sub-contract more work out to smaller units of production. In the opinion of some commentators, the earthquake did not inaugurate a new strategy, rather it helped speed up processes already underway.

The other face of recession and industrial restructuring noted in the literature is change in the organisation of work and working relations within small-scale production. Alonso (1982, 1983, 1988) has made several investigations of garment sewers who work as industrial home workers in Nezahualcóyotl, the conurbation that now adjoins Mexico City where garment production has thrived. Formerly, the large majority of seamstresses in Neza who took in sewing work for Mexico City firms had owned their sewing machines; a number were able to expand their enterprises by buying additional machines and began to employ wage workers. But the most recent investigations have revealed three new tendencies. First, a growing number of sewers are unable to buy sewing machines as they are now too expensive due to devaluations of the peso in 1976 and 1983. More home workers work with machines supplied by sub-contracting firms, losing the small margin of autonomy that machine ownership afforded. Second, in the few larger domestic enterprises, women are losing control over production to husbands or other men in the family. As male jobs diminish, so men look at domestic manufacturing with more interest. Third, the vast majority of sewers are facing growing impoverishment and worsening contract conditions. One result has been that more internal sub-contracting is taking place in Neza itself; there are now more local intermediaries and fewer have direct links with sub-contractors in Mexico City.

Few dispute that an advance of illegal, informal activities is taking place but the tendencies are being interpreted in different ways. Broadly, the right-wing emphasises the advantages and potentials of 'flexibility' and 'informality'. The persistence or re-creation of production structures of an informal type has sometimes been understood as a sign of people's resistance to commodification. Where informality evades market rules and escapes from obligations and organisational forms imposed by the State, this is seen to demonstrate a 'collective movement' away from universalistic regulations towards the resumption of 'particularistic values and behaviours' (Pinnaro and Pugliese, 1985). The thinking behind this view sees the 'collective movement' as powered by voluntary choice and the 'particularistic values and behaviours' as corresponding to a preferred ideal of social structures and relations. Both these assumptions can be challenged.

There are other types of positive interpretation which stress the 'rugged micro-entrepreneurship' as a lever for free market activity outside the sphere of legal and union regulation and see advantages in forming a more adaptable, flexible labour force. Such views have lain behind the resurgence of political action provoked most often by parties of the New Right in several Latin American countries (especially marked in Peru and Ecuador) in which the swelling informal sector is being treated as a new political constituency potentially with a stake in upholding the bourgeois State. The political platform of the New Right focuses on clearing away institutional/legal obstacles confronting owners/holders of property: from the shanty-town dweller, to the street trader, to the workshop owner whose rights to property are at present not sanctioned by law.[7]

Against these positive descriptions, one can set a vast mass of case study material that emphasises a more negative side: the exploitation and vulnerability of labour in situations of rampant capitalist growth where little or no protection is forthcoming from the State, or any other body. Many point to the long hours of labour time, low levels of remuneration and insecurity of employment whether this work is undertaken under conditions of quasi-autonomy (domestic enterprise) or through some form of labour relation.[8]

But when discussing particular instances in the Third World, a more complex view is required if the significance of informalisation processes is to be unearthed and distinguished in terms of the implications for relations of class and gender. The separate experiences of workers and capitalists and of women and men need to be reviewed in the light of the specific historical conditions (what was life like before?), the precise nature of the surplus appropriation and labour's relations with capital. The present general tendencies toward informalisation and disenfranchisement unleash feelings of concern, at least for those broadly on the 'left'. Workers' rights are being trampled upon; former victories won by the working class through class struggle have not been permanent. These defeats must be opposed. But when one moves to the local level and has a view from below, then the same feelings are not necessarily engendered. It is true that one can depict gross exploitation of labour. Nevertheless, new working classes are emerging composed of people who had never been given a chance of joining the old 'male' proletariat which had earlier led the confrontations with capital. The new working classes have not been passive but have been engaged in struggles of their own. In some circumstances they have forced through important changes in the social relations of production even within the 'clandestine' or informal sector. But what are the origins and prospects of these emerging working classes? How have pre-existing relations of gender and class, locality and ethnicity been drawn upon and reconstructed in the process of industrialisation? In this work, my principal focus is on the interplay between gender and class.

GENDER AND SOCIAL REPRODUCTION

An important discussion relevant to this research has centred on an understanding of how social relationships in a locality express dominance/subordination and how they are linked with particular forms of production. Up to now, more attention has been paid to petty commodity production than to other forms existing under capitalism and the theoretical problem has been pinpointed most clearly in the responses by feminists to recent Marxist debates.[9]

The version of the feminist critique most influential in guiding the approach taken here is by Roldán (1985) which she sets out by way of introduction to findings on industrial homework in Mexico City. Roldán defines the principal obstacle to theoretical clarity and rigour within debates on petty commodity production as being the prevalence of an 'economistic version of Marxism' which 'reduces the historical process to the mechanical operation of certain objective laws of material development'. This reductionism 'allows the concepts of classical Marxism to remain insulated and protected from feminist or any other critique which stresses the undeniable relevance of certain other dimensions of domination/subordination, namely those of race or ethnicity, or those relating to national and/or regional distinctions'. In spite of the well-attested preponderance of women in 'informal' activities, 'many Marxists have treated the sexual division of labour at best as a secondary issue and at worst as something both divisive and diversionary'.

More recently, greater notice has been taken of the association between present tendencies of industrial informalisation and the growing demand for women's labour.[10] The currently dominant development model of supply side economics, leading to an emphasis on export-led growth, cost-cutting (especially low wage strategies) and the deregulation of labour markets has major implications for gender relations in the labour force. As labour contracts and job stability are being undermined in the name of 'flexibility' so two tendencies can be noted. More household members must find income generating work in order to survive and this usually means that more women must come onto the labour market. And secondly, employment is being increasingly characterised by declining wage levels and by greater insecurity and dependency, forms of employment long seen as being more appropriate for women workers.

Roldán and other commentators hold out a wider theoretical challenge: how can relations of gender as well as other dimensions of domination/subordination be brought more fully into the identification and discussion of specific forms of production? To do this demands that we liberate ourselves from some of the analytical dualities so favoured by social science, such as between production and reproduction.

An emphasis on sectoral aspects of industrial change in specific economies has tended to obscure the implications of locational shifts: from city centre to shanty town and from large city to small rural town. One might perhaps argue that in the current period where small-scale units of production are being integrated within the more modern industrial sectors and where credit financing (including sub-contracting) is capable of overcoming 'distance' that geographical location is a dead issue. Yet if this were the case, why should well-defined industrialising regions, like western-central Mexico, emerge?

The concentration of industry suggests the need to engage in a broader enquiry concerning the contexts and meaning of location shifts so that attention focuses also on social reproduction in the regions concerned.

In an important article on the household's social reproduction Mingione (1985) explores the following situation (suggested by his knowledge of the rural industrialisation of Southern Italy). Workers in informal activities generally must labour long and hard for low rates of remuneration, and at the same time must combine income earning work with many other types of necessary labour to ensure reproduction (subsistence production, work to stretch the wage, domestic servicing work). Especially when women form the bulk of a labour force and also must meet responsibilities for ensuring the households' social reproduction, then the pressures on workers' time and energies become acute.

The outcome of this, Mingione connects in his analysis with the rise of areas where there are systematic concentrations of informal working activities. He states:

> In fact, in zones in which systems of small industrial concerns have developed, the presence of particular social conditions which assume a great importance in the context of reproduction have been noted... The combination of informal employment or, at any rate, of employment with a low ratio between working hours and income, and the need to dedicate relatively long hours to domestic activities implies the existence of particular organisational forms of the reproduction unit and the presence of solidarity at the level of the community, relations or friends (p. 32).

And he goes on to suggest that the demands of reproduction tend to 'confine the spread of economies with a high degree of informalisation to the areas where these preconditions already exist'. Thus although the direction of technological change may permit a 'mass' movement into industry, the boundaries of this movement will be set by the way workers' households are able to survive.

THE INVESTIGATION'S ANALYTIC FRAMEWORK

The introductory description of the region has already pointed to the existence of different perspectives within discussions of industrialising regions. The description drew upon the predominant local view which saw returning migrants as having voluntarily chosen to become pioneers of industry, turn their back on urban life and bring new livelihoods to depressed home regions. The chronology of the industrial movement supports the validity of this local interpretation. When the industrialisation began in the 1960s, the Mexican economy was rapidly expanding; the rise of regional industry predated the onset of economic recession. Furthermore, local industrialists have been able to go on producing profitably and expanding production because their flexibility allowed them to cater to a volatile market geared to consumer 'taste'. In the case of garment and shoe producers who supply a national (and international) 'fashion' market, their business has expanded as a result of the growth in the sectors of the consuming population who value 'fashion' apparel and are willing to pay for 'new' models and styles.

The description of the region also alluded to other features of the industrialisation which were present from the beginning: the association of the industrial branches with women's labour, the overwhelming preponderance of women in the labour force and the industries' clandestinity in the face of the law. These features, as later pointed out, have also been characteristic of the processes of informalisation accompanying recession and gathering momentum in Mexico from the 1970s. This interpretation throws a different light on the nature of the links between enterprises and the wider economy.

Underpinning this analysis of industrialisation in western-central Mexico are two principal perspectives. First, there is a need to explore the *form of industrialisation in the light of different models put forward concerning the origins and type of production*: the expansion of flexible, small-scale production of consumer goods as a result of greater national affluence, and the processes in connection with the informalisation of production, and industrial restructuring serving to undermine the autonomy and control of producers as well as the bargaining power of labour. Second, there is a need to explore the *form of industrialisation in the light of the processes by which production becomes gendered* linking this with the nature of the pressures within the realm of households' survival and social reproduction.

The translation of these more abstract perspectives into questions guiding research led to the specification of three areas of enquiry. These were explored primarily in a single centre of industrial production: Santiago Tangamandapio in the state of Michoacán, which developed a workshop-based sweater industry from 1960.

The first area of questioning focuses on '*origins*': put most simply, how and why do new forms of production appear, take root and flourish in particular time periods and places? This need not entail exploration into 'first ever' appearances; instead attention is placed on the introduction of different production forms in a locality and their co-existence with or displacement of pre-existing forms. The discussion of origins can be carried further for it is not purely of historical interest. In singling out the most important elements and relationships leading to the emergence of particular forms of production in a region, one is at the same time constructing hypotheses as to causation. Thus an analysis of the origins of specific industries in western-central Mexico emphasises aspects of regional and temporal distinctiveness which account for the rise of industry at that place as opposed to elsewhere.

The second area of questioning relates to the *relationships, forces and tendencies that surround a particular form of production*. Most of the analysis in this book focuses on one prevalent form, defined here as capitalised workshop production. Though in recent years many writers, especially on the 'informal' sector, have alluded to the proliferation of workshop activity, there has been little rigorous analytical treatment of workshop production as a separate form of production with its own dynamic and mode of surplus appropriation. It is generally seen as an 'awkward' form that sits uneasily in a plethora of production forms bounded on the one side by the classic expression of petty commodity production (where households hold property and also provide the labour necessary for production) and on the other side by 'fully' capitalist production. This indeterminacy together with the undoubted expansion of workshop production at the present time makes it particularly fascinating to study.

Capitalised workshop production, as its name suggests, is distinguishable from other types of workshop production that employ wage labour largely on account of investment strategy, the technology employed and close links with national and international commodity markets. Furthermore, it is usually unregistered production, flouting labour and tax legislation. This clandestine identity means that workshops are often lumped together with other 'backward' forms of production seen as constituting the 'informal' sector (Portes, 1983).

In some situations, highly coercive pre-capitalist types of labour recruitment and bonding typically underlie the rise of 'backward' forms of production giving rise to servile relations where workers are definitely not 'free'. But reliance on crude force cannot usually be sustained over a longer time period especially in those industries where labour is put to work with relatively sophisticated (and costly) machinery. More generally, workshop enterprises employ so-called 'free' workers, but they are low-waged, having been already classified as inferior bearers of labour. An understanding of why such a classification is in place, requires analysis of the dimensions of domination/subordination prevalent in a particular region.

The third area of enquiry focuses on *the implications of gendered production* and on the relationship between production and gender relations looked at in a wider context. The region demonstrates a tendency noted by many in recent years: women cluster in the most exploited forms of production. This clustering shows that a fundamental distinction remains between men and women as workers and that this endures over time leading to permanent disparities in terms of recognised skill, position in the labour process, wage level, and conditions of work. This points to the fact that men and women have a different relationship to the means of production and that relations of gender are transferred from society to the workplace and are reconstituted there. This transference runs diametrically against the hopes of the earlier generations of feminists that women's waged work 'of itself' carried emancipatory potentials. And it underscores the necessity of exploring 'the crossroads of class and gender'. As Cockburn (1983) has argued, all events can be read from a class perspective, and they usually are. But the same events must also be read from the perspective of gender relations if they are to have meaning. The gender perspective reveals the working of a separate system of human relationships which cannot be reduced to being a by-product of class relations. Only when both perspectives are integrated can events be understood.

The transference of gender relations as between society and workplace (and back again) demands that the relations of women and men are explored both inside and outside the workshops, at the level of household and of society. An evaluation of the significance of the expansion of wage work demands that some comparison is made between the lives of different generations of women to find out in what ways women's proletarianisation has been used to negotiate a different or a stronger position with regards men, their families, and the society in which they live.

A short discussion of the research investigation and fieldwork methodology is given in Appendix I.

Notes

1. The term was introduced by Feder (1977): see Arizpe and Aranda (1981) for a useful discussion of women's wage work in the strawberry packing plants in the Zamora valley.
2. A number of insightful studies of migration in the region are now available: López (1986), Leys (1987) and Massey *et al.* (1987).
3. Expansión, Mexico City, 16 January 1985.
4. See for example Pearson (1986) and Gordon (1988).
5. Uno Mas Uno, Mexico, 9 June 1986.
6. Excelsior, Guadalajara, 15 May 1986.
7. One influential book in this genre is by the Peruvian economist de Soto (1986); this combines detailed fieldwork analyses with a heavy political message.
8. This view is well argued in the contributions to the books edited by Bromley and Gerry (1979) and Redclift and Mingione (1985).
9. See Friedmann's reassessment (1986) of her earlier position on petty commodity production which she entitles 'Patriarchal commodity production' and Whitehead's critique (1985) of Gibbons and Neocosmos (1985).
10. See for example Roldán, (1987) and World Development, 1989.

2 The Region and its History

THE TOWN OF SANTIAGO TANGAMANDAPIO

The municipality of Santiago Tangamandapio lies in the hills above the humid irrigated valleys surrounding the town of Zamora in the state of Michoacán. Santiago is close to the old routeway that connects Jacona and Zamora to the south-east with Jiquilpan and Sahuayo to the north and eventually to the lake of Chapala and city of Guadalajara (see Map 2.1). According to the 1980 population census 6814 people lived in Santiago town (3488 women and 3326 men), while the municipal area had a total of 16 503 people (8372 women and 8131 men). But the census was renowned for its inaccuracy and the Santiago population was particularly difficult to enumerate given the numbers involved in short-term migration. The population of the town see themselves primarily as 'mestizos' without a specific ethnic identity: only a tiny minority in the town continue to wear local traditional dress. In the surrounding communities (known as 'ranchos') ethnic identity continues to be of importance; according to the 1980 census, some 4452 people in the municipality spoke the local language, Tarasco.

The people of Santiago as in many other parts of Michoacán pride themselves on the strength of their Catholic faith. In popular thought, the 'cristero' wars of the 1920s fought to protect the church and traditional forms of worship, were of greater importance than the Mexican Revolution. Families have long made sacrifices in order that their sons could be sent to the seminaries of Jacona or Zamora to train for the priesthood; and in the past many young women entered convents. The extension of catholicism into social life has meant that confirmation, marriage and baptism are extremely important and costly church occasions. Virtually all marriages are celebrated in church (according to the 1980 census only about 100 couples lived in 'unión libre'; and another 100 elected only a civil marriage). Divorce is almost unheard of: only six women and thirteen men were recorded as 'divorced' by the 1980 census.

The town has two churches; the new one built to commemorate the 'cristero' wars by the urban ward, Barrio Santos. The year is

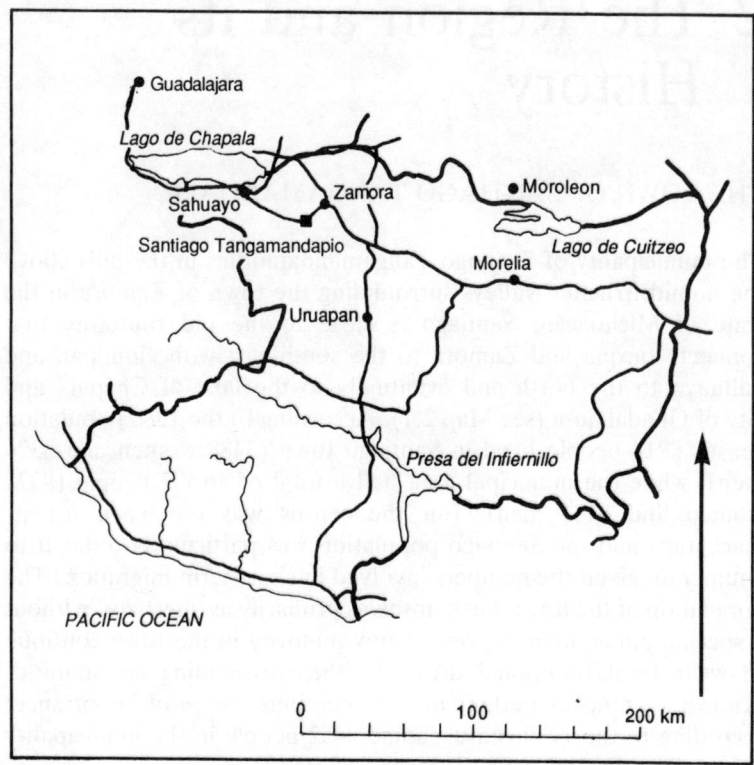

Map 2.1 Santiago Tangamandapio, Michoacán

marked by many elaborate celebrations of the Catholic calendar. Christmas time is the principal period of festivities culminating in pilgrimages to nearby shrines in which the different urban wards or *barrios* and *ranchos* compete through the costumes, music and tableaux prepared for the pilgrimage. At this time, many migrants return home from the US and in recent years have provided much of the money to cover the escalating costs. While Santiago society is imbued with Catholicism, distinctions can be drawn between an official, church-based religion and popular religious expression. The priest celebrates Mass in the two churches, but daily prayer meetings are held without priests in the houses of the poor in front of holy images that progress around the *barrio* population. In this society, as elsewhere in Mexico, the Virgin of Guadalupe is the most important figure in the everyday expression of religious faith.

Santiago serves as a market centre for the municipality's population having around fifty permanent food shops, twelve mills to grind maize flour, four *tortilla* making-plants and a weekly *tiangui* or market. Santiago borders irrigated valleys that have specialised in the production of strawberries for export but the district possesses only pockets of irrigable land which now grow vegetables for urban (and US) markets. The majority of the municipality's land is devoted to cattle raising while small rain-fed arable plots, *ecuaros*, are scattered over the hillsides, growing the staple foodstuffs of maize and beans. Over recent years the river water has become badly contaminated, but springs provide relatively clean drinking water for the town and some *ranchos*.

In the last ten years, major efforts have been made to 'clean up' the town and provide a better social infrastructure for its inhabitants. Piped water is now supplied to many houses in the town and most have now also been provided with electricity. House types vary greatly; the poor inhabit one or two roomed shacks in a central slum known as 'La Colonia'. The families of the old privileged, social strata still live in spacious adobe buildings in the old urban centre, while many families who have been in the US to save money for housing are constructing Californian-styled homes in all parts of town. The construction industry has been booming.

HISTORICAL PRECEDENTS

The state of Michoacán has a long history of cloth and garment production.[1] In the colonial period cotton and woollen cloth was manufactured by many urban workshops ('obrajes') for sale principally in the mining and commercial centres of the region. This Spanish-run industry was smashed during the struggle for Independence and many years passed before it could be revived. The mid-nineteenth century witnessed the rapid rise and later fall of a new textile industry, based on the local production of silk with mulberry trees grown and silk worms reared by many households in Michoacán. But there were obstacles hindering its sustained development and by the 1860s commercial interest was turning towards the reinstitution of a cotton and woollen cloth industry.

During the 1870s various groups of capitalists made plans to open factories to produce thread and cloth using imported machinery. Out of the various schemes mooted, three factories were finally set up; two in the state capital of Morelia and one in Uruapan. The output from these factories was bought by many small producers for manufacture into serapes and ponchos, saddle cloths and shawls. Workshops specialised in a range of goods: for example shawl manufacture predominated in the towns of Zamora, Jacona, Jiquilpan, Sahuayo and Tanguancicuaro, but it was not introduced into such small settlements as Santiago (see Map 2.2). The workshop and domestic production of cotton and woollen goods was usually combined with small-scale farming and was known as the industry of the poorer, more indigent social groups, while agriculture and stock raising were the pursuits of the rich.

Though textile and garment manufacturing was flourishing again in the late nineteenth century, by the 1890s the industry was subject to great swings of fortune. Local workshop and domestic production was being undercut both by the expansion of national factory production and by huge increases in the volume of imported textile goods, whose dissemination in the rural regions was facilitated by the railways. Small town production, especially of cotton goods, could be wiped out almost overnight. In response, the Michoacán state government offered all manner of incentives in an effort to attract investment capital to the region.

New investments were made in the factory-based production of cotton and woollen thread and cloth. In 1895 a new factory (financed by French, Spanish and Mexican capital) was opened in Zinapecuaro with 100 looms powered by electricity and in 1896 a similar plant was established in Uruapan. By 1896 the state's textile factories employed a total of 690 workers; output and employment then rose rapidly until 1910 when some 1458 workers were employed. For a few years there was a burst of renewed activity in the old textile and garment towns of the region where workshops and households continued to transform the factory made thread and cloth into shawls and blankets.

The renewed prosperity of the textile industry was short-lived. By the early twentieth century competition from other sources of supply from outside the region meant that the factories could no longer sell their output and furthermore, the price of local raw materials was rising. Once again the government of Michoacán offered incentives, this time to property owners to increase the area under cotton. This policy did not help much. Factories continued to diminish output and lay off workers. Textile production in western-central Mexico was in decline; capital was already being

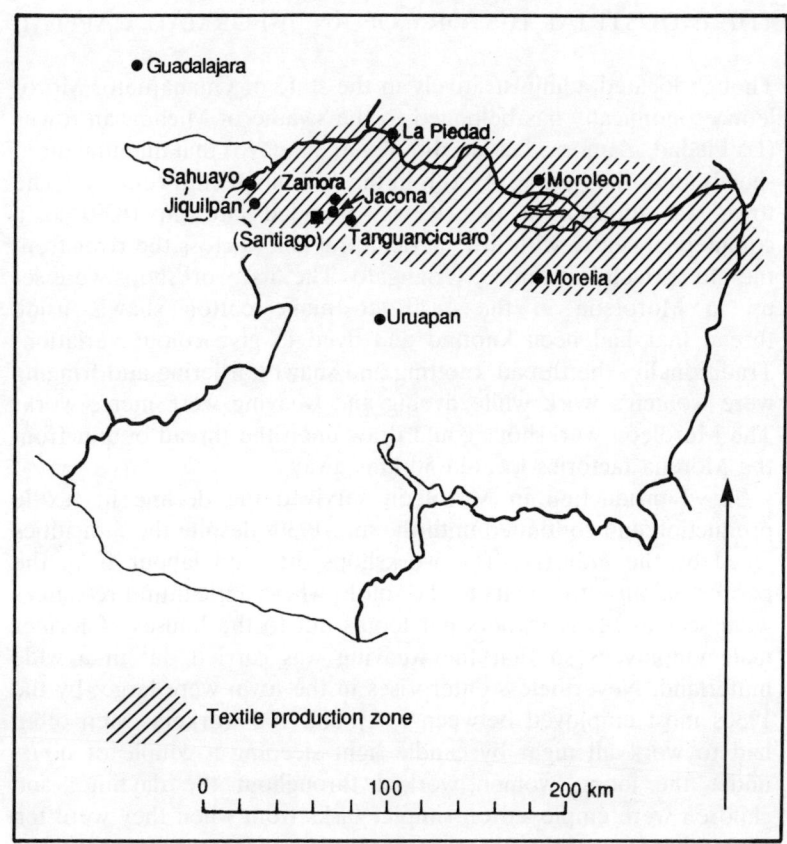

Map 2.2 Ninteenth-century textile centres in Michoacán

withdrawn by the time the country was engulfed in the Revolution of 1910. A few centres, however, were able to survive; they later were to have an important function in the 're-industrialisation' of the region from the 1960s onwards. From the perspective of Santiago, the most important servicing centre was Moroleón and this town has now become a booming 'capital' of the informal branch of Mexico's textile and garment industry. As no study has yet appeared on Moroleón, a few remarks will be made concerning its industrial background.

THE INDUSTRIAL HISTORY OF AN 'INFORMAL' CAPITAL

Though located administratively in the state of Guanajuato, Moroleón economically has belonged to the swathe of Michoacán towns (La Piedad, Zamora, Jacona, Jiquilpan, Sahuayo) that manufactured shawls and other goods of cloth in the mid-nineteenth century.[2] The town was unusual in that it was founded late (in 1839) as a commercial centre with little agricultural land, across the river from the old agricultural centre, Uriangato. The first workshops were set up in Moroleón in the 1840s to make cotton shawls using thread that had been knotted and dyed to give colour variation. Traditionally, the thread knotting and shawl bordering and fringing were women's work while dyeing and weaving were men's work. The Moroleón workshops could draw upon the thread output from the Morelia factories located 50 kms away.

Shawl production in Moroleón survived the decline in textile production and continued until the mid-1930s despite the difficulties faced by the industry. The workshops drew on labour from the poorer Indian settlements to the south, where agricultural resources were scarce. Many owners put looms out to the houses of former male employees so that the weaving was carried out in a wide hinterland. Nevertheless enterprises in the town were large; by the 1930s most employed between forty and 100 workers. Men often had to work all night by candle light sleeping a couple of hours under the loom; women worked throughout the daytime; and children were employed on simpler tasks from when they were ten years old.

In the 1930s despite the owner's employment strategy, a wave of union activity spread in Michoacán and Moroleón with workers demanding better pay and conditions of work. In that period profits had dwindled and owners tried to lower wages. The workers' movement strove to take over the factories and workshops and transform them into co-operatives. Even those former Moroleón employees who had later set up their own workshops in surrounding towns like Cuitzeo faced invasions by workers from Moroleón who wanted to carry off the looms. Depression and labour unrest meant that many shawl manufactures in the region went out of business.

The decline in cotton shawl manufacture did not, however, bring an end to Moroleón's textile industry. A new generation of entrepreneurs, often the sons of shawl producers, began in the 1940s to invest in different textile activities with simpler production processes, making bedspreads and towels from cotton yarn. These enterprises tended to be smaller, and they continued to be based on gender divisions of labour in which men worked the manually operated looms weaving patterned cloth while women sewed and finished the goods. Partly on account of the new possibilities for labour migration to the US (during the Second World War) and partly because of the smaller units of production, labour protest and union activity subsided. Moroleón's expanding production was reaching a largely rural population; this demand represented an improvement of the living conditions of the peasantry and the creation of new consumption needs but it also was undercutting rural women's domestic manufacturing.

In the late 1950s, Moroleón's industry diversified once again. The next generation of owners started the production of sweaters, made first from wool and later from acrylan. The growth of this activity was stimulated after 1964 when a thread making factory opened, Hilados Moroleón, using Italian machinery which Italian engineers installed and introduced to workers. In the early phase of the sweater industry, production was organised in workshops (employing at least three workers). At that time, a new demand arose to form a union. In 1964 workers went on strike in order to force owners to sign collective wage agreements, guarantee employment, pay a full week's wage (known as paying the '7th day'), provide medical attention and give paid holidays. But the movement faced many problems: the union lost support and leaders were accused of having sold out to the owners. No unions have been set up in the town since then.

By the late 1960s, it was the workshop owners who made more of their 'union' than workers. That year a group of sixty-eight owners went to the state capital, Guanajuato, to petition the Governor for help in opening up foreign markets for their products. Later some 200 traders re-installed the Moroleón Chamber of Commerce (first set up in 1935) under the slogan of 'la unión hace la fuerza' or 'unity gives strength'. One of the first projects of the Chamber was to campaign for the opening of a technical college in the town to train skilled workers. This project was finally realised in 1981.

Major changes were underway in the organisation of production in Moroleón during the 1970s. The large firms which manufactured thread and cloth became fully automated and computer-run, operating twenty-four hours a day employing a small number of workers and administrative personnel. A residual number of larger workshops remained, clustering in the town centre producing shawls, bedspreads, blankets and sweaters. But workshops employing wage workers were not expanding either in numbers or in volume of output. In comparison, an enormous growth was taking place in the number of enterprises defined as 'family run'; the 'household' production units were producing sweaters and sports shirts as well as new lines of women's 'fashion' clothing and underwear. According to the local tax office (in 1986) more than 2000 garment-making enterprises existed; of these 80 per cent were family organised and the remaining 20 per cent were workshops employing from fifteen to twenty workers. (The population of Moroleón was estimated at around 50 000 by the 1980 census.)

Many of the family run production units have employed a small number of wage workers as well as family members and they manufacture garments to supply their own independent commercial outlets – i.e. a shop that occupies a front room on the street where the goods are offered directly to customers.

Family enterprises have never expected to sell the whole output through the small shops, especially where houses are located away from the main selling quarters of town. In earlier years, there were two main types of linkage between small producers and traders. One was through sales made to traders possessing their own means of transport who distributed the goods throughout the country. Often the contracts involved an initial loan from the traders so as to get production going. The other variant tended to be more exploitative of the small garment producers and was based on sub-contracting. This was often part of a more complex relationship in which the small producers were indebted to a trader or to larger producers following the acquisition of machinery or inputs. In recent years, however, the prospects facing even the smallest producers in Moroleón have brightened immeasurably on account of the town's growing reputation as a centre of cheap clothing for the whole of the Republic.

Most family-run enterprises have now invested in modern, relatively expensive garment-making machinery. Some of those producing sweaters have installed computer-run Carrousel looms which 'automatically' knit complex weaves and colour patterns and cost some 25 million pesos (US$ 40 000) in early 1986.[3] A few have even acquired one of the most sophisticated looms on the market for 'household' production, costing 60 million pesos (US$ 100 000) which produces a tubular knit requiring no side seaming at the sewing stage. Many workshops produce sweaters only in the winter season, and make up fashion clothing from bought cotton cloth during the hot months. In the latter type of manufacture, the most successful have been those businesses where a family member has received some professional training in design and cutting. The capitalisation of production and increasingly technical skills of family members means that this type of production need draw on fewer wage workers than formerly.

The workshops and family-run enterprises that do employ labour prefer workers from the neighbouring (and reputedly backward) towns of Uriangato and Cuitzeo or from the surrounding *ranchos*. Some workshops send vans to pick up the workers every day. Many women take employment in Moroleón to learn a 'trade' with the idea of moving the family into town when they can set up an independent business. Workshops and family enterprises also put work out to women in the *ranchos*; in some cases sewing machines are placed in workers' homes; in others, the workers themselves own their machines.

Labour remuneration in the town appears extremely varied. Those recognised as 'skilled' have qualifications from the local technical college. Experienced loom operators (men) and cutters (women) expected to regularly earn 20 000 to 25 000 pesos per week (US$33 to $40) in early 1986. Women machinists and less experienced loom workers could hope to earn comparable weekly wages only in the winter months by working long hours (at least twelve hours a day). Wages are generally paid as piece-rates and in the case of the top rates, they amount to around double the legal minimum wage. At the other end of the scale, many apprentice or 'trainee' workers from outside town earn much less than the legal minimum wage. But though no unions exist, it appears that employers have been forced to concede to certain demands from workers. It is now well established that in the slack season workers have Mondays as well as Sundays free from labour (characteristically it had been hard to reassemble the full work force on Monday mornings); and 'fiestas' and holidays are also largely respected. For their part, workers have become suspicious of unions, fearing that they will put in jeopardy the possibilities open to earn high wages by working long hours.

Few workers in Moroleón see themselves as permanent members of a proletariat with life-long interests opposed to capital; instead they are aspiring members of a bourgeoisie hoping one day to become independent owners. Apparently very few cases of labour protest have been brought by workers against their employers (partly due to the owners' influence in Guanajuato). Where problems arise between workers and employers in the 'family' sector, workers usually resign in order to find better employment elsewhere. So large has this sector now become that workers have less fear of becoming 'black-listed' and refused employment.

Apart from the many garment producers who combine commercial activities, there are more than 300 specialised clothing distributors in the town according to the local tax office and the Chamber of Commerce now has more than 500 members. The commercial businesses cluster in new zones on the outskirts of town, with new 'walking streets' full of clothing dealers appearing annually. Alongside the stores, bank branches are opening to facilitate the transactions. The dealers of Moroleón buy up goods made throughout the western-central region and they move huge consignments of clothing between Moroleón and other major wholesaling and distributing centres in the country: Tlaxcala, Aguascalientes, Chiconcuac. In the town, greater specialisation is now appearing in the different selling districts, not only with regard to product type, also quality. Around the food market, for example, petty traders sell the cheapest clothing: defective shoddy goods, the 'waste' of the town's producers. In contrast, the newest 'walking streets' offer the best quality clothing, purporting to be designer-made, and complete with pirated trade-mark.

Every year increasing numbers of buyers are coming to buy stock in Moroleón. Market traders throughout Central Mexico buy on Fridays and Saturdays for sale at Sunday markets, and return to stock up on Mondays for the rest of the week. Retailers from distant cities such as Monterrey or Veracruz, charter buses to take them for a day's buying in Moroleón. Larger clothing wholesalers and retailers fly in from the industrial towns of the Mexican-US border; they have responded to the differentiated demand for clothing of the young women factory workers by buying cheap clothing in Moroleón for everyday wear and fashion clothing from New York and Los Angeles for 'best' wear.

In recent years, Moroleón is benefiting from a shifting of commercial and production capital out from Mexico City. This became especially marked after the 1985 earthquake which prompted capitalists to find less exposed, less politically 'hot' places for further investment. Paradoxically, outside of the garment business few Mexicans have ever heard of Moroleón.

For the scattered towns of western-central Mexico that have specialising in sweater production, Moroleón has been a vital centre. Though the town has not actively instigated the diffusion of garment production out to this broader hinterland, the services the town provides as the newly emerging 'capital' of 'informal' production has led to very important regional linkages. The town is central for the dissemination of technology and technical information; for the distribution of inputs; and channelling of products to national and international markets. Most knitwear producers in Santiago acquired their first second-hand looms and sewing machines in Moroleón and have returned later to buy new machines from dealers based there. They have always been dependent on the town for access to spares and repairs. Serious technical problems can only be handled by Moroleón's expert mechanics. Commercial travellers from Moroleón tour the region where small production flourishes selling thread and cheap cotton cloth and try to expand their markets through the offer of cheap credit. Moroleón is also the destination of a growing proportion of Santiago's output.

Moroleón's long and varied history as a garment-producing centre represents the exception rather than the rule in western-central Mexico. It is uncommon to find such continuity; other towns may have excelled in the production of certain types of goods at certain periods, but their fortunes rose and fell. Elsewhere there was not the same rapid replacement of declining activities with others for which the prospects were brightening. Moroleón was able early on to reach a sustained volume of production and level of sales, that secured the town a future through its supply, service and training functions, as well as through its well-established industrial 'culture'.

Notes

1. This historical summary is drawn largely from Uribe, 1983.
2. The material presented in this section derives largely from my own short appraisal supplemented by information from Patricia Arias and Jorge Durand.
3. The dollar–peso rate was changing rapidly during the fieldwork period, as shown by the table in Appendix II. The dollar equivalents have been calculated according to the quarter in which the observations were made.

3 Economic and Social Relations before 1960

QUESTIONS OF ORIGINS

The purpose of this chapter is to select themes from the history of Santiago up to 1960 that are most relevant for an exploration of the question of origins. How and why did a new form of production become introduced in Santiago? What particular conjunctures of social relations that had come to the fore by the early 1960s had allowed the new form of production to take root? The arguments will be presented in two main sections.

The first section examines the forces leading to *male long-distance migration and semi-proletarianisation*. *The history of violence and social disruption from the aftermath of the Revolution will be told from the perspective of Santiago*, bearing in mind that similar accounts would be forthcoming from the majority of small upland settlements in Michoacán, Jalisco and Guanajuato. The changes ushered in by agrarian reform and the subsequent erosion of rights to land and other resources for the mass of the population will then be explored. These themes provide the background for the discussion of the destruction of the subsistence base, meaning of poverty and increasing population mobility. As impoverishment deepened so men travelled further afield in search of cash earning work. Contrasting migration histories will be given of men coming from different social backgrounds and the conditions of their semi-proletarianisation described.

The second main section focuses on *family and gender relations as seen through women's eyes within the same period in the small urban society of Santiago*. The material is organised with respect to the different stages women of the present mothers' and grandmothers' generations passed through during their lives.

Economic and Social Relations before 1960

FORCES LEADING TO MIGRATION

Destruction and Social Upheaval: 1910s–40s

Nobody alive today in Santiago can recall any golden age of peace or prosperity. The older generations look back to nightmare years of famine and depravity that followed on the heels of the Revolution. The year 1917 was remembered particularly clearly on account of the death and hunger when many children died. But the deprivations of these years were overshadowed in people's minds by the terrifying memories of bandits. The most infamous was José Inés Chávez who had organized his first rebel forces during the Revolution and made forays under the flag of Pancho Villa. After the Revolution, he and his band (numbering between 2000 and 3000 men) adopted the motto of 'blood and money'. They scourged a large area of western-central Mexico, threatening in particular the more isolated upland settlements where they looted and killed, raped women and committed other excesses.[1]

The people of Santiago lived in constant fear of bandits. When they were in the neighbourhood, those who could escape left for larger safer towns or went up to the hills. Those trapped in town hid in the house roofs. On various occasions the bandits ransacked and burnt the town, using dried *chili* pepper to smoke out the remaining inhabitants. Every family had a horror story to tell of loved ones killed, or they remembered miracles when loved ones survived.

Olivia (now in her eighties) still sobs as she remembers watching her brother being tortured to death by Chávez's men – she was fourteen years old at the time. She saw many women abducted and raped for the bandits had an enormous appetite for women; women were beaten and tortured when they tried to retaliate.

Socorro recalls how her mother's family had escaped to the hills when news broke that the bandits were coming, but they had been forced to leave their mother behind tied up as she was suffering an epileptic fit. Miraculously the bandits left her alone and she had *tortillas* ready when the family returned.

Many Santiago people fled to Jacona. Ramiro, the pioneer of Santiago's sweater industry, had been born in Jacona in 1918, where his mother had sought sanctuary to escape Chávez. But Jacona with its large 'floating' population suffered major food shortages as the warfare and banditry disrupted production and trade. People tried to subsist on what they could find; months might go by without maize, and the arrival of a trader (such as Ramiro's father) with some sacks of corn was the occasion for great celebration.

Slowly the threat of the bandits subsided, the population started to return home to repair some of the damage and devastation. But the social upheavals were far from over. The demands for land unleashed by the Revolution had not yet found an answer.

The district of Santiago possessed relatively poor, limited agricultural resources and cattle raising had long been the more profitable activity. The two haciendas in the district and a few large private properties had amassed the better arable land. People from the district's *ranchos* were tied to the haciendas and other large properties as *peónes*. The grandparents of the present day look back with hatred not only to the monopolisation of the land by the landed families but also to crimes and injustice. The hacendados are pictured in stereotypical terms: as stern, arrogant, cruel men on horseback or flogging their *peónes* for the most minor of crimes. Women recall how hacendados used to abduct young, beautiful women when they took their fancy and murder their husbands if they were in the way.

During the 1920s demands were raised once again for the abolition of the hacienda system and the redistribution of land. Those making these demands were known as *agraristas*, and in Santiago, some forty men campaigned actively for radical agrarian change.[2] Some were known to be communists. Though the call for land distribution appealed to many, the political position (or suspected position) of the *agraristas* ran contrary to deep popular sentiments. In fact only limited direct support was forthcoming for a radical agrarian change; instead the demand for land helped unleash an opposing counter current that carried much stronger appeal for the rural population.

This popular movement grew strongly in western-central Mexico and drew support from a broad swathe of rural society. It coalesced in order to challenge the authority of the post-Revolutionary state which was seen as departing increasingly from the traditional values of the Mexican people. The traditional values associated with the Catholic Church were seen as put in jeopardy by the policy of secularisation pursued by the government in the mid-1920s. Owing to this religious identity, followers called themselves *cristeros* and their clash with the *agraristas* and the state resulted in the *cristero* wars of 1926–29.³

In the eyes of Olivia the *cristero* wars were sparked off by the arrival of 'foreign priests'. They were supposed to have been sent by the Government, but 'they really came from the Devil'. They set about closing the churches and ordering terrible penalties for crimes committed by the people. She described how men were executed for robbery and women were burnt to death for adultery (however there is no evidence to corroborate this). The whole people rose up and rejected the intrusion of these priests and demanded their Catholic faith be restored.

Santiago was strongly *cristero* in sympathy during the wars with the most fanatical supporters coming from the ward aptly named Barrio Santos. Most of the *agraristas* left the town. Although the churches had been shut by official decree and the ecclesiastical authorities had recalled the priests, the priest of Santiago remained officiating at services held secretly in people's houses. And children could still receive a Catholic education at the school run by nuns. In the region many men took up arms while women organised themselves into underground movements to support the priests who remained with their flocks and to take food and supplies to the *cristero* forces. Government troops invaded Santiago on two occasions; once again the richer inhabitants tended to leave for the greater safety of the towns while the poor (and the priests) made do with caves in the hills when the soldiers came. Although folk memory would like to credit Santiago with having been 'a hundred per cent *cristero*' in fact supporters of the Government were to be found among some of the wealthier, trading families (as well as among the remaining *agraristas*). A plot launched by these pro-Government supporters led to the murder of General Aguilar, a well known *cristero* leader, in Santiago.

The *cristero* supporters had greatly out-numbered their opponents in Santiago but by the time the fighting ceased in 1929, many 'ordinary folk' had lost heart in the *cristero* cause. Some of more privileged families had left Santiago to start new lives in Mexican towns or in the US. And in this new situation a growing group were prepared to listen to the *agraristas*. When Lazaro Cárdenas was installed as Governor of Michoacán, the people of Santiago thought more seriously about confronting the remaining landed elite in order to get land.

Agrarian Transformation and the Capitalisation of Agriculture 1930s–50s

After peace was restored the *agraristas* petitioned continually for the restitution of Indian land. In the early 1930s they were advised by the office of the Governor of Michoacán that they would meet with success if they filed a petition for a grant of *ejido* land. This was done, and eleven men signed the petition. Of these, only one was directly concerned with the land (a share cropper), the rest were townsmen with the following occupations; five basket-makers (the most 'traditional' artisan craft), two weavers (who made woollen ponchos and sarapes), two brick-makers and one baker. As a result of the petition, in 1932 Santiago was awarded a portion of uncultivated land that had belonged to the largest hacienda in the district, La Verduzqueña. The *ejido* grant was amplified in 1933–34 when the whole of La Verduzqueña was expropriated: this meant that a property of some 1000 hectares of rain-fed arable land and 800 hectares of pasture was handed over and reconstituted as *ejido* Santiago.[4]

The *ejido* grant was divided amongst a total of 135 beneficiaries. Many (probably the majority) who received land had not previously been peasants or share croppers. The peasantry had largely been kept out of the redistribution process, nor were they prepared to fight for access. The landed families had continued to threaten those who joined with the *agraristas* and in 1933 provoked terror at the time of the expropriation by murdering seven peasants. But outside Santiago neither the remaining *cristeros* nor the old landed families could find much support. The local *agraristas* had established close relations with Lazaro Cárdenas and were able to wrest control of the municipal Presidency away from the landed elite. The *agraristas* were then able to gain 'official' access to arms with which to defend their newly bestowed right to the land.

In 1937 a new initiative was mounted in the town to demand the expropriation of nine other properties including the second principal hacienda in the district bordering the *rancho* of Jerusalem. This hacienda possessed 14 hectares of irrigated land, 400 hectares of arable land and 800 hectares of pasture. On this occasion a group from the town who no longer identified with the *agraristas* petitioned for the hacienda in the name of the indigenous population of *rancho* Jerusalem. The land was expropriated in 1938/9 and distributed among sixty-three families, but only eight of these families came from the *rancho* (which at that date had a population of some 200 people). The old hacendado family tried to provoke resistance to the expropriation amongst their old *peónes* in Jerusalem and the reform was rushed through by the authorities so as to prevent further interference. The beneficiaries had to carry weapons to defend their plots while they sowed their first crops.

The former landowners sold their livestock and other moveable goods. (In 1930 there had been an estimated 2000 head of cattle in the district and 800 draft animals; most of these had been in the hands of the landed families.) With the proceeds they left the region to settle mostly in Guadalajara. As a result of the expropriations not only was the organisation of agricultural production rapidly changed, so too were cropping patterns and land use. One dramatic change was the switch out of sugar production when the haciendas were disbanded; the former cane fields in the valleys were planted with maize and fodder crops while the old *ingenios* were left to rot. But this also meant there was less seasonal work to be found locally. Dairy cattle raising was becoming the most important new activity: milk production being increasingly profitable when a new road was built in 1937 which allowed its transport to Zamora where it was bought by sweet manufacturers.

In total some 550 families received parcels of the expropriated land in the district of Santiago. The beneficiaries of the land reform included various social groups: there were urban artisans and traders, wealthier peasants from the *ranchos*, former hacienda *peónes* and poor share croppers. From the start beneficiaries who lacked resources were in a highly vulnerable position as the reform had failed to make inputs or working capital available to the *ejidatarios*. They had to turn to local traders for loans of cash and goods; soon many had become hopelessly enmeshed in debt. The poorer beneficiaries' access to land came under increasing pressure and they were robbed of it under a variety of pretexts.[5]

By the early 1940s the committees of both Santiago and Jerusalem *ejidos* had come under the sway of the wealthier members.[6] The committees (notwithstanding opposition from 'ordinary' *ejido* members) began to sell off portions of pasture land 'illegally'. The purchasers were mostly landowners whose properties had not been affected during the agrarian reform. This remnant of the old landowning stratum was busy accumulating property once more and increasingly made use of the *ejido* committees for that purpose. Before long, expropriated arable land was also being illegally alienated and purchased and used to grow fodder for dairy cattle. Many from this landowning stratum had accumulated properties well in excess of the 100 hectare legal maximum. Livestock numbers grew rapidly and soon surpassed the stock that had been kept in the old days of the haciendas. (An indication of this is the fact that more than 2000 head of diseased cattle were destroyed in the mid-1940s). But the cattle herds were in the hands of only a small group of farmers, the 'real' beneficiaries of the land reform.[7]

Throughout the 1940s the cattle-owners who had bought up *ejido* land and had acquired most parcels of irrigable land sought to take greater control of the *ejido* committees and use them for their own ends. They became known as 'new' *ejidatarios* ('los nuevos') and their political influence was growing at the expense of the 'old' *ejidatarios*, the first beneficiaries of the reform. The pre-eminent position of 'los nuevos' in local politics was assured in 1951 when the most powerful of the cattle owners was nominated by the PRI party apparatus (the ruling Institutional Revolutionary Party) as the municipal President on the strength of his good connections with the then Governor of Michoacán. For the next nine years he controlled the Presidency and used it to further the interests of the emerging group of capitalist farmers.

One of the tasks that fell to the municipal Presidency in these years was the administration and distribution of labour contracts for temporary work in the USA during the 'Bracero Program'. These contracts were being sold to the dispossessed, impoverished men whose lands and livestock the cattle-owners were usurping: it was a very convenient 'solution'.

Subsistence and Poverty

The picture given by the present generation of grandparents of traditional rural life (especially in those *ranchos* that were not 'under the thumb' of a strong patron) tends towards the idyllic. The horror of banditry and war is contrasted with the tranquillity of peasant farming. The independent peasantry lived predominantly in households comprised of three generational families which could collectively produce most of the maize and beans needed for domestic consumption. They might own a few head of cattle for milk and draught as well as some pigs and chickens. Wild game was still plentiful: there were deer and birds in the hills and at different seasons children scavenged for edible fruits and seeds growing wild.

Some families had specialised in types of domestic manufacture (producing cloth on wooden looms, baskets from local cane); others specialised in certain trading or exchange circuits (trading fish from the lakes of Chapala or Patzcuaro). The haciendas and other large properties recognised people's right to glean, so that even the poorest could scrape enough food together to survive.

Subsistence is a cultural matter, and in Santiago it was not evaluated solely in terms of an actual 'physical' intake of food. Certain foodstuffs and methods of preparation were considered essential if people were to realise a decent life. Fundamental to subsistence were the *tortillas* which formed the basis of every meal of the day. A meal lacking *tortillas* could not be considered adequate as food. It was men's work to grow the maize, caring for the plants throughout the growing season, eagerly awaiting the time when the first cobs could be harvested, and even more the time when a large pile of cobs lay stored in the household for the year ahead. Women processed the maize first into flour and then into dough spending many hours in the early morning to make the day's *tortillas*. Men secured the lime that was added in tiny amounts to the dough and women gathered wood from the hillsides for the fire on which to cook the *tortillas*. Men and women saw their identities partly in terms of their relationship to the maize food staple.

> Genoveva considered that her grand-daughters were not yet women although they were fifteen and seventeen years old – as they could not make their family's daily ration of *tortillas*. She thought they were neither strong enough to work the long hours in the early morning grinding the corn nor clever enough to produce perfect *tortillas* with regard to thinness and taste. No machine-made *tortilla* could possibly match those made by a woman after a lifetime of experience.

Maize was the basic food, but only the most indigent were forced to subsist on *tortillas* alone. People might consume beans that had been stewed with pork fat and flavoured with salt and *chili*, young green *nopales* gathered from the cactus by the house or from the hillside, cheese, rice boiled with onion and tomato, fried eggs or vegetables. Children were recognised as needing milk daily until they were nine or ten years old. Meat was a luxury good though a necessary one with which to celebrate a family or religious festival. Certain choice dishes were associated with different seasons or dates in the year; others were produced infrequently as a treat to offer other households. Food was often discussed and appraised, it remained a source of pleasure and wonderment despite the time and labour its production demanded.

For the people of Santiago the adequate production of the staples maize/*tortillas* and beans for domestic consumption brought independence and social respect and the ingenuity behind dietary variation was a source of pride. The disposession and impoverishment suffered by most in the first half of the twentieth century was registered most profoundly in terms of food decline and it carried wide connotations.

As households lost access to land, so they had to compete to rent *ecuaro* plots in the uplands on which to grow maize and beans for consumption. Rents for even the most marginal lands rose, and share croppers were forced to accept ever worsening deals, paying back as much as two-thirds of the maize harvest in return for the land. Gleaning rights were suspended by the 'new' *ejidatarios* and the hillsides were cleared of game. Grandmothers recall their desperate struggle to find enough food for their families, and the situation was deteriorating through the 1940s in particular. Diets were reduced to *tortillas* with a little salt, occasionally made more appetising with *chili* or *nopales*. Fresh meat, eggs, vegetables and milk were out of reach. The only meat available for the mass of the population was from the carcases of dead animals that were dried and salted for future consumption. Malnutrition especially among children worsened, and child mortality apparently rose as children weakened by hunger were carried off by disease.

Social Disruption and Population Mobility

One dramatic response to social unrest and agrarian transformation was a greatly enhanced mobility of population. Indicative of this mobility is the fact that few parents of the present generation of grandparents had been born in the *municipio* of Santiago. Furthermore, one distinct social class, the old landowning families had disappeared by the end of the 1930s. Many kinds of mobility can be listed. Families from Santiago and its *ranchos* periodically fled to the towns to escape bandits and soldiers, some never returned. *Peónes* were being thrown off the haciendas expropriated during the 1930s. Those without access to *ejido* land wandered away: some coming to Santiago from the former haciendas of Sahuayo, others leaving the *municipio* following the expropriation of La Verduzqueña

Economic and Social Relations before 1960 43

and Jerusalem. Many left the *ranchos* in order to settle in the town, perhaps after an intervening period of wandering. And increasingly men from Santiago district migrated from the region to find waged work elsewhere.

In the period 1920 to 1960, some thirty *ranchos* in Santiago were completely abandoned. In the earlier years, the unrest and invasions had prompted many to leave the more isolated settlements, but latterly the out-migration was more closely connected to the changes underway in the agrarian system. In several *ranchos*, water was becoming an increasingly acute problem: scarce, contaminated or not available at all in the dry months of the year. Men and mules had to travel long distances to bring back drinking water. The reason for the shortage was usually linked to the usurpation of water by the emerging capitalist farmers who diverted water in order to increase their land under irrigation or to build small reservoirs so as to water their dairy cattle throughout the year. Water shortage was even more pressing than land shortage in forcing people to finally move away from home and fields. This rural-urban movement was by no means haphazard.

The people leaving a particular *rancho* elected to settle in the same *barrio* or ward in the small urban centre of Santiago. Thus kin and social ties were being transferred more or less intact and reconstituted in a new environment. This meant that the four *barrios* of Santiago town were credited with quite distinct social characteristics stemming from the different origins of their inhabitants.

Movement into town did not solve the problem of how to survive. Relatively few waged jobs were available, many families were competing to find places as share-croppers despite the highly onerous conditions and many paid high rents for patches of barren upland soil to grow maize. In the town, women took on whatever work could earn them money or food within domestic services and domestic manufacturing. But increasingly men had to look outside the *municipio* for work. Now that the local sugar industry had come to an end, there was no longer much seasonal wage work available in the vicinity. Instead, men migrated seasonally to the sugar harvest in the Los Reyes district (some thirty miles away), spending several weeks there each year. But these earnings were rarely sufficient to tide over families who now required far greater cash resources to enable them to survive.

Underlying the complexity of the population mobility was one striking constant. No tradition was instituted in that part of Mexico involving the mobility or migration of women on their own. Unlike the situation in many other regions of Mexico (and Latin America in general), women from Santiago rarely went to distant towns to find work as domestic workers or as market sellers. Women moved with their families and then stayed at home – whether in the *ranchos* or in the urban *barrio*, while it was the obligation of their menfolk to travel far and wide to find a livelihood. Only under exceptional circumstances did women take domestic work in nearby Zamora. Social disruption and labour redundancy had not led to an expulsion of women.

Male Migration and Semi Proletarianisation

Recent studies of long distance migration patterns over time in western – central Mexico stress their complexity, but also suggest that certain trends have predominated. Especially marked in Santiago and elsewhere during an early period (from the turn of the century to 1940) was the migration of men and families from wealthier, most privileged social backgrounds.[8] Their reason for leaving was more often connected with a search for personal security and an escape from feuds and vendettas at home. This stratum was more likely to possess the resources necessary for travel, contacts in other regions and greater knowledge and know-how of life in the towns. Male out-migration from this group continued after 1940 but it was no longer predominant and the underlying motivation was more varied and multi-faceted: the search for higher education, adventure and experience of the world. The young single men were not pressed to support parents or siblings back home, but they were expected to help out with cash now and again.

Men from more privileged social backgrounds in Santiago tended to move to the larger towns in Mexico or the southern US where they looked for wage work. But despite their years of schooling and advantages (as seen through local eyes), the openings encountered by this group were relatively limited. Most Santiago men had to struggle to enter urban wage work and they began 'at the bottom', the majority remaining in unskilled or semi-skilled manual work with insecure employment conditions. Few found they could join a stable urban proletariat. Even fewer were able to achieve social mobility through higher education: one migrant rose to a senior position in the Ministry of Education and another became personnel manager in a large metallurgical consortium in Mexico City – both returned home to Santiago on retirement. But in general, migration to the towns led to a temporary, insecure or incomplete incorporation into the urban working class of Mexico or the US; contacts with Santiago were not broken.

The life and work histories of men from this group are complex and revealing. To exemplify the experiences of migrants from this social background the biography of Ramiro Espinoza has been selected.

Ramiro Espinoza, who later started Santiago's sweater industry, was born in Jacona in 1918 (while the bandit Chávez was sacking Santiago). He was taken by his parents to make a new life in California in 1924. The Espinozas had been traders; but then family members found themselves on opposite sides in the conflict between *agraristas* and *cristeros*, which prompted Ramiro's parents' decision to leave. Ramiro, his two younger brothers and sister spent their childhoods in the US, but only he attended school and learnt 'to speak like an American'. Ramiro's father found permanent waged employment, but in 1931 was killed in a motor accident. His widow came back to Santiago with the children and with the 4000 dollars she had received in compensation bought some land and cattle.

Ramiro had no wish to remain 'buried' in the backward Mexican countryside tending his mother's cows so he left 'without a coin' in his pocket and set off for Mexico City. As a fourteen year old, he found it hard to get work. He first made his way to the central market where he lived off scavaging and occasional portering jobs. Finally he managed to secure more permanent work as a chemist's assistant in a German-owned firm that manufactured patent medicines. The firm was shut down following Government expropriation during the Second World War and Ramiro went back to California in 1943, as an illegal immigrant. For the next ten years Ramiro worked as a foreman on the Southern Pacific Railroad; he never bothered to get his immigration papers and due to his 'good' American accent was never troubled by the immigration authorities. He interpreted his overseer position as one of protecting his gangs of illegal Mexican workers against the 'migra'.

Fed up with the spartan life as a railroad worker, Ramiro returned to Mexico in 1953 and married Alicia López, from

Zamora. They settled in Mexico City where Ramiro took a job as a machine operator in a box factory. Meanwhile, his younger brother Jesús had also come to try his luck in the city. He was living with an uncle and worked as a market seller, collecting ladies' underwear from factories for sale in the weekly markets around the capital. Through this work, Jesús was beginning to build up useful contacts in the garment sector. Recognising his own growing commercial flair, Ramiro's mechanical skill and Alicia's prowess on a sewing machine, Jesús proposed that they set up a family business in the capital to make sweaters. This project they began in 1954.

The character of the predominant migration flow from Santiago changed abruptly in 1940. Due to wartime labour shortage, the US Government signed an agreement with the Mexican Government to establish a Farm Labour Programme. Mexico was charged with recruiting and transporting workers to the border. Once across the border, the men were settled temporarily in camps (known as concentration camps) until they were contracted out to individual employers for stipulated periods of time. In Santiago as elsewhere, labour recruitment was put in the hands of the municipal council which illegally sold the contracts or distributed them among chosen clienteles.

A flood of impoverished men took advantage of the Bracero Program (as it became known) to earn money in the 'north'. Some took labour contracts for certain months each year, most alternated between taking formal contracts (and paying for them) and crossing the border illegally to look for work once they knew the ropes. Migration and agricultural wage work thus became available to a much wider social spectrum. But once again women and children remained in Santiago. The main variation in the migration experiences and patterns to be found among this group of men rested on the length of time they elected to remain away from home. But the following life history of a Santiago *bracero* is illustrative of many:

> Jaime Gonzáles, a married landless agricultural labourer, went to California every year between 1948 and 1956. When he could afford it, he bought a contract from the municipal council which charged some 300 pesos for a forty-five day contract and up to 1000 pesos for longer contracts. At other times, he went 'under the wire'. The men possessing labour contracts had to make their own way to collecting points (which could be as far from Santiago

as Monterrey) where they were loaded on to railway cattle trucks and dispatched with minimal food and water. Crossing the border entailed first the indignities of fumigation and delousing and generally humiliating treatment by the frontier guards and then the dawning realisation of the racial discrimination in the US against Mexicans.

On formal labour contracts, Jaime only once had a chance to intervene in the decision as to where he was sent to work; he volunteered to go to Fresno (because he thought that the place looked nice). Otherwise he was directed to perform all kinds of agricultural work for all kinds of employers. Sometimes he lived in crowded bunk houses full of violent men who were prepared to steal the shirt off his back. Once he found himself alone on an isolated farm with only dogs for company, the owner only coming once a week to give him instructions. Most of the time, Jaime worked for a daily wage of US$3 to 4 dollars from which some $1.50 was deducted for food.

As an illegal, Jaime only very occasionally made use of kin or social networks. Usually he travelled alone or with one companion, and every journey was fraught with danger. Everybody knew several men who had died on the journey. The illegal migrants had to walk huge distances to avoid the immigration authorities guarding roads and railway; they might spend two or three days without food or water crossing desert land; they had to learn how to find food 'off the land' and cure themselves when ill. During the 1940s the independent Mexican workers had been given a better reception, Jaime thought. At that time he used to walk from one farm to another looking for work and people were generally quite helpful and friendly; sometimes a car would stop to offer him a ride – though he never learnt to communicate in English. By the 1950s, he felt discrimination deepen; by then very few Americans were prepared to help a poor, ragged Mexican on the road.

For eight years in succession Jaime went north, returning home to visit his family for a few months at a time. He was never once given Social Security, though one US employer of Japanese extraction had been prepared to 'arrange his papers' so that he could become a legal immigrant. He was reluctant to do so partly as that would have meant confessing he was unable to read or write. Jaime was painfully conscious of his illiteracy and the problems this posed for maintaining contact with Genoveva, his wife. He sent small sums of money back with a note written by a friend. But when he had been incarcerated on the isolated farm, six months went by before he could get a note and money out. Similarly, he often had to wait some weeks before he encountered a Mexican he knew well enough to ask to read his wife's letters to him.

Jaime had never been a physically strong man and he had periodically suffered serious ill-health while in the US. His memories as a migrant veered from excitement to great anguish. He had felt guilty at leaving his wife, children and parents and had never been tempted to abandon them. He deeply resented how the Mexican state had been willing to 'sell' him and so many others to a foreign country and how the experience conspired to rob him of his own sense of dignity and worth. He went 'north' out of acute economic necessity and was relieved to end his migrant life when agricultural wage work opened up near to home. From 1957 he became an agricultural labourer in the Zamora valley which was rapidly developing strawberry production for export to the USA.

Labour contracting under the Bracero Program continued until 1964. It had opened the way to mass out-migration, but at least officially it was limited to only temporary durations. The US wages (however miserable they were in a US context) had attracted many to go north but heavy social and psychological costs were involved. This was a crude and violent form of labour contracting and largely through drinking men found some collective solace.

The lives of the women left behind were also harsh but their sufferings remained more hidden and individualised, and there were strong barriers preventing women from fully recognising and airing their grievances. The worlds of women and men had become very different. Genoveva, Jaime's wife, was very explicit about the hardships she suffered by being a migrant's wife:

> Genoveva had eloped with Jaime when she was fifteen years old, against her parents' wishes. As was customary she went to live in the house of her parents-in-law, being obliged to remain there after Jaime started his migrant life. Until Genoveva had borne three children, Jaime sent back the remittances always to his mother and since Genoveva's relations with her were strained, she found it difficult to get hold of any of the money returned. She lived as a virtual prisoner, not allowed to leave the house;

only once a month was she allowed to visit her own parents and then she was accompanied by a sister-in-law to ensure she did not gossip about her new family. Genoveva devoted all her energies to securing the survival of her growing number of children (fourteen pregnancies and ten surviving children). Jaime usually left her with maize grown on his *ecuaro* plot and some item that might be sold in case of emergency. Genoveva prided herself that she never had to sell, but always managed to make do. Jaime did not like handing money over to his wife, but whatever she was able to save, Genoveva put towards the purchase of a plot of land in order to get away from her mother-in-law's house.

Apart from Jaime's 'miserliness', Genoveva's complaints about being a migrant's wife revolved around two issues: her husband's addiction to drink during the months he spent in Mexico and the absence of communication when he was away (this not helped by Jaime's illiteracy). The direct problems arising from her poor relationship with her mother-in-law were difficult to tackle or express to her husband. By and large a situation of stalemate developed with Genoveva refusing to appreciate the dangers and difficulties faced by migrating men, and Jaime refusing to appreciate the difficulties of surviving at home.

By the time that strawberry production began in the Zamora valley Genoveva's eldest daughter was old enough to be left in charge of domestic work. This allowed Genoveva to take seasonal wage employment in the nearest strawberry packing plant, La Estancia, during three to four months of the year. And once the sweater workshops arrived, Genoveva was among the first to take on embroidery out-work.

The two migration streams that developed in the twentieth century showed the existence of different social classes in the country towns like Santiago. First, there were migrants who came from families still possessing resources – some plots of land, a few head of cattle and whose position of relative privilege was reflected in their higher educational level and in their better contacts and knowledge of the world outside. Some migrants from this propertied class became 'target workers', taking on wage work so as to earn enough to invest in and develop activities back home. But while some cattle owners fell into this category, there is little evidence to suggest that target work was a route taken by men who later became owners of the sweater workshops. Second, there were the migrants drawn from an impoverished, increasingly landless class who were already forced to sell their labour power and depend on wage employment. They were able to avoid agricultural labour in the US only when changes in the international division of labour brought US-style (and predominantly US-owned) agri-business within easy reach of Santiago, with the rise of strawberry production.

The two classes can be distinguished on the basis of access to means of production. But although the progressive impoverishment and loss of resources suffered by the one class could be laid squarely at the door of the emerging propertied class, busy accumulating and reorganising production along capitalist lines, these two classes had not been brought into open confrontation. There were several mechanisms that militated against this outcome. Chief among them was the intervention of male long-distance migration and semi-proletarianisation. Landless migrants on labour contracts were more likely to blame the Mexican state or US employers for their plight than local capitalising farmers, especially since they had often shared at one time or another an identity as 'foreign' migrants. The shared migration experience served to cut across and obscure local class differences and generate certain bonds and common interests among men. This gave some basis for understanding, if not unity. By the same token, migration and semi-proletarianisation drove a wedge into relations within households separating those who had migrated and worked under capitalism from those who had not. This meant that divisions of a different nature were being created and superimposed as between migrants and non-migrants, and thereby between men and women.

Although the people of Santiago could recount several cases of husbands and sons who had 'disappeared' in the north, none the less the overwhelming impression is of the tenacity shown by the people of Santiago towards the family as an institution. Some men had lived apart from their wives and children for over forty years (as Genoveva's father had done while working as a cook in Mexico City and the US) but had not failed to send money back. Though placed under great strain, the family appeared to be surviving.

FAMILY AND GENDER RELATIONS IN HISTORICAL PERSPECTIVE

The discussion of family and gender relations will focus primarily on the experiences of the grandparents' and parents' generations after they had abandoned the *ranchos* and had come to live in the small town of Santiago. Though kin and social networks were transferred from country to town as newcomers settled in the *barrio* 'belonging' to their former *rancho*, nevertheless, the move transformed much of the social and economic context of people's lives. Recapturing the content and quality of the 'old' life in the *ranchos* was extremely hard for those who had moved to town as children. Generally speaking peasants from the *ranchos* forced through impoverishment to move to town continued to lament the loss of their world, while the families of former hacienda *peónes* associated settlement in the town with some degree of emancipation. A short summary will be given of the main features of gender relations in rural areas as can be gleaned from statistical sources and from the comments made by the grandparents' generation. This will be followed by more detailed discussion of particular aspects of household and family relations in the town of Santiago before 1960.

HOUSEHOLD RELATIONS IN THE RANCHOS

Patrilocality had long been the custom in the countryside: women moved as brides to the houses of parents-in-law and stayed there for many years if not for the whole of their lives. Sons customarily worked alongside fathers. The relative position of women under patrilocality can be said to partly depend on age of marriage and on the degree of endogamy; a more favourable situation for women generally ensues when (i) the age of women's first marriage is relatively high, (ii) there is little age gap between the spouses, and (iii) where most marriages take place between people of the same community. Some estimation of these data can be discerned from the marriage registers of Santiago district.[9]

In the *ranchos* of Santiago women's age at first marriage was relatively high. From the earliest records of 1926 until 1960, the overall average age was 18.6 years though there were substantial annual variations over the period. In the decades up to 1950, the average age was around 19 years (the highest annual average being 19.8 years), but during the 1950s the average age dropped to just under 18 years (the lowest annual average being 17.6 years). Thus the average age of women's first marriage appears to have been declining – the change taking place during the 1950s prior to the establishment of the sweater-industry. The men they married were some three years older. The average age of men at first marriage was 21.7 years and although the annual average varied over the years, this was less marked than in the case of the women. The registers reveal in addition, that there had always been a number of women who married men younger than themselves.

With regard to endogamy, the records suggest that the majority of women married men born and raised in the same *rancho* as themselves. Presumably as wives they came to live not so far away from their own parents and siblings. This pattern, however, varied markedly over time. During the 1930s only 60 per cent of *rancho* women married men from their own *rancho* and marriage patterns tended to reflect the social turbulence and population mobility of the time. Later the percentage of endogamous marriages rose to between 80 and 90 per cent during the 1940s but fell again during the 1950s to around 75 per cent. All but a very few who married men from outside their *rancho* stayed within the district.

The grandmothers of the present day who married into relatively wealthy independent peasant families in the *ranchos* look back with nostalgia to those days. They had generally not been allowed by their parents to marry until they were experienced in all aspects of women's domestic labour. Acquisition of these skills marked the transition from girlhood to womanhood, and furthermore a girl's mother wanted to retain her daughter's assistance for as long as possible. In addition, young women were expected to take with them the domestic articles they would require in their new homes. Both these factors tended to result in the relatively late marriage of women, some years after puberty.

Although young brides were brought to live in the household of their parents-in-law, among the wealthier strata there was usually place enough for a son and his new wife to set up a 'sub-household'. The three generational households resembled compounds where each son and his wife lived in their own room and cooked on their own hearth. Elderly women remembered enjoying their early married years as each couple had 'a nest of its own'. In these extended households, men tended to labour in common in the fields to provide the bulk of the foodstuffs needed. Under the authority of the father, food was distributed to each sub-group living in the household. Thus the chief responsibility of men was to ensure sufficient production of the staples, maize and beans, and maybe also milk for household consumption. The chief responsibility of women was to transform and process the produce into food, and women's independent activities could include pig and chicken rearing in the compound.

While men's work was generally collective, women's work tended to be individualised; there was little sharing of tasks among daughters-in-law or between them and their mothers-in-law and sisters-in-law. Each wife assisted by her older daughters ground the maize daily by hand and made the day's ration of *tortillas*. After their preparation, wives would generally take the midday meal out to their husbands where they were working in the fields, and then stay to work in the fields before returning home. Though virtually all women made this contribution to agricultural production, it was not depicted as 'work'. Some women talked of helping out, most recalled it as an enjoyable break from domestic labour.

HOUSEHOLD RELATIONS AFTER RESETTLEMENT IN THE TOWN

Growing Up in Santiago: Girl's Work before Marriage

The vast majority of the women of the Santiago *barrios* had worked for cash remuneration before marriage. Those who had not directly earned money usually explained how they had been obliged to take over the bulk of the domestic labour in order to release their mothers or sisters for income earning work. Settlement in the town had been accompanied by a certain commoditisation of women's domestic work. In one variant, girls from poorer families went to work for the señoras of wealthier families; and though this was in effect employment of one class of women by another, recruitment and the ensuing relationship between señora and servant was usually couched in terms of kin or social ties. In the second variant, domestic labour was exchanged among women from the same impoverished class and cash was used occasionally in compensation when this was more convenient than an exchange of goods. Only latterly in the

1950s did a third variant appear: women's work purchased by outside capital and reimbursed with cash wages.

Girls were put to work by their mothers from when they were some nine years old; for the vast majority, this meant the end of any hope of schooling. Cash returns to girls' work were derisory. As one woman commented: 'We had no idea how to charge in those days. I could spend a whole month embroidering and get a handful of centavos at the end of it.' Most girls could only hope to earn sufficient to buy some cloth to make new clothes for the annual feast of the town, and so relieve their mothers of this burden.

From the 1930s to 1960 there were four main types of activity where unmarried girls might find employment: domestic manufacturing, domestic servicing, agricultural labouring and, beginning in the 1950s, out-work.

Domestic manufacturing

This type of work had the advantage that girls did not have to leave their own house. There were several possibilities. Wealthier women placed orders with poor women with several daughters at home especially for embroidery. A few girls from basket-making families surreptitiously learnt the craft and sold their output via brothers or fathers. Food processing and preparation was often done by young unmarried women for neighbours; girls might grind maize or make *tortillas* for a neighbouring wife whose work took her away from home (e.g. clothes washing).

Domestic servicing

This work was usually undertaken by poorer girls for wealthier women; it was less often exchanged among the poor. Some girls did general housework and though cash payment was small, many recorded the importance their mothers gave to the food they could consume in the wealthier house. A few señoras were prepared to allow 'their' girls to attend school (El Colegio, run by nuns) so long as they worked for them before and afterwards. Occasionally an exceptionally diligent pupil would be offered work as a living-in servant at El Colegio in order to continue to study up to the end of primary level. Only on very rare occasions did young women leave Santiago to work as domestic servants elsewhere. Virginia (now a workshop owning wife) had this experience.

Virginia's father died when she was seven years old leaving nine children. She went out to work first with rich señoras in the town, then as her elder brother wanted to train for the priesthood, she and her younger sister were sent as servants to work in the seminaries of Jacona and Zamora so as to pay for his education. Virginia was twelve years old when she began work in Jacona and twenty-four years old by the time her brother had finished his studies.

Agricultural labouring
Some young girls from Santiago found paid work in the fields before the 1950s even though this was seen as 'men's work' and it was more difficult to supervise and protect them. But necessity sometimes pushed widows and wives to take on agricultural day labouring with all their children. With the rise of strawberry production in the Zamora valley in the late 1950s, fathers often took all their children with them as labourers.

Out-work
During the early 1950s, shawl production was revived in Zamora. A Santiago man who had settled there started to bring silk shawls to the town and distribute them among women for finishing and fringe plaiting. Many young girls found themselves sitting and plaiting the fine black, silk threads of the shawls, especially for poor widowed mothers. The work was intricate, time-consuming and ruinous of eyesight; a 'family' of women was usually able to finish one shawl per day, for which they were paid 75 centavos. In this case also, the activity had the perceived advantage of being undertaken at home.

Courtship and Marriage under Gender Segregation

One reason behind the greater demand for young women's domestic labour in town was the tendency towards the greater seclusion of women. There was nothing new about women's seclusion in Hispanic society especially in this most conservative, catholic region of Mexico. The years of banditry and social upheaval had only made the tendency more pronounced. Women from wealthier families rarely left their houses. This was made possible when domestic work outside the house (especially fetching the daily water requirements in huge earthenware pots from the town's springs and washing clothes and household articles) could be handed over to other women. Seclusion was a highly 'visible' signifier of status but only for a minority of families.

The majority of urban families needed daughters to perform the heavy domestic labour that took them outside the house and this over-rode other social pressures. Since seclusion was an impossibility for most, then extreme gender segregation was the next best option. This found expression in the inordinate fear parents had of their daughters' contact with men. But the greater the enforcement of gender segregation, the more explosive the situation was to become. The worst fears of parents came to pass in Santiago in the 1950s: the years of the 'robberies'. Before discussing these, the earlier history of courtship and marriage will be explored using the statistical evidence available in the marriage registers and points made in women's life histories.

Analysis of age of first marriage of women from Santiago town shows a bi-modal distribution prevailing in the 1930s to late 1940s. This meant that women tended to marry either when they were between sixteen or seventeen years old or when they were around twenty-two years old; relatively few women married while they were between eighteen and twenty years of age. It appears from informants' comments that contradictory pressures surrounded the age of women's marriage in the 1930s and 1940s. Many parents still wished to arrange marriages for their children or at least determine the age at which daughters should marry. By and large parents pressed for daughters to remain relatively long at home before marriage: not only were traditions of the *ranchos* perpetuated in the town but the cash earnings and domestic labour of older daughters were increasingly important for the survival of parents' households especially when men were dead or absent. However, despite extremely intense supervision and protection of unmarried daughters, there were still possibilities open for independent contact with men.

There were two recognised meeting places for the young: the spring and the church. Men looked for possible brides among the girls fetching water from the *barrios*' springs. As each *barrio* had its own water source, this meeting place had the advantage of keeping contact within the *barrio* community. Just as marriage in the *ranchos* had been generally endogamous, this pattern was carried over into the town. Up until recent years, cross-*barrio* marriage brought social condemnation. The other meeting places were connected with the Church. Virtually the whole population attended Mass on Sunday evenings and might then take a turn around the Plaza in family groups. Here initial contact could be made, and it could be furthered during the annual religious pilgrimages organised on the basis of the *barrios*.

Fetching water from the spring and the pilgrimage usually gave rise to the first meeting with a future husband. But gender segregation put almost insurmountable obstacles in the way of courtship. Maybe a few whispered words could be exchanged, or a purchased 'love note' left in a secret place. But courtship was more or less confined to looking, though while a man could look at a woman, she was not supposed to return the attention. Parents, grandmothers and older siblings were constantly on the watch and daughters were beaten savagely for any encouragement given to a suitor. After the minimal and most secret contact a young man presented himself to the parents to ask for the hand of their daughter. Though families in the town knew of each other, the young couple would marry as virtual strangers.

In contrast to the heavily controlled 'formal' courtship there had long been a counter current most strongly associated with indigenous society. Couples did defy a woman's parents and mutually agree to elope; it was a common occurrence particularly among young girls of particularly harsh, brutal parents.

> Jaime had first seen Genoveva collecting water at the spring, and for months had watched her go to and from Church with her mother and siblings. Her mother was extremely strict. As Genoveva was only occasionally allowed out of the house he had given her a purchased love-note a couple of times. She was fourteen years old when at the celebrations of the feast of Santiago, she walked with her sister once around the Plaza to see the lights and the stalls and came back with confetti in her hair. Furious that she must have flirted with the young men, her mother hit her hard in public and took the whole family home as a punishment. Genoveva, mortified, got a message to Jaime appealing to him to take her away. They eloped and were married immediately by a civil ceremony, her mother refusing to attend. Reconciliation with her family took six months, after which the marriage was celebrated in the church.

The records suggest that women's age of marriage in Santiago changed abruptly in the early 1950s. No longer can any bi-modal distribution be detected, instead a skewed normal curve shows that the majority of women married between the ages of sixteen and seventeen years of age. Furthermore, the evidence shows that the overall average age of marriage in the town was now lower than in the *ranchos* (the opposite of what had been the case in the previous decades). These data alone suggest that a major change had taken place in courtship and marriage.

The 1950s and early 1960s are remembered in Santiago as in many other parts of Michoacán as the years of the 'robberies'. Though elopement with mutual consent had previously been given the name of 'robbery', now this meant abduction by force. For the women who were robbed, it was the most traumatic event of their lives. Two experiences of robbery will be given in detail: Concha and Amalia.

>Concha, now in her fifties, recalls how she was robbed at the age of fourteen years; the same week eight other girls were carried off at gunpoint. Her family had been relatively prosperous before the deaths of her father and eldest brother; and she still lived with her mother and sisters in the large family house near the Plaza. They continued to farm and tend their dairy cattle. Sometimes she sold milk to neighbours from the front room of the house and this was where her abductor first saw her.
>
>Though he was the son of a neighbour, he had lived in the US for the previous six years and she did not recognise him. He was twenty years old and made a deep impression on her; she was conscious of him gazing at her from street corners. But frightened of his attentions she refused to work in the shop alone again. In the shop he asked her sisters where the beautiful girl with the long plaits had gone. When she found out his identity she lost interest. With hindsight Concha rationalised that her family had disapproved of his brother for beating his wife and she had promised her mother to have nothing to do with the family. At this stage Concha talked to her mother about his unwanted attentions. They took the threat seriously, especially as there was no father or brothers to protect her. Concha's mother locked the children up in the house when she went out. But then the family heard that the man had gone to Mexico City and they thought they could relax their guard.
>
>When Concha was returning with her mother from collecting water and were just passing the church deep in conversation, two

men came up beside them. They said 'Good evening' and then one grabbed Concha, saying 'By your leave Señora' to her mother. Concha threw the pitcher of water at her abductor and her mother threw herself at him to free Concha. But five masked men stepped out from behind the bushes, restrained the mother and allowed the man to escape with Concha. He carried her off to the hills on horseback where his father was waiting. The father asked Concha whether she was willing to marry his son and she, terrified, agreed. She then spent the night in the father's house and was married at a small civil ceremony early next morning.

Concha's mother came to her neighbour's house where her daughter was held mid-morning. After the abduction she had rushed to Zamora to bring back police with her, knowing that the local police had been paid off in advance not to intervene. She claimed that the marriage was illegal as Concha was under age and refused to give her consent to it. Meanwhile Concha was locked in a room. First she talked to her 'husband's' mother and then to her own. Her 'husband's' mother explained that her son really loved her and wanted to look after her; she also warned that although many men might think her beautiful and want to go with her, none would marry her after this disgrace. Her own mother showed her an alternative was possible. Concha could go immediately to Durango where she had relatives and settle there so nobody would know her past. Already there was a car waiting in Zamora for her escape. She said she would give Concha half an hour to decide; she would not oppose the marriage if that was what she really wanted, but she insisted she should feel no obligation to marry.

Concha weighed up her future. She remembered that the man had sworn in front of the police that no matter where she hid he would pursue her till he found her. He had also publicly declared that he would marry nobody else. In the end with a heavy heart she agreed to a church marriage. Concha remained in the house of her husband's parents until the wedding. On the night of the wedding she saw that two pistols had been left out in her husband's room and felt an overwhelming urge to kill the man she had just married. But there were four brothers in the house, and she knew she would never get out alive. Her husband watched her look at the guns then picked them up and locked them away in his trunk.

Concha recognised that there was a deep division within herself;

all her life she felt angry at her 'capture' and 'robbery' but admitted that her husband had been a good and loving man though life had become hard when he had taken to drink. He respected her. He was handsome, well dressed, from a wealthy family. He was affectionate and considerate towards her. Until he started drinking, all his earnings he handed over to her and he taught her how to cook, iron, do housework – skills she had never properly learnt but which he had mastered during his six years in the USA. Concha thought she could have done a lot worse: many girls in that period were being abducted by 'Indians'.

Amalia's history was quite different from Concha's:

Amalia, now in her early forties, was born into a poor family. Her father had been a hacienda *peón* in Jerusalem but received no land after the expropriation and had moved into town from where he worked as an agricultural labourer. Amalia was rarely allowed to go out of the house except to Mass. She was nineteen years old and was secretly courted by a man from her *barrio* when a stranger whom she was not aware of ever having seen before carried her off on horseback from the doorway of her house. He rode with her to his parents' house in a different *barrio*, banged on the door and said to his father: 'I've brought Amalia'. The man then rode away and Amalia spent the night under his father's roof. For the next nine months she lived with his married sister as her own father would not have a disgraced daughter back but by this time her abductor had regretted his 'capricious whim'. Finally both sets of parents forced them to marry and after two years living in his parents' house, Amalia's husband went to the US and did not communicate with her for the next nine years.

In the 1950s and 1960s abduction was widespread. Santiago people now claim that the violence had been worse in other places: men did not dare take their young wives out of the house, they said, in places such as Cienega or La Barca (on the Michoacán/Jalisco border) for fear of them being raped. Local people are also certain that abduction by force occurred in Santiago only for a particular span of time, dying out during the 1960s.

It seems logical to suggest that the diminishing age of women's marriage in the marriage records of the 1950s was a direct outcome of the prevalence of abduction. Parents did not dare risk their own or their daughters' honour by delaying marriage. So even when women did not experience the trauma of robbery, they tended to start out in married life younger than their own mothers and grandmothers and having been more 'sheltered' by them.

The life stories given above suggest that abduction lay behind an increase in feuding. Some men colluded with each other with respect to the robberies. Sons were supported by fathers who could buy the silence of local male authorities. But blood feuds could well develop for the sake of an abducted daughter or sister. Though as in Amalia's case, fathers tended to push for the marriage of a disgraced daughter, relations with the abducting family could be strained to breaking point. In the face of male violence, mothers increased their guard and vigilance of daughters, married them off at an earlier opportunity and only very occasionally (as in the example of Concha's mother) struggled to find an alternative for an abducted daughter.

In speculating about the robberies, one is tempted to see them as an echo or reverberation of the chaos and disruption of society. Endemic violence sanctioned in so many other areas of life had come to pervade and brutalise relations of gender inside local society (outsiders such as soldiers, bandits and hacendados had long been guilty of raping and abducting women). Thus one can point to the propensity for violence as a backdrop to the outbreak of the abductions by force. Men had been socially permitted to develop ways of thought and modes of behaviour that were more in line with cruder expressions of 'machismo'. Women were turned into victims prior to becoming wives and marriage relations were more greatly infused by force and brutality.

But one can also suggest that the rise of the abductions was connected with the intensification of male migration to the US. In the first place, men went young to work in the north, they returned infrequently and tended to lose contact with their home society. As few women of Santiago origin were encountered in the north, young migrants had to search for brides during their brief visits home. However, given the seclusion of women, they could not hope to select a bride through any open courtship. In the second place, the US had become a place of escape for men; they could easily disappear north instead of living with the consequences of irresponsible actions. Third, the migration experience itself enhanced the more brutal forms of machismo already rooted in society. Working and living conditions of Mexican men in the US were dangerous and humiliating;

migration was a brutalising experience and had repercussions on how men behaved towards women.

The numbers of abductions were diminishing during the 1960s and ended around 1970. What brought the robberies to an end? There were several civilising tendencies at work, especially in the spread of education. Important though these influences were one should not let it obscure how women reacted against their role as 'victims' and fought back. Mothers fought on through their daughters and daughters drew on the experiences of their mother's generation to refuse a 'victim' role. This resistance was assisted by the rise of wage work for women and the opening of the sweater workshops.

Patrilocality in the Context of Urban Life

Abandonment of the *ranchos* and resettlement in a Santiago *barrio* changed the type of residence, but the tradition of patrilocality was transferred from countryside to town. What this meant for most women was an early married life in a corner of a poor cramped house, usually sharing a hearth with their mothers-in-law, husbands' sisters and the wives of their husbands' brothers. Furthermore, young wives were more often left alone in their in-laws' houses under the ever-watchful eye of the mother-in-law while husbands went 'north'.

> Beatríz moved to the house of her parents-in-law after she married at the age of nineteen years. There she lived for nine years with three other daughters-in-law. The women shared a kitchen, each having a small space to keep their food and all shared the fireplace to heat *tortillas*. But they never prepared food together although they cooked and ate in the same room. She felt a prisoner not being allowed out to see her mother and there were many conflicts and tensions in the household.
>
> Maria lived four years with her mother-in-law after marrying at sixteen years. She remembers being shocked for she had not realised that families had such different customs. The couple had a tiny room as had the other son and his wife. But the father-in-law slept in the corridor outside their rooms – this she felt was very strange. All the women of the household shared the kitchen, but young wives had to wait until after the mother-in-law had finished cooking before they could prepare their husbands' food. Sometimes when the mother-in-law went out, she put out the

fire so no *tortillas* could be warmed until she returned. María tried to break down the barriers by offering food to the others, but this was never welcomed. A timid, nervous woman she never answered back while living with her parents-in-law but deeply resented their treatment of her and their refusal to let her see her own family.

After Amalia was married by force, she felt rejected by her parents-in-law. Her mother-in-law continued to prepare food for her son, but did not offer her any. Her husband rarely gave her money and was seldom in the house. Every day, Amalia had to escape to her own parents' house where she was given *tortillas* to take back. On occasions her husband took Amalia back to her parents saying he did not want her any longer, but her father forced her to go back to her husband. She returned to her mother to give birth to her first child, but had to go back again to her husband. By the time Amalia was pregnant again, her husband went north; they had been married two years. When no money came to support Amalia, her parents-in-law threw her out and she was able to move back to her parents' house.

Only very infrequently could young wives move to a house of their own; Concha, despite being abducted, was one of the fortunate few. And only a tiny minority of wives seem to have forged affectionate and lasting relationships with their mothers-in-law. Wives endured many years living with their parents-in-law; four, nine or twelve years even when relations were sour. Not only was it economically beyond the means of young couples to acquire a plot of land and build a separate house, migrant men and their mothers refused to let wives live independently. The older generation considered it 'natural' that sons should live with them and were affronted by any plans they might have to move away. The eventual separation was often intensely conflict-ridden.

The response of women to this continuation of patrilocality in the town was that they scrimped and saved every centavo they could especially of the money sent back from the US. They cut back on food, especially their own consumption, in order to put aside enough money to win their liberation from their parents-in-law. But to do this they had to confront their husbands as to the distribution of cash within the household.

Changes in the Distribution of Goods and Cash within the Household

Increasing landlessness, the move to the town, expansion of the cash economy and labour migration to the US all carried far-reaching implications for the way goods and services were exchanged in households. By changing the terms of intra-household exchange, pressures were also put on the conjugal relationship. The intra-household distribution of cash had become an extremely sensitive issue and was a major battleground between men and women.

When families resettled in town, households could no longer function as a unit of production and consumption as they had done previously in the *rancho*. There was no complete break, however. Sons might continue to help their fathers as share croppers or on an *ejido* plot or by sowing an *ecuaro*. But this often demanded seasonal rather than full-time labour and could only provide limited output. There was still consensus generally as to the obligation of men to produce and hand over maize and beans for family subsistence. The problem arose as to how the ever more vital cash was earned and distributed. The conflict was played out partly between generations (mothers and daughters-in-law) and partly between husbands and wives.

With respect to relations between husbands and wives, it appears that two contrasting patterns had grown up earlier in response to the expansion of the cash economy. In some cases, men handed over their entire cash earnings to wives for them to administer: this pattern was more common where men took local wage work and did not go to the US.

> After Olivia and her husband moved from *rancho* Jerusalem into town, they continued the practice they had started in the country. Her husband gave her all his earnings from agricultural labouring and she handed back a small sum for him to spend on himself. As he neither drank nor gambled, he only required 'pocket money' for cigarettes. Olivia recalls that he was 'a fine man' and they never quarrelled over money.

In other cases, men insisted that their sole marital obligation was to provide maize and beans and that cash earned by each partner remained individual, not family property. Again this pattern could really only be maintained where men stayed in local wage work or could sell agricultural produce and where married women could also get access to cash.

> Marta, now in her late 60s, and her husband have always possessed separate funds. She has found ways of earning money in the town (having a small front-room shop and embroidering)

while her husband, a share-cropper, managed to sell some surplus and with the cash pay for his own clothes, drink and tobacco.

Neither of these two contrasting patterns of intra-familial cash distribution provided an appropriate model for households where men left for long periods to work in the US. While most migrant men considered they should have full control over the money they earned at the cost of such hardship and humiliation, their wives also believed they had rights to this cash as it was a family resource. This was especially true when wives had given the money a man needed to travel north or buy a labour contract. Wives considered that financial reimbursement from their husbands was a just reward for their own difficulties and sufferings while their men were away. Though most men tried to send a trickle of money back to their wives when they could, they liked to return to Santiago with a large sum.

The struggle between men and women over migrants' earnings often resulted in an oscillating distribution pattern. Men emphasised their right of control over money by alternating between giving and denying wives a share. The legitimation for this in the eyes of male society was that men should be free to pursue their vices: drinking and gambling. Among informants whose husbands took part in the Bracero Program some 15 per cent of husbands were without vices who regularly handed over all or most of the cash they earned; some 20 per cent received virtually no cash from their husbands, and the rest were forced into the most insecure position, sometimes receiving cash and sometimes not. As Beatríz put it: 'There was no tradition here that said wives had any right to their husbands' money; and they always complained of how their wives misspent what they were given.'

The contrasting patterns of cash distribution inherited from earlier times overlaid by the spread of labour migration to the US created many contradictions and confusions that found expression at an ideological plane as well as in everyday life. There was no clarity as to who was 'a good man' or 'a good parent'. If a man handed over his earnings to his wife, then he was seen as a responsible husband and parent, but he would tend to lose face within migrant male society as he had allowed his wife to 'dominate and give the orders'. But men who withheld money from their families so as to pursue their vices, ignoring their wives' and children's distress also risked losing social respect as they were no longer benevolent heads of household.

Ramiro Espinoza, a notorious drinker for many years of his life, described Santiago as 'one hell of a town' in the 1950s and 1960s. There were bars everywhere and men were frequently shooting each other in the streets. Few could remember when and how they started drinking or when they changed from being an occasional drinker to being an habitual drunk. But most men had started to drink in the US and had joined in the drinking bouts when men returned home to Santiago with money.

Concha's husband had been respectful and affectionate for the first ten years of their married life; but during his first visits to the US began to drink. Most of the time he still managed to send a little money back to her from the US (except when he lived with another woman for one and a half years). But in Santiago he gave her no money when he was drinking. Drinking spells could last several months. He shouted a lot at her when drunk but never hit her. She hated the drunkenness but then increasingly felt sorry for him.

While Socorro's father was in the north, her mother saved all the money he sent so as to buy a plot of land. This she planted with cane – a long and difficult enterprise. But when her husband returned he sold the cane and spent the proceeds on drink. He then divided up the land she had bought and sold it using the proceeds once again to finance his drinking.

Susanna's husband had been going north from when he was 15 years old and had worked all over the US. After they married he went north mostly at harvest time but usually returned with no money whatsoever as he had drunk his wages in the US. There was not even enough to pay off the debt for the ticket she had bought him to get to the border.

When a husband developed 'vices', the security of the whole family was put in jeopardy. Nevertheless women carried on saving what they could from the money handed over by husbands.

By the 1960s family incomes were rising and even poor women were improving their houses and acquiring basic household goods that had not been seen outside the wealthier social strata before. They bought beds for the first time, chairs, wardrobes, metal kitchen utensils and pans, plastic buckets to carry water and clothes. They also put cash into savings; carrying on the tradition of raising pigs to sell at a time when they needed immediate access to cash.

Though women claimed cash from husbands their rights of access were highly insecure. Men were killed or maimed or went 'missing' in the US; only some were on US Social Security; there was a strong likelihood husbands would turn out to be drunkards or gamblers, or become extremely mean about money. Most women were in reality pushed into the position of being responsible for raising the cash the household needed for daily survival at least some of the time. Wives struggled to find cash earning activities for themselves and their daughters.

Most women brought up in the town worked for cash returns before marriage and as wives they continued to do so. Domestic manufacturing undertaken by wives included the preparation of more elaborate food products. These might be sold from the house or taken round the neighbourhood by young children in wheel barrows. Clothes were made for sale as well as embroidery done. A few married women took on residential domestic work with rich families in Zamora, while their mothers looked after the children. Many wives took in washing, some worked an *ecuaro* or were employed as agricultural labourers. They also continued to take in out-work, though often in secret from their husbands. Wives struggled to earn cash so as to lessen their impoverishment and their dependence on the fortunes and whims of husbands.

Beatríz stressed how mortified she felt asking her husband for cash. Her husband was by no means a poor man; he earned well from the agricultural land he owned and found comparatively well paid jobs in the US. Yet he refused to give her a regular sum for house-keeping. She continued sewing and embroidering for sale all her married life so as to avoid the quarrels that inevitably followed her requests for money.

Angelina who had been an out-worker adorning shawls before marriage insisted on carrying on after despite her husband's opposition. She continued sewing and plaiting shawl fringes with her unmarried sister and taking her share of the proceeds. She confessed that the enjoyment of the work and the companionship were as important to her as the money it brought in. As her husband was often away, in the sugar harvest at Los Reyes or the US, it was not hard to conceal her income from him. He had never brought in enough money to meet the household expenses and she felt morally justified in defying him. Even now, when Angelina and her husband are both in their late sixties, the memory of her insistence on continuing to work is a source of pride.

Out-work for shawl manufacturers was the first 'new' employment opportunity for women in Santiago, and it was greeted by men's opposition even though the work was done in seclusion at home. Men had not intervened previously to oppose women's income earning activities when these were connected with the exchange of domestic goods and services whether this took place across class lines or through networks of women of the same class. Taking in out-work from a male intermediary, even though a local man, was work different in meaning from that identified under the heading of domestic labour. Men were uncertain about it.

Once women had managed to extricate themselves from the house of their parents-in-law and a daughter was old enough to make the daily *tortillas* and look after younger siblings, then wives were pressing to take on a wider range of work as and when it became available. Married women whose husbands were in the north were amongst the first to take work in the strawberry packing plants in the Zamora valley; only later did this become more solidly identified with being 'daughter's work'.

Gender Relations within Marriage and Parenting

The quality that women in the grandmothers' and mothers' generations stressed time and again in family relationship was respect: from husbands, children and society at large. Without respect, many women said love and affection was impossible. It was seen as a natural right for all who had been decently brought up; they did not feel they should earn it in adulthood through any specific way of behaviour. Only by overturning the conventions set by society would they risk losing it. This way of evaluating respect was important for it allowed women to hold on to an ideal of moral righteousness in the face of social upheaval and their husbands' failings. But if women found it heartbreaking living with feckless, disrespectful husbands, men could also find it hard living with self-righteous women who constantly called the Virgin of Guadalupe to their side. The potential polarisation in terms of the right to and negation of respect constituted another battleground in marital life.

Many of the mothers' generation had been married young and even when not actually victims of robberies, they were 'innocent' at marriage. As young wives, most had had to suffer their husbands' long absences and their brief return as virtual strangers who still expected their wives' sexual compliance. This seems to have provoked great tensions. But it took a very strong minded woman to refuse to have sex with a returning husband, no matter how many years he had been away.

When Amalia's husband returned to Santiago after nine years, she consented to go with him to a hotel in Zamora because he was still her husband. A third child was conceived, but he later refused to accept paternity.

The repressed yearnings and frustrations of migrants' wives were compounded by prevailing attitudes towards women's sexuality. Many had to confront daily allegations as to their infidelity levelled by fathers-in-law in particular and often repeated by their husbands once they returned. For some women, a husband's jealousy was the worst and most dangerous vice of all. Men's demand to control their wives' sexuality seems to have become more violent when men could no longer hope to act as heads of household as under the old agrarian regime. Migrants could not protect their wives' or daughters' virtue. Furthermore, a woman's passivity towards a returning 'strange' husband could be interpreted as an indication of submission to other men.

Beatriz suffered acutely from her husband's jealousy; she would have preferred him to have been a drunkard or a gambler like her own father. All their married life he accused her of going with other men, of being an old whore. He constantly foul-mouthed her to his family who spread the rumours about her infidelity.

Men's jealousy and drinking have gone hand in hand with physical violence. Many wives were beaten up by their husbands and there was a comparatively large group of battered wives from the mothers' generation forced to 'accept' the frequent beatings. Some women saw male violence as being directed towards them particularly as reproducers: pregnant women often being in greater danger of attack. Even if this was not so prevalent as some women made out, their interpretation is of interest in itself.

The response of many women had been to seek the solace of religion. Women especially from the poorer parts of town frequently attended daily prayer meetings held in neighbours' houses. Women prayed their men would mend their ways; but this religious forum did not permit women to take a more firm or confrontational stance. Women were born to suffer, that was the message that catholicism continued to preach. The struggle for respect was not conducive to the formation of any kind of women's solidarity to confront male violence or irresponsibility. Battered women did not receive much support from neighbours or even from their own family.

In contrast to the histories of violence, one can point to a handful of older couples who openly profess their 'luck' at finding each other and say they have lived happy and fulfilled married lives. In most of these cases husbands never went north to work and never developed 'vices'. But no wife no matter how 'fortunate' saw herself as occupying a position equal to her husband in the household. As Socorro remarked: 'The husband is like the President in the family; he is the boss but I am his second in command.' Nevertheless much stress was put on the importance of mutual respect between husband and wife, and on the unity and complementarity of gender roles in the household.

The relationship of couples forced into prolonged separation through labour migration inevitably became attenuated and distorted. The majority of women of the mothers' generation saw themselves as having been 'unlucky' in marriage, but with no other option but to carry on. Divorce in Santiago is still out of the question; men abandon wives by 'disappearing' in the US, but wives at home cannot abandon husbands. Wives locked into unsatisfactory marriages have had two responses. The first has been to take on an identity as suffering victims throughout their lives. The other has been to transfer desires and yearnings to motherhood. The two responses are linked, and together with the pursuit of social respect in a highly catholicised culture make up a form of female behaviour described sometimes as 'marianismo' – the counterpart of 'machismo'.

Women from the mothers' generations bore large numbers of children; many more than in previous generations survived to adulthood. The mothers whose life histories are recorded in this book (and who have reached the end of their child-bearing years) produced on average ten surviving children after fourteen to sixteen pregnancies.

It was not possible to draw conclusions about how husbands and wives have viewed fertility or explore divisions between them as to the desired number of children. In explaining their own views some women took refuge in the Catholic teachings, saying that it was sinful to limit conception as the Bible taught that God wanted people to multiply. By doing this, they could also legitimise their own desire to produce large numbers of children. Other women said that in a 'machista' society it was always the men who wanted many children so as to carry on their families' names.

The impression given by a mass of indirect evidence was that women of the mothers' generation actively wanted large families but they were rarely entirely passive to God's or their husbands' wills. Many reasons can be given as to why child bearing was important to them. Children could give them greater 'presence' in their mother-in-law's houses and eventually could be used to justify separation to form their own households. Child bearing showed that some semblance of family life prevailed despite social breakdown. Women used children to make their husbands feel involved in the household. Children gave women an important weapon to wield so as to get cash from husbands. Some women claimed they never thought of the financial expenditures required to raise children. But even where women did begin to calculate the burden of child raising, they still did not necessarily opt to have smaller families.

Eva disputed that the money saved by parents in having smaller families would ever benefit women. She saw that men only spent the money saved on themselves to drink or gamble more. Women might well be financially better-off bearing more children and forcing their husbands to hand over more cash.

Very few men revealed their thoughts about fertility: possibly their views were more equivocal than their wives believed.

Ramiro possibly spoke for many when he talked of the frustration he felt when confronting his wife's desire for children. Ramiro, brought up in California and married late, claimed he had wanted an 'American-style' family of two children. But his wife refused to 'protect herself' on the grounds that God would punish them by taking away the two first-born. She went on to have sixteen pregnancies from which twelve children survived. The main reason Ramiro put forward for his lack of financial success as a workshop owner was the size of his family.

The violence of men in the fathers' generation towards pregnant women and their frequent challenges to wives as to the children's paternity perhaps point to men's deep anger at being locked into a society that put strong cultural emphasis on procreation at a time when the continuity of family life was deeply threatened.

For women, the survival of many children has been double edged. Emotional satisfaction may have been won but the costs have been high. For mothers, the struggle to feed, clothe and educate large numbers of children has placed enormous burdens on them and they must seek remunerative work for virtually the whole of their lives.

Mothers seek strong enduring relationships with children as they grow up but greater authority and protection can usually be exerted over unmarried daughters than over sons. However, patrilocality has always meant that marriage brought a violent rupture in mother–daughter relationships. Grandmothers and mothers recall the enormous bitterness of this separation, especially cruel in the cases when daughters faced ill-treatment after marriage. But few women of the mothers' generation felt they were able to overturn the conventions even though they brought such pain. In this the powerful self-image of the 'suffering woman' played a reinforcing role. Terrible and poignant histories were recounted by some mothers over the fate of their daughters.

> Olivia wept and cursed as she remembered her 'robbed' daughter, Amalia's treatment at the hands of her husband and parents-in-law; yet at the time she had not stood up to her husband to offer Amalia any refuge until after she had been abandoned.
>
> For Beatríz the fate of her eldest daughter was still uppermost in her mind. When she went to visit her brother in Tijuana she 'came to grief' by getting pregnant. After giving birth to a daughter she married an older man from the *rancho* Jerusalem who was told the whole story of her past. Later the husband tried to drown his step-daughter in the well, fighting off his own mother. The mother managed to save the child, who was sent to live with Beatríz. The husband frequently knifed and beat his wife and ill treated their two children. Her health suffered severely and she developed heart problems. Beatríz managed to get her away from her husband and to Guadalajara for medical attention. Afterwards she tried to insist she recuperate in her house, but the husband came for her. Beatríz was too frightened to prevent him from taking her back to Jerusalem where she died. Beatríz knew that the husband had killed her, but never complained to the authorities 'through fear'. The husband took another wife and forbad Beatríz to see her two grandchildren.

Economic and Social Relations before 1960   73

WOMEN AS A POTENTIAL LABOUR SUPPLY

One aim of this chapter has been to offer some insight into the intense and dramatic way that people in a rural district of Mexico have been exposed to and thrown around by currents of history which offered them limited choice or negotiating space. The themes discussed have mostly reflected the topics that older people wished to address when reviewing their past lives. People's sense of loss and vulnerability provide a background in which to place the later efforts made by different groups in local society to find an escape route from a fate as 'victims' by struggling to secure alternative livelihoods which at the same time drew upon and reconstructed material and ideological structures and relations existing but under enormous threat.

The other important objective has been to build up a picture of historical events from a class – gender perspective, so that class and gender are seen as inseparable from each other in the interpretation of the dynamics of socio-economic change. With this focus, the chapter has attempted to explore the expressions and meanings of these dynamics at both a societal and household level.

One central argument has been that in the period prior to 1960 women had little opportunity to leave Santiago compared with men and their economic insecurity, feeding into an emotional insecurity, had greatly worsened as a result of male out-migration. In the urban *barrios*, daughters and wives had long been forced to sell their labour to earn cash in order to provision themselves and their families. Male semi-proletarianisation had done little to arrest this cash need as few women could count on adequate, regular or permanent financial support from husbands, fathers or sons. This failure by men to provide regular remittances arose partly from the particular employment and working conditions faced by men, but it was exacerbated by men's responses to the social and economic dislocations of their lives and by the condoning of 'vices' by masculine society.

Women desperately needed cash. Their need did not stem solely from a demand for purchased basic consumption goods. Most married women living with their parents-in-law were also strongly motivated to save in order to establish their own independent households. In town this demanded considerable cash payments to purchase a plot of land, provide building materials necessary even for a simple dwelling and acquire basic domestic goods and utensils. Coupled with this yearning for greater independence under the new urban conditions, many mothers held out the hope that the lives of their daughters would not be so hard or bleak as their own. The image of the 'suffering woman' was not necessarily one that mothers wanted daughters to inherit. Mother–daughter solidarity was a potential strength, but it had been thwarted especially by the survival of the patrilocality tradition in the town.

Before 1960 women had shown their willingness to take on new forms of income paying work and pursue these despite male opposition. Already Santiago women had gained experience of outwork from the silk shawl manufacturers of Zamora and had taken on seasonal work in strawberry picking and packing in the Zamora valley. There was a deeply held collective belief that a 'good woman' was one who strove to support her family as a daughter or a mother. But the returns women could get for their labour were still extremely low. Locally, the returns still reflected the low value given to the commoditisation of women's domestic labour, and this had determined the payment offered to outworkers. Though some women were working in capitalist agribusiness, most were employed as 'family workers' in the fields meaning that their wages were paid out collectively to the male family heads; women's labour was not recognised as having its own independent value.

Women's relations with the sweater workshops developed out of the pre-existing differentiation of women's work and out of the networks through which domestic labour had been exchanged for cash. Young, unmarried women were seen as eligible for service in a señora's house and as under the tutelage of an older woman. For them workshop employment brought no great discontinuity, but it did demand that owning wives fulfill the same role as the señora, taking charge of training, management and protection of workshop workers. For the older married women, the hand sewing and adornment of sweaters represented a new possibility for domestic out-work.

Notes

1. González, 1968, pp. 161–8.
2. I am grateful to Pedro Luna, 1985, for allowing me to use his working papers from which this information derives.
3. For a comprehensive history of the *'cristero'* wars, see Meyer, 1973.
4. Material on agrarian reform in Santiago was made available to me by Don Luis Ochoa, former municipal President, who is preparing a commentary on the history of the district.
5. This process has been analysed in some depth in the neighbouring district of Chavinda in the thesis by Alarcon, 1984.
6. Luna, 1985.
7. Ibid.
8. See Massey *et al.* (1987) for a discussion of migration patterns in western central Mexico, and Leys (1987) for an analysis of migration history in the case of Santiago.
9. See Appendix I for discussion of data sources and their analysis. The data are presented only tentatively here, being used to support information on changes coming from other sources.

4 The Rise of a Rural Industry

It is common to meet the assumption that workshop production is relatively static; that the small enterprises persist in a relatively unchanged form over long periods, unable to grow and reluctant to retreat into domestic production. This assumption is not borne out by evidence from Santiago. The advantage of taking workshop activity within a small town is that it provides information about a bounded population. The characteristics of workshop production are thus methodologically easier to explore than where workshops are more scattered. A review of Santiago's workshop history can therefore be expected to give some insights into the dynamics of workshop production in general by revealing how individual enterprises alter over time, how differentiation comes about within a single industrial branch, what form differentiation takes as seen from a comparison of individual enterprises (in terms of size, technology, markets, etc.) and what relations link enterprises within and across 'class' boundaries.

This chapter focuses on *workshop ownership and production*, using material provided primarily by owners. The topics under discussion here relate first to workshop foundation and growth over a twenty-seven-year period and the changes in ownership characteristics over time; and second to the patterns of production and labour process in workshops of different sizes seen in relation to changing technology and markets. These topics are initially sketched out in general terms under separate headings, then the elements are reassembled to give a more holistic impression of conditions of workshop production using selected enterprises as examples.

INDUSTRIAL EXPANSION AND WORKSHOP OWNERSHIP

The Espinoza family had been responsible for taking the sweater-making industry to Santiago in 1960. Many kinsmen and neighbours who had worked on Espinoza's looms, later separated to form their own workshops; there were twelve operating in the mid-1960s. The growing prosperity of the 1970s provoked both a greater capitalisation of workshop production and a faster rate of enterprise formation. And the first 'official' list of workshops compiled in 1981 showed that there were then six large, twelve medium-sized and twelve small workshops; a year later the total had grown to forty; and by 1986 there were more than fifty workshops.[1] All these enterprises employed at least three wage workers. The first signs of industrial recession were becoming apparent by 1986 largely on account of the rise in the cost of thread, the largest variable cost. By 1987, some workshops were closing and producers generally were being forced to react to the deteriorating conditions. Thus during its history the Santiago knitwear industry has gone through a number of phases. These will be explored in greater detail under the following headings: the Espinoza family business; the first proliferation of enterprise in the 1960s; the wider spread of the workshop activity in the 1970s; and finally the start of industrial decline.

Industrial Beginnings: The Espinoza Return to Santiago

The agreement between Ramiro Espinoza, his wife Alicia, and brother Jesús, was that each should learn their own respective part of the sweater-making business and start production in Mexico City. While still employed as a machine operator at the box factory, Ramiro set about learning how to work a wool knitting loom. He paid a friend with a job in a sweater-making factory to take him along at night so he would try out the looms and watch the machine repairs being done. Through this agreement, Ramiro also found out about wool suppliers and dealers in machine parts. In 1955, the Espinoza used capital saved to purchase an old manually operated loom and a second-hand overlock sewing machine. They also bought sweaters of every adult and child's size in order to make wooden patterns to guide cloth cutting until Ramiro and Alicia could do this by eye. They spent the next year practising; and many months went by before they were producing sweaters of high enough quality to sell. Meanwhile, Jesús, taking no part in production, concentrated his energies in seeking out potential customers as he toured the weekly markets.

Once the family dropped their other jobs and dedicated their labours to sweater production, the business did well. Ramiro had become an innovative and skilled mechanic, able to repair and modify machines so as to produce many different knitted effects;

Alicia was a fast and good sewer, and Jesús developed his flair as a salesman. Before long the workshop could invest in more looms and overlocks, buying them from larger businesses and paying off the costs in sweater production. The workshop could now employ wage labour. Among the loom operators employed was one who later caused Ramiro 'great trouble' which led to a skirmish with a labour union. Ramiro came to see unions as 'mafias' and 'extortion rackets' whose activities were harmful to both the working man and to small producers like himself. He decided to only appoint relatives from Santiago to take on the men's work in the workshop. Two brothers-in-law joined them to work the looms and two cousins helped distribute sweaters. Alicia found no difficulty in employing women from the neighbourhood for the sewing jobs, and there was no 'trouble' as unions were not interested in intervening in women's employment. But even though the workshop avoided 'interference' by the labour unions, less could be done about the inspectors who toured the districts of backroom workshops rapidly growing in the capital. The workshop's move from Villa de Guadalupe to Mixcoac was partly an attempt to avoid the inspectors demands for bribes which were particularly damaging for small struggling businesses.

Many considerations entered into the Espinoza's decision to take their workshop home to Santiago. Ramiro's principal explanation on hindsight was that he was fed up with the unions and inspectors. It was a rotten and corrupt system and he wanted out of it, even though economically the workshop did well. He was also conscious of the impoverishment and great need for employment opportunities back home. While future owners (including his brothers) saw this need primarily reflected in cheap labour, Ramiro genuinely wanted to do something for his community's welfare. Alicia's reasons for leaving were different. A cramped workshop in a poor urban district was not a good place to bring up her growing family – she already had six children to look after – and she wanted to go home to Zamora, a town with many more facilities and advantages than Santiago. Jesús and the other family members would have been content to stay on in the capital.

Santiago in 1960 was not an attractive location for small industry. Like thousands of other rural centres there was no electricity or telephones; no piped water or sewage disposal; only the main street was cobbled while the rest were of earth which turned into a sea of mud in the rainy season. The only advantage possessed by Santiago was that it lay close to the road from Zamora and Jacona to Sahuayo and Guadalajara. The social infrastructure was equally unprepossessing: the many bars and gambling dens catered to the 'vices' of the returning migrants, the streets were full of drunks and shooting incidents common.

On returning to Santiago, the Espinoza first set up their workshop in their mother's house but later moved to more spacious premises on the main street, Calle Madero. The male relatives moved back with the workshop and for a time continued to work for Ramiro and Jesús, so that the immediate burden of training new workers fell on Alicia who had to recruit women workers for the sewing room and for embroidering the garments. She drew on her husband's family and neighbourhood networks to find workshop workers: they included old school friends and former domestic workers – women who were accustomed to come to the Espinoza's houses. Married women, especially those with husbands in the north, were more eager to take on the embroidery out-work, but Alicia found many problems. The women did not lack skill with a needle, on the contrary, so proud were they of their ability they resented Alicia giving them instructions on designs to embroider. For over a year, Alicia battled with the embroiderers so that they performed the work the workshop required of them.

Before leaving Mexico City, Ramiro had developed good relations with one of the firms selling wool. Now Ramiro could entrust his orders (given by phone from Zamora) to a friend who dispatched the balls of wool in cardboard boxes by freight bus to Zamora. Jesús, meantime, had to develop a new market for the sweaters in a region of Mexico unknown to him.

The Early Proliferation of Enterprise in the 1960s

The Espinoza had come back to Santiago with experience in the sweater-making trade, and also important personal contacts especially with the wool supplier. These contacts could not easily be transmitted to or built up by others. The proliferation of the knitwear enterprises in Santiago during the 1960s needs to be seen within the context of a rapidly changing national economy which opened up a series of new prospects that could be grasped by would-be producers even in an isolated spot like Santiago. Chronologically, the most significant national changes were the following:

1. the change-over from wool to acrylan as the preferred sweater

fibre which thereby opened up new sources of input supply;
2. the interest on the part of thread suppliers and/or clothing dealers in entering contracts with producers of knitted goods;
3. the greater use of hire purchase as a sales policy by machine distribution firms so as to expand the market for new looms and sewing machines;
4. the increased quantity of second-hand garment-making machinery coming into the market as a result of the adoption of more efficient looms and sewing machines by larger enterprises;
5. the changing policies pursued by banks offering easier loans to small scale enterprises.

The first phase in the proliferation of enterprise resulted from the opening up of new sources of inputs when acrylic thread began displacing wool. In the early 1960s, acrylan was still more expensive than wool but it washed better and could be produced in a wider range of colours (including 'pure' white). Popular demand grew for garments made from acrylan. Producers only needed to make a simple adjustment to their machines for them to work the new fibre. The major change that transference to acrylan brought was the breakdown of the former dependence on wool suppliers in Mexico City. Acrylan could be purchased directly from the new chemical industries springing up throughout Mexico (the nearest producers of thread to Santiago were the factories in Aguascalientes and San Juan Potosi) or from commercial travellers coming from Moroleón. Easier access to thread allowed the already trained loom operators to consider separation.

Within a couple of years of returning to Santiago, the kinsmen of Ramiro and Jesús who had worked their looms left to establish their own enterprises. One brother-in-law opened a workshop in the small town Ecuandureo while another set up a workshop in Zamora. The two cousins left to open workshops in Santiago, as did Ramiro's youngest brother Manuel. Though the partnership between Ramiro and Jesús had worked well in Mexico City, major differences between them surfaced after the move. At first profits had been divided equally between them but in Santiago, Jesús demanded a larger share to cover his costs of travel, food and hotels while away from home finding markets for the sweaters. Ramiro objected to these expenditures and felt increasingly dispirited at being tied to the workshop. He began to drink heavily and after a particularly violent quarrel with Jesús, left for California. Alicia left behind with seven children was forced to carry on working with Jesús while earning a small sum for the 'rent' of her machines.

It appears that some of the new enterprises were able to start up through contracts negotiated with the suppliers of thread or clothing dealers. Through such contracts second-hand machinery was forwarded to the new enterprise and paid off in product. But subcontracting was accepted as a temporary expedient rather than a chosen future linkage. Ramiro and his cousin, José, both remember their dissatisfaction and frustration with the sub-contracting system. The contracting firms imposed very stringent demands with respect to sizing; they would not accept to pay for garments that departed from exact size measurements. This level of precision was difficult for workshops producing knitwear to attain, as the cloth always stretched in the sewing and pressing stages. (It was far easier technically for manufacturers using woven cloth to meet the exact size requirements.) Sub-contracting therefore carried risks and penalties so that the proceeds from the sale of sweaters could fluctuate. More importantly, owners saw no point in handing over profits from the commercial side of the business to an outside firm unless the contract was absolutely necessary. Most owners aspired to be independent producer/merchants and aimed to leave contract work as soon as possible.

The proliferation of workshops now meant that several owners drew on male relatives and neighbours, training them to man the looms. These workers were seen primarily as 'apprentices' learning the trade; their wages were low but there was usually an understanding that separation would come about sooner or later. The twelve workshops struggling to survive in the mid-1960s were linked to the Espinoza family, they sometimes competed and sometimes collaborated with each other.

Sweater production constituted a new form of capital accumulation. The activity had first spread through links of kin and neighbourhood so that workshops were concentrated in the centre of town. An already privileged social group had been in the best position to take advantage of the new opportunities; however, the Espinoza and their relatives were not from the class of 'new *ejidatarios*', the capitalist farmers accumulating land and cattle in the 1940s and 1950s.

The early owners came mostly from trading families who had prospered earlier and built large town-houses but who had subsequently suffered a decline in their fortunes. Declining profits from regional trade had led many from these families to migrate to the US (before the onset of mass migration), or in search of urban waged jobs in Mexico. But they still possessed social and material resources at home. The chance to enter independent workshop production offered them an escape from further incorporation into the urban proletariat. They could now return to Santiago to reclaim their higher social status and emerge as a local industrial bourgeoisie. At the same time, their formation and experiences as urban workers in Mexico stood them in good stead as producer/merchants for they had become familiar with the organisation of city life and factory production.

The Wider Spread of Workshop Activity in the 1970s

Several new workshops were opened in the 1970s by families who were no longer closely connected with the Espinoza clan. One such example was Mario who came to own one of the largest workshops.

> Mario, born in 1943, was the son of the secretary of the municipal council who though of humble origin (a shoemaker) had been rewarded by the cattle owners running the Presidency in the 1950s. Having accumulated some plots of land and cows, he could afford to offer his children a better education. But Mario fought to leave school early, and bored with working his father's land decided to migrate to the border town of Mexacali. He could not find the kind of work he wanted there nor in Tijuana and as he did not want to join the mass of Mexican 'Indians' now crossing the border to the US, he went instead to Mexico City. After a long search he was taken on by a small plastic-making factory as an unskilled worker. He later manned a machine and later still was given a supervisory role. Mario enjoyed the increase in wages and status this gave, and strove to be taken on in the sales department. After consistent refusals, Mario left and finally achieved his ambition by joining another small firm producing wire and twine for packaging. He was able to visit and observe conditions in a very wide range of enterprises through selling and he became particularly interested in the way certain Jewish families organised their business activities. He yearned to copy their example of sharing investment and risk among several family members and in 1974 convinced his brother and brother-in-law to join him in a joint venture in Santiago through which he would

manage a sweater-workshop and they a dairying enterprise.

There were several routes to workshop ownership opening up particularly in the late 1970s and early 1980s and workshops began proliferating outside the town centre. By the 1980s small and medium-sized workshops could be found in all *barrios*. The origins of the most recent generation of owners were diverse. Some owning husbands had been waged loom operators for many years in the established workshops (but not connected by kin or neighbourhood ties with the owners). They could separate due to easier access to machinery (especially when larger workshops were capitalising production and selling off old machines), and cheaper credit. Some formed independent enterprises with the support of their old patrons, others had to look elsewhere for help. Some new owners were men who had returned after many years residence in the US and could invest their savings in knitwear production. Other new owners had been well educated and held professional qualifications but judged workshop-based industry to be the more lucrative occupation. Only in the last few years have children of the new *ejidatarios*, the wealthy cattle owners, entered the knitwear industry.

Relations between owners of older workshops and the new generation of owners have varied. A few were linked through ties of *compadrazgo* and money lending; others were linked through local subcontracting deals when work was occasionally put out by the larger workshop to the smaller. But in general, these do not seem to have been common. Especially once the larger enterprises were attempting to improve quality, sub-contracting even to former loom workers was not so attractive and many small producers lament the 'egotism' of their former patrons in not providing them with work. Small workshops often had to rely on large workshops for thread, but most were exploited rather than assisted by the conditions of purchase. Perhaps the most important direct service that the owners of the older workshops did perform was in the field of training loom operators; Ramiro Espinoza in particular had helped many in this way, and claimed to have taught more than 100 men.

In sum, the growth of workshops in Santiago was due to an underlying social 'will' in the community at large to establish and work in workshop manufacturing. The pioneers had lit a spark and the fire had spread. The activity had been able to spread partly on account of favourable conditions in the external economy amongst which the switch to acrylan, access to second-hand machinery and easier credit facilities were of fundamental importance. But there were also internal reasons for the spread, not least the obligation of the owners of older workshops to help their loom workers to become independent and sometimes helping them with loans and sub-contracts. Not in every rural centre could workshop production catch hold as it had done in Santiago. Though a pioneering workshop had been opened in Ecuadureo in the early 1960s, to this day it remains the only one in existence.

Sweaters or Sports Shirts?

All the early workshops made sweaters, at first using wool and later, the thicker, more expensive type of acrylan. In Mexico the demand for sweaters has always been highly seasonal. The warmer garments are purchased primarily in the colder, wetter months from around August to January, business getting increasingly lively towards Christmas time and then rapidly falling off. For the rest of the year, sweater orders are intermittent. Given that the garments are responsive to fashion swings, both producers and traders have been reluctant to stock too many in advance for future sale. Many have made mistakes by doing this and at the start of the 'season' find they cannot get rid of out-moded colours and styles. The response of many sweater workshops has been to close for several months in the slack season during which time the labour force must 'rest'.

Seasonality of demand has posed problems for both producers and workers when the workshop's plant lies idle for months on end. This prompted several workshops to experiment with different kinds of knitwear that were less susceptible to market fluctuations. In the 1970s, the production of sports shirts greatly expanded; using cheaper acrylan thread, these garments could be made on the same looms and by the same workers and they could find some market throughout the year, although demand was still peaked. Sports shirts are more difficult to sew and need several additional steps in the labour process. Nevertheless, because of the cheaper thread the finished garments sell for lower prices than the sweaters. This means that not only can some garments be sold all year round, buyers tend to belong to the lower income sectors of the population who buy two cheaper garments instead of one more expensive sweater.

Given the different production and demand characteristics of sweaters and sports shirts, one tends to find that choice of product is related to size of workshop. The larger, longer established enterprises have kept their specialisation in sweaters, but they close for part of the year. Medium-sized workshops have often tried to combine the production of both articles, sewing the more profitable sweaters in the busy season and filling in with sports shirt production from February to July so as to keep the machinery and workers occupied for most of the year and an income coming in. Small workshops have concentrated on sports shirts, supplying the lowest income markets and hoping to sell a basic minimum quantity each week.

More recently, there has been a tendency towards greater diversification of production, largely through the buying in of woven cotton cloth. In some workshops extra sewers are now employed to sew cotton garments which are then offered for sale along side the knitwear. A couple of workshops have made no investment in looms and the whole output of children's trousers, or women's 'fashion' clothing is sewn from purchased cloth. This type of production has been boosted in the last few years, as a result of the increasing cost of acrylan thread, and therefore the relative cheapening of the price of cotton cloth. But competition is very high in that branch of the garment industry, and workshops in or near the large cities are better placed than Santiago to respond to more volatile fashion changes within different parts of that clothing market. Furthermore, technical competence especially in the cutting stage is at a premium, and the Santiago producers cannot easily transfer from their specialisation in knitwear to one in women's fashion clothing.

Gender Complementarity and Ownership

Santiago's sweater manufacture had been organised so as to perpetuate an image of gender complementarity: the husband on the loom knitting cloth and the wife on the sewing machine making up garments. All the early workshops started that way. This appeal to complementarity was especially important for women. Underlying it was a distant memory of the greater valuation put on women's labour under the old agrarian system of the past. None of the owning wives interviewed thought they had been forced by husbands to become 'unremunerated family labour'; on the contrary, they identified themselves as owners and managers and saw their work load as a consequence of the responsibilities of ownership. Women's sense of partnership, however, extended only to relations inside the workshop; external contacts and negotiations were invariably handled by husbands.

The presence of owning wives in the workshops has been crucial for the recruitment of women's labour, organisation of production and development of specific forms of labour disciplining and control. Up to the late 1970s workshops could not have been established without an owning wife present (or represented). The presence of owning wives was not solely a reflection of the wife's labour input in production (though this was in itself important), at a more profound level it was linked with how workshops could gain access to and control over women's labour in a society based on gender segregation.

'Ideally' under gender segregated production, the male loom operators have worked for owning husbands and the female sewers for owning wives. However in practice, no such complete or symmetrical division has ever occurred. Owning women were not expected to direct loom operators nor spend a working day in the 'male' part of the workshop. But owning men were able to direct women workers and perform tasks alongside them by adopting the identity of a 'father'.

In recent years, owning women have tended to withdraw from taking an active part in workshop activity. From the mid-1970s workshops were being established by men with minimal intervention from their wives so that now the management situation is mixed. In some workshops women retain their former position as working partners; they work every day, manage all workshop business when husbands are out of town, and remain responsible for labour discipline and control in the sewing room. But in other workshops wives are now absent.

Several processes have led to women's retreat from active management. First, it must be remembered that men had always taken charge of the commercial side of the business; only owning husbands travelled to make deals concerning the supply of inputs or marketing of output. While owning husbands faced a choice as to how much time to allocate to production and commerce, women were confined to the workshop. And though one might posit the argument that owning wives would become more vital as managers when men travelled most frequently, in practice the opposite seems to have been the case. Higher profits could generally be realised through attention to commerce rather than through devotion to production and with increasing wealth greater pressures seem to have been placed on wives to become housewives demonstrating by their consumption habits the owning family's adoption of a bourgeois life style. The fact that owning wives can now choose whether to remain active in the production or become housewives demonstrates the passing of an early model of production relations and its replacement by another model in which gender complementarity in management is no longer relevant.

The Start of Industrial Decline

The knitwear workshops have recently faced very serious problems due not only to general recession, but most specifically because of the rising cost of thread. The Santiago owners were taken by surprise by the sudden increase in the cost of thread which more than doubled between December 1985 and June 1986 (from 1200 pesos to 3050 pesos per kilo) and doubled once again between June 1986 and June 1987. Thread is the largest variable cost in sweater and sports shirt production and the workshops are acutely dependent on the pricing policy of the Mexican chemical industry.

Potential producers wanting to set up workshops can still find ways and means of acquiring machinery without great difficulty, but the main stumbling block is the need to purchase four or five months stock of thread in advance, cash down, with which to begin production. Very few workshops have started production since 1985. On the contrary, since that date several workshops have closed. Some older owners have decided to 'retire' early rather than struggle under deteriorating conditions (such as Manual Espinoza); others have turned their attention to different branches of commerce, though not necessarily selling their knitwear-making machinery. Only when thread prices stabilise do producers foresee that business will thrive again.

Workshop Ownership in Perspective

The main arguments coming through from the discussion on ownership are the following.

The national economic and technological developments of the 1950s were opening up possibilities for a greater proliferation of the knitwear branch of the garment industry. Though garment-making in general had always been a workshop activity, the production of knitted cloth and sweater manufacture had previously been organised primarily on a factory basis. The proliferation was first registered in the large cities. Though some relocation took place to rural areas, this movement was facilitated by later economic tendencies, especially the growth and decentralisation of the chemical industry and the growing use of synthetic fibres.

From the start, sweater workshops were jointly owned and managed by wives and husbands. This ownership form, harking back to images of domestic enterprise and gender complementarity, was part of the process by which relations of gender were being transferred and reconstituted at the workplace. But although the organisation of production has remained gender segregated, a study of the shifting position of owning wives demonstrates an important aspect of the interplay between class and gender. The active presence of owning wives was necessary to establish and develop workshop production in rural areas, as their involvement expressed the continuity of gender relations as an organising principle and the protection and legitimation of women's waged work. In time, however, societal pressures towards a new expression of class differentiation and the ascendance of a 'modern' bourgeoisie mounted. Membership of the bourgeoisie was not only seen through ownership of capital but also through the life-style of those owning it. This had major implications for the gender identity of women in this class: managers or housewives.

Workshop owners have originated from several social strata. The pioneers came from old trading families which although 'eclipsed' had retained some property and social position in the locality. Newer entrants came both from the ranks of wage workers without propertied or privileged backgrounds (e.g. former loom workers or migrants in the US), and also from wealthy land and livestock owning families. Underlying class differences have not necessarily diminished over time. Instead, the different origins and resource base of workshop owners have contributed to relatively permanent differentiation found among workshop enterprises.

PRODUCTION, LABOUR PROCESS AND TECHNOLOGICAL CHANGE

The production process in the workshops has been organised into three distinct phases: cloth-making, garment sewing and garment adornment. This division was mirrored in the labour process so that men manned the looms while women were employed in all other phases of the labour process. Garment sewing in the workshops involved cutting, tacking, seaming, hemming, sometimes button sewing and button holing (for sports shirts), pressing, labelling, finishing and packing. Made-up garments were then put out for adornment to women home workers. The three phases have characterised production from the start.

At the beginning workshops were relatively small enterprises. But once initial problems were solved and profits rising, workshops could hope to expand to become medium sized and then larger enterprises. Through this development, workshops came to differ in many important respects. The divisions were at first registered in volume of output (determined largely by loom number and capacity), quality of product and type of market supplied. In later years this differentiation has been reflected in the capitalisation of production, technology employed and in the changing relations of capital with labour. These processes in turn have had implications for the kind of relations workshops have with the wider economy as well as with each other.

This section will explore some elements of workshop production and differentiation seen first from the perspective of the effect of technological changes on production and labour processes and second from the kind of market supplied. After a general discussion of the elements, strategies of accumulation (and dis-accumulation) followed by a selection of specific workshops will be explored.

Workshops as Gendered Places

The concealment of industrial activity has long been associated with 'clandestinity'. Even walking down Santiago's main street today, there is little to indicate that, behind the facades, workshops are in full swing. Doors and windows are boarded up, if the workshop is near the street; most workshop buildings are not in view. But 'clandestinity' provides only a partial explanation; it is not wholly convincing. For a long time the proliferation of small scale industry was an open secret in the region. Since 1980, Government inspectors have periodically visited the town. At first producers hid their machines and gave workers a 'holiday' when inspectors came. But even after workshops, as a result of various pressures, became more 'legal' this has not necessarily led to more 'open' industrial activity.

One can argue that workshop concealment has been as much to

do with the desire on the part of the owners to continue emphasising the 'domestic' or 'household' nature of industrial production as with clandestinity per se. This has been integrally connected with the importance of women in the labour process.

Most workshops began in backrooms of the old houses in the centre of town. As business expanded, sweater making activities spilled into the passageways and central patios. Later, an expanding workshop would either acquire property next door or construct new brick buildings at the back of the house. The vast majority of workshops in town still combine domestic and business premises but a new trend is emerging: three large enterprises have now separated the workplace from the house. The separation has been associated with changes in the organisation of labour and management relations as well as with the withdrawal of wives from production.

Emphasis on the 'domestic' and a rigid gender division of labour have gone together with the gendering of space inside workshops so that male and female wage workers remain segregated. Looms are placed inconveniently in passageways rather than occupy the women's sewing room. The male and female parts of the labour process may occupy different buildings, rooms or floors. The gendering of space extends beyond the workshops. Young women are generally allowed to go with girl friends to and from the workshops. But these same women are not allowed to travel without a suitable escort outside the town. The sanction against young women travelling presented Manuel and Jesús Espinoza with a problem when they decided to shift their workshops to Zamora in 1984. If they were to continue employing workers from Santiago then they could not expect the young women's parents to let them travel alone by bus. The workshops would have to arrange the transport. Furthermore, the transport could not be handed over in any permanent way to a male employee; nor was it seemly that their wives drive. The brothers chose to retain a wholly Santiago labour force at the cost of personally fetching and returning the workers every day. Only in this way could the alien space between home and workshop be negotiated.

Labour Process and Technological Change

Men's work: the production of knitted cloth

In the early period, only manually operated looms could be worked in Santiago. They produced some three dozen garments per shift of eight hours. Small enterprises usually possessed three looms. This represented the minimum number required for efficient production. As thread was the most costly input and re-threading the looms time-consuming, the most efficient way to produce cloth was to devote the different looms to knitting different parts of the garment. Minimally, therefore, one loom was needed to knit sweater bodies, finishing off each garment length with a welt of different stitch and producing pieces of suitable dimensions for different garment sizes; a second loom was devoted to knit arm lengths and the third, bands for the neck.

Production on the manual looms could be expanded first through an increase in the number of shifts worked. Some workshops insisted on running a three shift system, others made do with two shifts. But looms could also be worked at a faster or slower rate; an owner hard pressed to complete an order could produce more than employed workers. Loom breakdown was a constant hazard, repairs cost time and money and mechanics had to be summoned from Moroleón when faults were serious. Some owners chose to devote themselves more to problems arising in production and became skilled mechanics, others bought in this expertise so as to concentrate on sales.

By the early 1970s, owners invested in motors to power their old manual looms or could purchase larger capacity motor looms coming onto the second-hand market. One man could then oversee two machines at a time and so produce on average six dozen garments per shift. But while Santiago lacked a reliable electricity supply, workshops were prevented from investing in more efficient looms. The need to increase output was a major factor which brought workshop owners into local politics so as to fight for their interests against the cattle owners who remained in control of the Presidency. Cattle owners had directed public funds largely into the provision of irrigation and small reservoirs for their own benefit; the industrialists fought to improve the local electricity supply sufficiently to allow them to purchase new machinery. Larger capacity looms were wide enough to knit two bands of cloth adjacent to each other and labour productivity was increased even more.

The final phase of technological change in cloth production began in 1978 when the first Carrousel loom was introduced to Santiago. This larger, sophisticated loom not only produces a much greater output per shift (cloth for at least thirty dozen garments) it could knit more intricate designs with different weaves and colours. A loom operator on a Carrousel could produce ten times the output of an operator using a manual machine.

Technological change in cloth production has led to two main tendencies: the redundancy of male workers and more clear demarcations between different categories of workshops. Among those male loom operators made redundant were some who bought the obsolescent machines they had worked and swelled the numbers entering the ranks of small-scale producers. This kind of 'retirement' policy not only made economic sense for the larger workshops, it kept alive an ideology that the way was open for all men to move from wage labour to capital ownership. But for most, the barriers preventing further growth turned out to be insuperable.

Before the introduction of the Carrousels, workshop size differentials were reflected largely in the numbers of machines in operation. But the changing technology of cloth production has been associated with a more profound and permanent division (as later sections will demonstrate). At present, small enterprises with two to three motorised looms produce some five to six dozen garments per day. (There are very few manual looms still in operation in Santiago, though some are still working in Ecuandureo). Medium-sized enterprises have six to twelve motor looms producing some fifteen to twenty-four dozen garments. Large enterprises can now be defined as those which have invested in at least one Carrousel and produce minimally thirty dozen knitted garments per day.

No enterprise has entirely dispensed with motor looms in Santiago. Even large workshops with Carrousels retain some old looms to perform particular tasks (such as knitting sweater neck bands) or to substitute for the large capacity looms when thread is limited or orders are few. Those workshops which in the late 1970s and early 1980s possessed twelve to fifteen motor looms, in general dismissed some five or six men after acquiring a Carrousel. They might continue to employ one or two occasionally. The medium sized workshops have tended to employ young men on the motor looms who are willing and strong enough to work extra shifts and long hours or they have kept on older workers after a lifetime's service. In the small enterprises usually the owner or a family member produces the bulk of the cloth output.

It is generally reckoned to take a year to train a motor loom operator though it takes a much longer time for a worker to master the skills necessary to do repairs. Operating the Carrousel requires different skills and a much longer training period. Only young, literate, technically oriented men have entered this specialisation; and apprenticeships have been hard to secure as owners are very wary as to whom they will let near such a large item of investment. In 1986 there were only six recognised Carrousel operators in Santiago.

For most of the industry's history, loom operators were paid piece-rates according to how many sets of garment parts they produced during the shift. This form of reimbursement is now less common; workshop owners mostly pay workers a fixed weekly wage. No evidence was found of trained loom operators receiving wages less than the official minimum. Motor loom workers earned a basic wage of between 10 000 and 12 000 pesos in early 1986, though the take-home pay could be higher in the larger workshops on account of overtime. The few skilled Carrousel workers could command much higher wages: from 13 000 to 16 000 pesos as a basic wage and up to around 20 000 pesos per week including 'regular' overtime.[2]

The changing technology of cloth production appears to be leading to two tendencies which may well become more pronounced in future. A growing number of male owners have decided to learn the techniques of cloth production or hand the work over to a son rather than trust and pay a worker. Sons may be pressed to follow a technical training so as to understand the new technology and develop the workshop. This tendency implies a decline in the employment of male wage labour and an increasing involvement of family labour. Thus, it is in the larger, most technically sophisticated workshops that one finds a movement towards family enterprise.

The second tendency refers to the future use of motor looms by workshops where the bulk of the knitting is done by Carrousel. Several owners have expressed an interest in making these jobs 'female' in future when elderly male loom operators have retired. Thus, high technology loom work will continue to be associated with men's work, but other loom work might well be taken over as lower paid 'women's work'. No women are known to work looms in Santiago, but already there are female manual loom apprentices at work in Ecuandureo, an experiment looked at with interest by some Santiago owners.

In the future development of the industry, one can foresee that men will cease to find employment in the Santiago workshops. As wage levels rise, so men's loom work is being squeezed out by the greater use of family labour on the one side and by restructuring the gender division of labour on the other.

'Women's work' – the garment sewing phase
Cloth coming off the looms is passed into the sewing room. After being pressed flat, garment pieces are cut into shape before sewing. Cutting involves the shaping of shoulders, arm holes and neck pieces, jobs that cannot be done automatically by the looms. Cutting has been acknowledged as a critical stage in the production process and has often been performed by an owning husband or wife; otherwise a woman wage worker will cut in the sewing room. Cutters train by using wooden pattern pieces as guides but this is slow. The more experienced cut by eye. In most workshops large scissors or shears are used; only a minority have invested in electric presses or motorised shears capable of cutting through greater thicknesses of cloth. Part of the hesitation to invest has been due to labour opposition; few workers are prepared to operate the highly dangerous unguarded machine cutters. Several owners believe a better cut is achieved when the cloth for each garment is cut individually.

The cut garment pieces are then tacked, pressed and handed over directly to the overlock machinist. Overlock sewing has been the preserve of the more experienced women and an owning wife is expected to operate the overlock sewing machine when rushed orders must be completed. The majority of overlock sewers work in the workshop, but some owners place overlocks in the homes of skilled sewers after they marry. The most skilled overlock sewers combine many qualities: they sew fast and accurately; they produce minimum waste thread and rarely break needles; they know how to diagnose and repair faults in their machines. A fast sewer can seam ten dozen sweaters during a four-hour stretch; an average sewer produces less than this quantity in a full working day of eight hours.

In the production of sports shirts, the sewing phase is more complex as collars need attaching at the neck, buttons sewn and button holes made. In addition, the thinner acrylic material is not finished off by the knitting loom and needs hemming at the sewing stage.

Technological change in sewing has not led to such labour redundancy as in cloth-making. Instead the changes have led to the replacement of manual labour by machines and by more divisions of the labour process in the sewing room, especially in the case of sports shirt production. In sweater manufacture, the most important technological improvement has been the use of a specialised seaming machine which can sew neck pieces to sweater bodies using needles that enter the cloth horizontally and therefore produce a less visible stitch than the overlock. Operating this machine is now a separate part of the labour process and workers are employed all day on this tiring exacting work.

In sports shirt production, after seaming on the overlock, a worker fits and sews collars on a small overlock, another does button holes, a third sews buttons and a fourth hems the garment. These latter three tasks were formerly done by hand but now most of the larger workshops have invested in specialised sewing machines for each separate stage. In the final stages of the sewing phase, garments are finished off and checked, being repaired if necessary; then labelled by hand or machine and pressed. Smaller workshops still use domestic irons for pressing while larger enterprises have invested in steam presses.

Formerly, there was a marked division in the status and remuneration of workers on the overlock and others who sewed by hand or performed other more menial tasks. But processes of capitalisation in the sewing room have challenged definitions of skill and positions in the wage hierarchy. Generally, young women entering the workshop as trainees are given jobs such as carrying sweaters between the specialised sewers or labelling. In the past this work might not even be paid, and in early 1986 would be reimbursed with around 4000 to 5000 pesos per week (after an initial week or two at even lower wages). As sewers left and new trainees taken on, so workers advanced to manual sewing and to simpler machine work such as button-sewing and button-holing or to operating the steam press. This work would command a weekly wage of around 6000 to 7000 pesos in early 1986. Finally, workers who showed aptitude were put to work on the overlock, earning between 7000 and 8000 pesos per week in early 1986. The most experienced overlock sewers, usually women in their late twenties, could earn higher wages, sometimes being paid on a par with motor loom operators, at around 10 000 pesos per week.[3]

Wage differentials of this order are common in the workshop sewing room, but the size of the differential cannot be 'explained' with arguments as to attributed skill level. In the case of overlock sewers, for example, among the medium-sized workshops there can be a difference of 25 per cent in the wages received by 'average' workers; i.e. not including the older most skilled sewers. In the past all sewers were paid according to piece-rates, but now a fixed weekly wage has superseded this practice in all but a few workshops and for all in the sewing room (except in the case of the most experienced overlock sewers).

In Santiago today, a few large workshops have dispensed with the complexity of wage hierarchies and have begun paying sewing room workers the same wage pegged at the official minimum level. This labour policy has only been realised where workshops can off-load the costs involved in training workers. Thus there is now a marked tendency for small and medium sized workshops to pay lower wages and train workers who will subsequently leave for better remunerated work in a larger workshop.

'Women's work' – the adornment phase
In the past, the distinguishing feature of the Santiago sweaters was their embroidery. This phase of the production process has always been put out to home-workers. But in recent years there has been a diminishing demand for hand-sewn adornment for several reasons. First, the switch to sports shirt production has limited the use workshops have made of home-workers for the only additional sewing required on these garments is the fixture of a 'trade-mark', such as the pirated Lacoste crocodile. Second, many consumers demand simpler designs using striped or textured cloth. Only in certain branches, principally baby and children's clothing, is embroidery still considered essential. The old sweater workshops have remained faithful to the practice of embroidery out-work and put out to women they have employed for many years. But other large sweater producers have taken the decision to end out-work.

The workshop owners who stopped putting out to home-workers explain their decision on the grounds of efficiency. The old system had demanded that somebody at the workshop was constantly on hand to supervise the distribution and collection of garments; often the garments came back dirty, or badly done. Producers found it difficult to force home-workers to meet deadlines especially when work had to be rushed; inevitably home-workers came with excuses as to why the work was unfinished when pressure was greatest to get the output delivered. And there was always the danger that garments would go 'missing', or be sold on the side.

The Rise of a Rural Industry

Some of the larger workshops, trying to improve quality of output, saw the continued dependence on embroidery out-work as anachronistic and inefficient and so changed their styles and production system accordingly. This did not necessarily mean that Santiago home-workers could never find work; since they had gained the reputation for being conscientious and honest workers they were in demand by garment producers in Zamora and Jacona. Payment for embroidery out-work varied very greatly in early 1986; in part this reflected the amount of embroidery required per garment. But there was also a gulf between 'good' and 'bad' payers: a bad payer was offering at that date 240 to 360 pesos per dozen garments while a good payer was giving 600 pesos.[4]

MARKETS, PROFITS AND WORKSHOP DIFFERENTIATION

Workshop Size and Market Supplied

The older owners confess they began producing cheap goods for sale in the lowest priced markets. Over time they managed to greatly improve the quality of their garments. Workshops beginning production now must achieve a relatively high quality from the start or they will be unable to compete. Producing quality knitwear has been a matter of pride for most of the older owners; some managed to achieve high quality garments on the old looms and machines. But it was the search for higher priced markets that partly lay behind the decision to capitalise production. At the present time, Santiago workshops supply a variety of different markets: size of enterprise being connected with quality achieved as well as type and location of market. The following are the main markets now supplied.

To this day, *small enterprises* produce poor quality sports shirts for the local weekly markets. These are workshops with low output, minimal investment in machinery, no owned means of transport. Producers sell to market traders living in Santiago who then hawk the goods around the local market circuit (Chavinda, Los Reyes, Purépuro, Zamora, Tanguancicuaro). Some reimburse producers before and others after the goods are sold. Some owners spend one day a week taking their output by bus to sell to traders in a nearby town (Guadalajara, Sahuayo, Uruapan).

The small workshops operate on the narrowest of margins. They cannot afford to buy thread in bulk or store output. They need to dispose of their output each week in order to continue in production. Specialisation in sports shirts gives a more regular income than sweaters but even so, manufacturing is often combined with other income earning activities. In recent years, efforts have been made to start a co-operative among the smallest knitwear producers to facilitate thread buying and develop market outlets so as to better survive the slack season. To date nothing has come of these attempts.

The preferred sales policy of several *older medium and large workshops* has been to sell relatively small quantities of garments to a great many urban retail outlets. Some leave their goods on a sale or return basis but most sell on the understanding that the money will be transferred to the producers within the space of fifteen days. Seeking out, supplying and chasing up the bad debts from the multiplicity of outlets is time-consuming and owners must possess transport. But this marketing strategy carries the great advantage of risk diminution. Over the years workshop owners have built up extensive networks of customers in towns within a day's reach of Santiago: Guadalajara, Uruapan, Sahuayo, Morelia; others go further afield where prices are higher: to Manzanillo, Tepic (Nayarit), Colima, Zacatecas (see Map 4.1)

Usually, the owner sets out in the slack season or when the workshop closes (from January to April) to visit customers, search out new buyers in the same market area, show samples of the new stock and take orders for the following autumn season. Orders usually cover a six-month period. A great standby of this market is school uniform sweaters which change little over time. Though producers try to work to orders agreed in advance, clients frequently demand new rushed orders in the course of the busy autumn season. Given the level of competition among sweater producers, workshops cannot afford to refuse clients requests for that could lose them future business.

Workshops supplying wholesalers in the large cities fall into a number of different groups. A few produce under fixed contract, though no Santiago owner will openly admit to it. This form of sub-contracting where decision-making and control passes entirely outside the workshop is no more favoured now than it was in the pioneering days. More commonly, a workshop receives regular orders from a particular wholesaler or supermarket chain during the busy season, and may if lucky also be able to sell some output to this client during the slack season. The seasonality of demand and

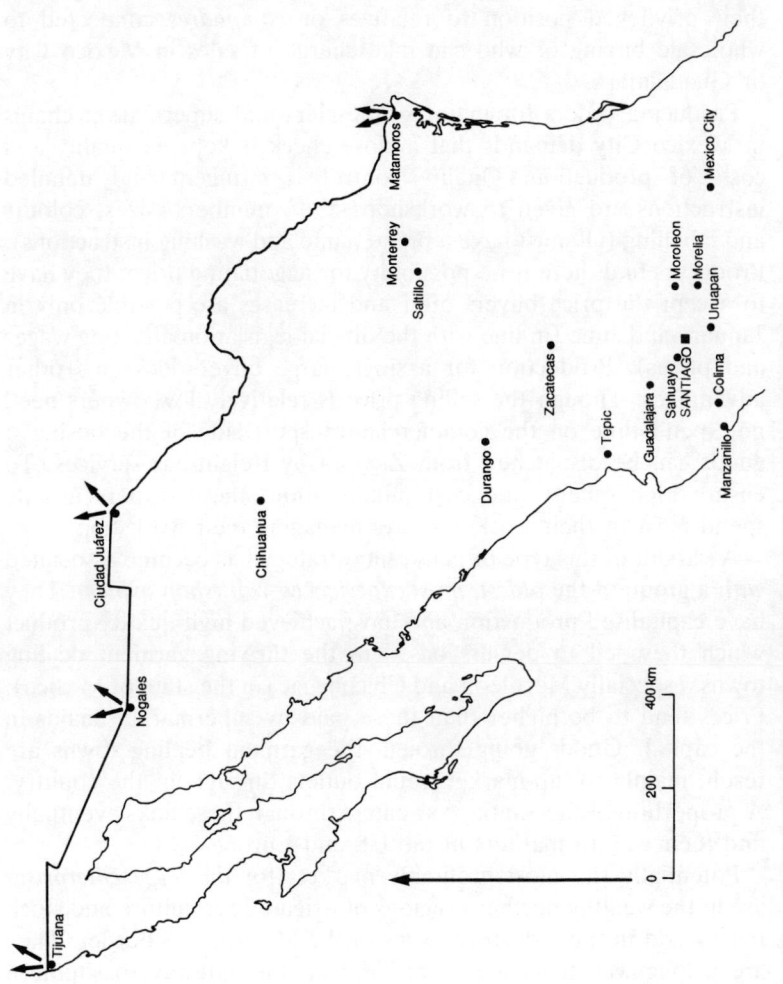

Map 4.1 Long-distance markets of Santiago workshops

style changes in this more fashion-conscious market mean that wholesalers are not very interested in maintaining contracts all year round. Workshops with greater market security have generally owed their privileged position to relatives or *compadres* connected to wholesale buying or who can take charge of sales in Mexico City or Guadalajara.

Producing orders for major wholesalers and supermarket chains in Mexico City demands that a close check is kept on quality and costs of production. Quality control is stringent and detailed instructions are given to workshops as to numbers, sizes, colours and labelling (all must have a brand name and washing instructions). Producers find there is no possibility for negotiating price; they have to accept the price buyers offer and increases are possible only in January and June (in line with the official legislation affecting wages and prices). Production for a single large buyer does give other advantages. Though the selling price is relatively low owners need not spend time on the commercial/transport side of the business: goods can be dispatched from Zamora by freight/bus services. To ensure high quality and cost minimisation, these owners usually spend most of their workings days managing their workshop.

A variant of this type of marketing strategy has become associated with a group of the *oldest, most experienced workshop owners*. They have capitalised production and have achieved high quality product which they sell to dealers based in the thriving garment dealing towns: especially Moroleón and Chiconcuac (in the state of Mexico). Prices tend to be higher than those paid by supermarket chains in the capital. Goods going through the garment dealing towns are resold mainly to 'up-market' retail outlets throughout the country. A proportion of the Santiago sweaters through these links eventually find their way to markets in the US and Europe.

Potentially the most profitable markets for *the large enterprises* are in the wealthy northern regions of irrigated agriculture and stock raising and in the industrial towns of the Mexican-US border. They are a long way from Santiago: Tijuana, the gateway to southern California, lies some 1800 miles away. Supplying the northern markets is a young man's activity. Some owners have built up networks of customers in the northern towns of Chihuahua, Durango, Saltillo, Monterrey; others take their goods all the way to the border towns of Ciudad Juaréz, Tijuana, Nogales, Matamoros (see Map 4.1). Wages and costs of living are highest in the north and export agriculture and industry have generated a strong demand for consumer goods produced in cheaper regions of the country.

By taking goods to the border towns, workshop owners can negotiate sales to the intermediaries who supply the illegal export trade to the US. These intermediaries are usually resident in the US towns close to the border; they often buy Mexican-made goods that faithfully copy US styled clothes and may even affix a 'Made in the US' label to them before resale to outlets in the southern US. A sweater selling for $US3.50–4.00 in Tijuana (in the spring of 1986) could be resold for $US7.00–8.00 across the border in southern California. (A final stage in this foreign trade may be the re-importation of the same garments back into Mexico; everybody in Santiago has a story to tell of a friend who had been duped into buying a re-imported Santiago sweater for 'ten times' the original price). Supplying the high priced northern markets carries costs not only in terms of transport and owners' time but also in the risk of delayed payments and bad debts. While the 'normal' repayment period in Mexico is between fifteen days and one month, delays of two to three months are common in the northern (and especially the illegal export) deals.

The price differential between Mexico and the US has stimulated another very different type of export trade: one that is less visible and smaller in scale. Women from around Santiago, possessing the coveted 'mica', a permit giving them freedom of entry to the US, have specialised in buying up relatively small quantities of Santiago garments to take with them on trips north. They have specialised in taking women's and children's clothes which are then sold through networks of Hispanic immigrants. Some men also take part in this type of trade and sell the goods to lower priced clothing chains. Through the activities of these small-time occasional traders, all workshops of Santiago have been given the opportunity of 'exporting' goods though the volume is impossible to estimate.

The future perspectives of supplying the US market are complex. A few of the Santiago families who have settled more or less permanently in the US (especially Merced, in the Californian Central valley where over 200 Santiago families now live, and Los Angeles) have been inspired by the garment industry back home and have opened workshops in the US.

Costs of Production and Profits

The most difficult area in which to gain an overall impression has been the costs of knitwear production. The variable capital costs, thread and labour, have not generally been difficult to estimate; much more problematic are estimates of the 'real' costs of machinery investment and the costs of evading 'legality'.

In the spring of 1986, a 'simple' Carrousel loom cost in the region of 10 million pesos (US$25 000) and a small electrically powered loom cost on average 2 million pesos (US$5000). Second-hand small looms cost 500 000 pesos (US$1250), as did new overlock sewing machines. Though the Santiago producers have been investing in Carrousel looms since 1978, none has yet been able to purchase the more modern computer controlled models capable of producing far more complex weaving and colour designs, now found in workshops of Moroleón.

A list of selling prices does not, however, give a useful picture of the actual costs as these have been affected by the different deals open to producers in the acquisition of machinery. Up until 1984/5, machinery could be purchased on hire purchase with varying conditions of down payments and monthly sums; this had allowed relatively small-scale Santiago businesses to capitalise production. But with the growing restrictions on credit, machinery importers and suppliers have demanded cash down payments in full and producers have had to turn to banks and private lenders for loans. Some have found it easier to borrow from banks than others even though official Mexican policy has been to give credit support to small and 'micro' industry. Thread or clothing dealers may also forward capital and then demand repayment in product through a temporary contract.

The largest variable cost for the Santiago workshops has been thread. A large workshop with two Carrousels producing on average sixty dozen sweaters per day will require some 12 metric tons of thread per eight months' season. Once again restrictions on credit have meant that in recent years neither thread dealers nor the chemical plants have been willing to offer credit in the purchase of acrylan (which they had done throughout the 1970s). The factories now will only sell loads of over 40 metric tons at a time. The credit difficulties have tended to enhance the differences between workshops: large enterprises can buy in bulk direct from factories and achieve considerable savings in the per unit cost of thread; small workshops have not the liquidity to buy up thread or store it but must pay higher prices per unit for the small quantities they regularly purchase from dealers or other workshop owners. Certain large and medium-sized workshops in Santiago have thus specialised in a subsidiary business trading in thread. These enterprises have been able to buy in bulk at the start of a season and at regular intervals sell off thread to small producers at ever-increasing prices.

To the great consternation of producers, the price of thread soared during 1986. In December 1985, 'ordinary' quality yarn bought at discount prices from the factory cost 1200 pesos per kilo. The price rose to 2100 pesos per kilo in January 1986 and to 3050 pesos per kilo by June 1986.[5] With the June leap in price, owners found themselves stuck with orders agreed with purchasers for the forthcoming season that had badly miscalculated the costs of production. Even large producers knew they were powerless to renegotiate the orders.

In 1986 all owners were lamenting the declining profitability of knitwear production. By then, the cost of the acrylic thread was rising fast; credit was hard to secure; customers were cutting back their orders and taking longer to pay or falling into bad debt. Stuck with production contracts that had been negotiated on the basis of an erroneous assessment of thread costs over a future six-month period, by late July 1986, owners were fearful of a major drop in profits. Owners' fears proved justified. By July 1987 the price of acrylan thread had risen to 7000 pesos per kilo (more than doubled in the year), and producers found that their profits had been seriously squeezed.

Until recently, profit margins have been consistently high for medium and large-scale producers. Some workshop owners in early 1986 thought their profit had been around 300 per cent. One owner of a medium-sized workshop illustrated how he had arrived at this figure with reference to his own production. If he produced some 1000 sweaters per week (about fourteen dozen per day) which sold for 1000 pesos each his gross earning was 1 000 000 pesos (in March 1986 prices). His principal expenditures were 70 000 pesos per week for acrylic yarn and 50 000 pesos per week for wages for two men and three women. (He did not include remuneration to himself, his wife or his daughter, all of whom worked full time). Transporting the goods represented a cost of around 40 000 pesos per week while the amortisation of his machinery (seven old second-hand motorised looms, three overlock sewing machines, an ordinary sewing machine and a button holer) came to around 40 000 pesos per week. He had managed to keep the enterprise out of the municipal records and paid no taxes; living in his parents' house, he paid no rent. But in

1986 owners began to be extremely pressed by the rising costs and the increasing difficulties of getting credit. This owner could still claim a high profit rate, but only because he had bought and stored thread when the price was much lower, and offset the rising cost by selling profitably to small producers.

From 1960 until the early 1980s, no Santiago sweater workshop paid taxes, nor were they harassed by government inspectors whose task it was to check up on compliance with tax and labour legislation. For many years the word was passed around when inspectors were expected and owners warned in advance gave their workers the day off and arranged to transport looms and sewing machines to neighbours' houses. They also offered bribes of several thousands of pesos to ensure that they were not bothered by surprise investigations in future. In the first twenty years, the view predominated among the more prominent citizens that the initiative and endeavour fomenting Santiago's industry should not be penalised, nor should it fall victim to control or harassment coming from 'outside'. The state apparatus representing central government or Mexico City interests was not popular.

In the early 1980s, a group of younger, more politicised professionals (with the tacit support of the President) began to take up the cause of workshop workers, denouncing their exploitation and the non-compliance of labour legislation. This group invited the state governor to send inspectors to enforce legality in Santiago. The more vocal opposition came from within the ruling party, the Partido Revolucionario Institucional (PRI), and was hard for the workshop owners to brush aside.

Up until 1981, the workshops paid no local taxes but at that date a levy was imposed on all enterprises to be paid in cash or in goods so as to improve local public works. The local President suggested what amount each enterprise owner might pay on a 'voluntary' basis and this was fixed according to size of business. The levies were continued throughout that particular President's term of office and were subsequently replaced with a regular tax.

The institutionalisation of local taxation has been resented by most owners, even those with deeper commitment to the community. From 1985 to 1986, taxes rose 70 per cent and precipitated serious economic difficulties for several owners. A new tax assessment was enough to make one workshop close down. Other owners, especially of the medium workshops, resent the growing injustices whereby larger enterprises can negotiate better deals with the municipal authorities than they can themselves.

Differentiation among Workshops

To summarise the previous discussions, processes of differentiation within workshop production has led to a three-fold division whose characteristics are depicted in Table 4.1.

(1) At the bottom rung are small workshops with two or three motorised looms and a single sewing machine producing some five or six dozen garments per day. The majority produce sports shirts sold through local intermediaries in nearby markets. Wage workers assist family members only on a seasonal basis. Some are in an early stage of growth, and may have become blocked from entering the medium-sized category by the deteriorating economic climate; others are at a stage of dis-accumulation, due to the advancing years of the owners and the family's lower financial needs. But there is also a large group of more or less permanently small businesses, in which only limited investment has taken place. The majority have limited direct relations with larger local workshops. Poor quality output means that few find orders through local sub-contracting deals, though some are forced into buying thread locally. More acutely, this group has suffered from indirect pressures exerted by owners of larger workshops to prevent them from forming a co-operative to acquire thread and sell product.

(2) Medium-sized workshops possess six to fourteen motorised looms and produce twelve to twenty-five dozen garments per day; at least one loom is kept as a stand-by in case of breakdown. Most have diversified the machinery of the sewing room. By and large, workshop owners in this category are the most energetic seekers after profit; their workshops close for only short periods in the slack season. Men with a flair for machine management and repair who like experimenting and innovating tend to concentrate on production with the aim of producing the highest quality/lowest cost knitwear; those with a flair for commerce and financial management try to produce cheap and sell dear, travelling far and wide to search out the most lucrative markets. Amongst this group are risk takers and heavy exploiters of labour who pay low wages, and demand long hours of work.

(3) Large workshops have invested in at least one Carrousel (no workshop had more than two Carrousels in 1987). Output ranges from around forty to 100 dozen garments per day sold through more regular outlets (than in the medium-sized group) in large cities, wholesale clothing centres, and on the Mexican-US border. Work-

Table 4.1 Characteristics of selected workshops in mid-1986

	Output dozens per day	Starting year	Looms		Workshop wage workers		Family workers		Home[1] workers	Total[2] labour
			Motor	Carrousel	Women	Men	Spouse	Children		
Rafael	7	1981	3	0	0	0	1	5	0	7
Toribio/Rosa	9	1982	3	0	3	1	1	4(pt)[3]	0	6
Ramiro/Alicia	10	1960	3	0	3	1	1	0	5	8[1/2]
Yolanda	12	1982	6	0	5	3	0	1	8	14
Jorge	15	1982	7	0	3	2	1	1	1	9
Raul	25	1979	12	1	8	3	0	0	0	12
Carlos/Virginia	40	1979	3	1	10	3	1	0	0	15
Miguel	55	1962	3	2	8	4	1	0	30	29
José	60	1970	4	2	9	3	0	1	0	14
Hernández	100	1982	12	1	27	9	0	0	0	38

Notes: [1]Home workers are estimated as working 1/2 a working day
[2]Total labour includes owners as workers
[3](pt): part-time in which four workers are reckoned to do the job of one 'full-time' worker

shops in this group have faced strong pressure to alter relations with labour and this had led some to pay wages set at or above the official minimum. Unless owners have begun with considerable resources, workshops in this category are also among the longest established.

STRATEGIES OF ACCUMULATION

Typologies give only a rough indication of the similarities and disparities among enterprises; relatively little can be inferred about the relationships existing within and between the different size categories. To go deeper into these requires the presentation of information on the histories and present conditions of individual workshops. In this section the situation of seven workshops drawn from the three size groups will be described. Comments on the relationships between enterprises will be given by way of conclusion.

A Family Workshop

Rafael started his workshop in 1981 in a small room of his poor adobe house at a distance from the town centre. He had previously worked ten years on the looms in Mario's workshop, was tired of it and saw no prospects in remaining a *peón* for the rest of his life. He had only 6000 pesos saved, but was fortunate in being able to borrow 30 000 pesos from a cousin. With this capital he made downpayments on a second-hand loom and overlock from Guadalajara. By working day and night, he and his wife and children were able to pay off the debt of 20 000 pesos owed for the machines in six months and then began to repay the cousin's loan. Repayment was postponed in order that Rafael buy two additional small looms from a Santiago workshop. By 1986, it was unclear as to whether Rafael still owed money or not.

With three motorised looms, this workshop can produce cloth for between five and seven dozen garments per day. Rafael took the decision to produce only sports shirts as this entailed lower expenditures on thread as well as the possibility of selling some output all through the year. Though sports shirt manufacture is more demanding of labour time, the workshop employs no regular wage labour. Rafael's wife and daughters take turns on the overlock and perform all the other tasks of the labour process: sewing buttons, button holes and hemming. In 1986 the women insisted that the workshop acquire a second-hand button hole sewing machine to relieve them of some of the burden of hand sewing work.

Each week Rafael carries the workshop's output by bus to Guadalajara where he sells it to small-scale traders who supply the markets in the towns surrounding the city. Prices in Guadalajara are usually higher than those offered by local traders in Santiago. Though Rafael has built up a network of trading contacts, there is no contracted work or forward buying. Each week he has to negotiate a price in an effort to cover the rising production and transport costs. He is selling in a highly competitive market and fears having to return home with his output unsold. He also fears being robbed of his earnings on the way home.

Rafael speaks bitterly against the owners of the larger workshops in Santiago. According to his experience, they have no wish to help small producers like himself. He would be willing to work under sub-contract to a local workshop and thereby avoid the long risky selling trips to Guadalajara. But nobody wants to draw on his poor quality sports shirts. As a small producer, Rafael had been interested in the plan to start buying thread in bulk and to market goods collectively and was disappointed when the initiative came to nothing.

A Small Expanding Workshop

Toribio and Rosa bought two second-hand motor looms in Moroleón in 1982 and started to produce sports shirts. Toribio had already twenty years experience working looms, first for Ramiro's sister in Zamora and later for a *compadre* in Santiago. He saw himself as one of the few mechanical experts in the town, second only to Ramiro Espinoza. He believed that the other producers, especially those who concentrate on the commercial side of the business, waste much money buying in this expertise while his skills had given the small workshop a chance to succeed. The workshop was too small to purchase its own thread in bulk; however, Toribio had arranged to buy small quantities for a relatively low price from his *compadre's* workshop where he formerly worked in return for occasional emergency help with loom problems. By 1986, the workshop had three motor looms packed into a passage way outside the sewing room which were kept running for two shifts (of eight hours) each day manned by Toribio and a young loom operator who did the evening shift.

Matching Toribio's skills on the loom was his sisters' prowess on the overlock. Teresa had agreed to 'help out' in the workshop from when it opened. She has been greatly in demand as a sewer but it suited her to work part-time for her brother while taking a course in hairdressing in Zamora. She was producing some twelve dozen sports shirts per four hour stint and insisted on being paid piece-rates which brought in some 8000 pesos per week in spring, 1986 (at a rate considerably higher than the minimum wage). Not only could Teresa work fast and accurately, as an 'artisan' sewer she produced very little waste thread (which represents a substantial cost for workshops training young sewers). The waste there was, Toribio recycled in the cloth making stage. But relations between Teresa and Rosa, the owning wife (who cut the garments), were often strained. Teresa's sewing was essential for the workshop to gain a reputation for quality and build up a clientele in the early stages, but she crossed Rosa's efforts at managing the sewing room through her demand for piece-rates and for coming to work 'in her own time'. This, Rosa believed, set a bad example to the two other young women employed on the many other sewing room jobs. These women were treated as unskilled and paid wages well below the minimum legal wage.

A further advantage this small enterprise possessed was good contacts to buyers in Mexico City. A brother-in-law employed in a retail clothing firm had taken over the distribution of knitwear and had usually arranged regular orders even through the slack season. As the workshop did not own a vehicle, boxes of garments were taken by bus to Zamora and then freighted to the capital. Toribio had no interest in seeking out new markets in the north, but given the workshop's ability to produce good quality garments from the outset, it has been able to gain access to higher priced city markets.

The owning couple saw their rapid success as being primarily due to Toribio's lack of vices – he neither drank nor gambled – and to an ethos of hard-work and sacrifice in the family. To instil the latter, all five children have been expected to work after school and at weekends on workshop tasks appropriate to their ages (from around seven years). The owners have taken the workers' requests for higher wages as a personal affront and have consistently refused increases; they had a similar reaction to the pressures that they pay taxes, for which they were legally liable having three looms and three and a half workers.

The deepening recession from 1986 to 1987 forced change but has not yet threatened the workshop with closure. The rising price of acrylan together with the workshop's insecure command over this input led to a decision to limit the output of knitted cloth in the slack season and to produce garments cut and sewn from purchased woven cotton cloth. Toribio and Rosa have been able to purchase a small second-hand van, and make a garage for it. Once Toribio learnt to drive he could buy cheap cotton cloth in Moroleón and possibly offer the garments for sale there after sewing. But the change of product led to Teresa's resignation because working the new material slowed down her pace. Instead of producing the twelve dozen shirts per four hours, she could only manage seven dozen shirts when using cotton cloth. Toribio asked her to work longer hours to make up the quantity, but she did not like the idea and she left. As a producer of cotton clothing, the workshop now finds itself in a highly competitive market and the best it can hope is to survive. Should the market for knitwear recover, then the future would brighten again because of the particular advantages possessed by this workshop.

A Declining Small Workshop

As a business, Alicia and Ramiro's pioneering workshop has always been hard to place; in some ways progressive, yet it never expanded sufficiently to join the ranks of the medium-sized enterprises. Ramiro returned penniless from California in 1963 and for a number of years, he and Alicia continued to work for his brothers until they could get back into independent production. Ramiro remained the most technically expert and innovative among the Santiago producers and also enjoyed bargaining and negotiating with suppliers, buyers and competing producers (including his brothers). Yet while his brothers successfully expanded their enterprises being known locally as 'millionaires', and moved out of Santiago to palatial residences in Zamora, Ramiro's workshop remained small.

The progress of Alicia and Ramiro's workshop was baulked by a lack of investment capital for two main reasons. The first was their determination that each of their twelve children should be given a higher education that preferably would lead to a profession. This offer was open to the girls as well as the boys and all of them completed secondary school and 'Preparatoria' before taking a university or technical education. The workshop's proceeds were used for 'social investment' and the upward mobility of the children, not for business expansion. The second reason for a shortage of investment capital was Ramiro's alcoholism; not only was money spent on drink and gambling, Ramiro was absent for lengthy periods leaving both the production and commercial sides of the business in Alicia's hands. After years of struggle, Ramiro finally quit drinking in the mid-1970s (and then sponsored an alcoholics anonymous branch in the town).

In later years, the workshop possessed three motor looms (bought second-hand in Moroleón, and replaced with Swiss machines bought from the brothers) and has employed one loom operator. Alicia continued to sew, seaming sweaters in the busy season and making a variety of garments out of faulty/waste knitted cloth in the slack season. Some two or three young women were employed in the sewing room and the workshop continued to put sweaters out for embroidering, employing regularly some five home-workers and drawing in a further six or seven home-workers during the busy season. Ramiro generally took charge of cutting and managed the sales and distribution. He preferred a policy of selling garments to many small retailers in the towns of central Mexico and over the years built up a network of clients in Uruapan, Guadalajara, Morelia.

Throughout the workshop's life, Ramiro gained the reputation for being the most considerate and 'respectful' of employers. Alicia has always been viewed as the much tougher manager. Though small in size, the workshop was the first in Santiago to comply with minimum wage legislation, provide workers with social security and pay the officially recognised holiday time (two weeks). In mid-1986 weekly wages of some 15 000 pesos were paid to the loom operator and 10 000 pesos to the sewers; the home-workers were receiving some 600 pesos per dozen sweaters embroidered, the highest outwork payments in town. Furthermore, the workshop has paid a relatively high tax from the start. Ramiro's more enlightened attitude to labour and to the community's welfare at large has been criticised by his brothers and neighbouring sweater producers. He had not been forced into greater legality by the government inspectors, nor by a protesting labour force; his fellow producers saw his behaviour more in terms of 'bloody-mindedness'.

Ramiro and Alicia are now old and weakened by declining health but they have kept the workshop going. Their need for cash has diminished as only one child remains in education. The effect of the deepening recession on this workshop has been to push it into domestic production. The waged workers were dismissed at the end of the 1986 season and a loom and sewing machine sold. Ramiro still tinkered with his looms, produced cloth and enjoyed his conflictive relationships with brothers and neighbours. Alicia divided her time between sewing sweaters and garments from cotton cloth and visiting her family. Domestic workshop production has become a retirement occupation.

As parents, Ramiro and Alicia had held out high hopes for their childrens' future; they were not expected to enter the workshop. However, the skills and know-how picked up by the older children have stood them in good stead now that jobs in the 'formal' economy have become so hard to find. By the summer of 1987, three of the children had already launched their own independent garment producing workshops – assisted now and again by their parents. Two workshops located in Guadalajara are devoted to making jogging suits. The largest workshop is owned by a lawyer son in Zamora who started as a student to sell his parents' sweaters in Guadalajara.

A Woman's Workshop

The only woman to have opened a workshop on her own is Yolanda, a relative of the Espinoza. In the late 1970s she had agreed to work in partnership with a cousin: he made cloth and cut out garments, while she sewed on an overlock in her own house. They shared the profits between them. She discovered a flair for colour and design especially of children's clothes and in 1980 decided to acquire her own looms and sewing machines. Yolanda's husband continued to look after his few cows and sell milk; he never participated in the workshop. Yolanda (now in her fifties) believed she confronted major difficulties that have prevented her from expanding out of the class of medium-sized producers.

Her workshop has produced a wider range of garments than any other: apart from sweaters and sports shirts, she produces children's and infant's clothing and women's knitted suits. She pays great attention to style and adornment and her garments are much sought after locally. In 1986 the workshop possessed six looms on which cloth for twelve to fourteen dozen garments was produced each day. She employed two or three loom operators (depending on the season) who were paid some 10 000 pesos (in spring, 1986). She and a daughter worked full time in the sewing room where another five women were employed paid at different rates. The worker with four years experience in Yolanda's workshop cutting and finishing was paid a weekly wage of 7500 pesos; the steam presser received 6000 pesos; and the unskilled trainee sewers received 5000 or 5500 pesos.

Although Yolanda has the reputation for paying low wages her workshop has never lacked labour. On the contrary, a stream of young women are brought to Yolanda by their mothers in the hope that they can receive a training. This has been a mixed blessing. While in training, workers tend to be slower, more wasteful of thread and more negligent of their machines. Yolanda has responded by becoming a hard task mistress. But the workshop finds it hard to keep workers; once they have reached a certain level of proficiency many leave to find better paying jobs in the larger workshops. With the stronger differentiation among enterprises especially in terms of wage policy in recent years, this tendency has increased. As a result, Yolanda decided to secure a more experienced, and costly, overlock sewer to boost production and agreed to pay her both the minimum wage and give her social security.

Given the importance of individually styled and adorned clothes, Yolanda has drawn on many home-workers. In the past, her garments carried such heavy embroidery that home-workers spent up to two days on each garment. Now, in line with changing fashions, the embroidery is more discrete; by 1986 some adornment was being done inside the workshop with a recently acquired machine. Some eight home-workers were regularly employed, paid at relatively low rates.

Not only does Yolanda's choice of product and position as a training workshop have a bearing on the social representation of women, she has also confronted a distinct marketing situation when compared with her male counterparts. Given her class and generation, not surprisingly Yolanda has never considered driving a vehicle. But even if she had overcome this obstacle, social barriers would have still prevented her from travelling on her own as a younger woman to create a network of clients in the distant higher-priced zones of the country. Instead she built up a clientele among the retailers in Guadalajara, personally taking samples around on Sundays and later dispatching the orders through the freight/bus companies. She also tried to develop contacts amongst the supermarket chains in Mexico City but found herself unequal to the accounting procedures and paperwork demanded. She was aware that as a woman she had been more exposed to tricks and deceits in the course of her commercial dealings. Selling in the 'outside world' was a constant source of anxiety.

In later years, Yolanda's reputation has meant that the largest number of clients now come themselves to place and pick up orders from the Santiago workshop. Buyers have included retailers from the nearby towns, local traders and many women who buy up the most original of her clothing to take to the US for sale. The development of these essentially female, long-distance marketing channels gave Yolanda a new lease of life and she began to negotiate a bank loan of 2 million pesos so as to purchase more specialised sewing machines (never considering, in her case, investment in a Carrousel loom).

At that point disaster struck. On the night of 24 June 1986, a flood swept through part of the town causing much damage. Yolanda and her husband nearly drowned as the flood waters broke down doors and overwhelmed the house. The looms and sewing machines were clogged up with silt and the thread and finished garments were sodden and dirty. Neighbours and workers shared the task of cleaning and repairing what could be saved; but for many months, Yolanda was unwell and unwilling to re-open the workshop. She tried to get a government grant to help repair the flood damage, but although promised, the grant never materialised. The shock which finally led her to start work again was the decision of her twenty year old son, then attending Preparatoria, to leave school and go as an illegal migrant to San Francisco in order to no longer be a financial burden on her.

By the summer of 1987, two looms were back working in Yolanda's workshop manned by a single loom operator. She was able to re-employ her experienced overlock sewer who now took on the job of cutting in addition to the sewing and still received the legal minimum wage. Three young trainee sewers were employed for the other workshop tasks on wages below the legal minimum. Production varied daily between some five to eight dozen garments, depending on the orders received. But Yolanda was more hopeful of the future and had recently managed to get a private loan to enable her to buy a specialised machine to 'invisibly' sew neckbands onto the garments. Given Yolanda's involvement in an export market, albeit not the most profitable part of it, there is reason to suggest that she can build up her workshop once more.

A Medium-sized Workshop Struggling to Accumulate

Jorge had spent many years in California as a factory worker. He lived with his family in Merced, until in 1981 they decided to return home. The first work Jorge found in Mexico was selling plastic goods. But through Manuel Espinoza and a rich *compadre* in Zamora he was able to raise enough capital to start a workshop in 1982. He took over his parents' house and started producing both sweaters and sports shirts on three second-hand motor looms and an overlock. The workshop expanded: by 1984 another four motor looms had been acquired. But the last purchase of a new Italian motor loom had brought difficulties in that finding no source of credit, Jorge had to pay 1.2 million pesos in cash for it. Given the withdrawal of credit, Jorge by 1986 had despaired of being able to expand further. He saw his workshop as being 'stuck' in the medium-sized class.

Jorge was able to produce cloth for some fifteen dozen garments per day using six looms while the seventh loom was on hand in case of breakdown. He employed two or three loom operators, depending on the season, paying them 12 000 pesos per week in early 1986. From the start his wife has sewn garments on the overlock while three women have been employed on unskilled sewing and other sewing-room work. With the expansion of loom capacity, Jorge persuaded Julia, his niece, to become an out-worker and he provided her with an overlock in her own house. She sewed some forty-eight dozen sports shirts per week and on her insistence was paid piece-rates, which gave her a weekly wage of around 10 000 pesos (in early 1986). Partly by putting out sewing work, Jorge has claimed to be a family enterprise, not liable for taxation.

Though Jorge was competent at cutting and operating a loom, he recognised that far greater profits lay in developing the commercial side. He spent most of the time 'on the road' in the van he had bought before leaving the US. He experimented with selling in all types of markets. Sometimes he dealt with trading firms on the Mexican-US border and though he could easily sell his garments (faithfully copied from current Sears and Roebuck catalogues) his was not a large enough enterprise to easily withstand the delays in payments. Sometimes he joined with other Santiago producers to send garments to the traders of Moroleón. The most reliable and lucrative market he found in towns such as Zacatecas, Nayarit, Colima where he sold to both retailers and traders. Though Jorge had for a time employed a transporter to take goods to clients, he found that this delegation lost him business. He saw personal contacts as essential for the building up of a regular clientele and for prompt payment.

The area of business where Jorge had greatest hopes of increasing his rate of profit was in the purchase of thread. All the larger Santiago producers were interested in the possibility of collective purchase so as to bring down the unit price. Jorge wanted low cost thread not only for his own manufacturing, but also for sale. He developed useful contacts in the San Luis Potosi factory and offered to take charge of the purchase on behalf of neighbouring producers. The deals went through, though not without considerable suspicions being raised as to what Jorge's full gains were from the operation. Jorge was able to keep aside for use and future sale a large quantity of thread.

The flood of June 1986, ended Jorge's hopes of profiting from thread deals. The waters destroyed about 1 metric ton of acrylan, worth at the time an estimated 3 million pesos. This heavy financial loss prompted Jorge to leave the garment sector completely. Although the looms have not been sold, they have not been at work since October 1986. Instead, Jorge has become a dealer in kitchen equipment, acquiring cut-price liquidisers, pots and pans through a *compadre* in a factory in Monterrey for sale around the same circuit of towns where he had previously sold his garments. Maybe when the prospects for garment manufacture improve he will resume production.

A Large Workshop Struggling to Accumulate

In the early 1980s children of the rich cattle owners began to take an interest in the garment industry in Santiago. Their entry has tended to come later when other prospects for social advancement appeared more limited. In the case of the Hernández, one brother had practised as a lawyer for some years but judged he could live better as an industrialist and so went into the business with his brother who had already worked in the garment trade in Guadalajara with his sister. Family wealth meant that large workshops could be set up from the start; they did not need to progress from the small scale in an incremental fashion.

Family quarrels in the first few months led to temporary closure. The sister left and took away the sewing machines in order to start an independent workshop making women's clothes from purchased cloth. Some six months later the brothers re-opened the workshop and called back the labour force. Though the workshop was established in Santiago, the brothers preferred to live in Zamora. Due to this separation between home and work, the wives have played no part in workshop management. After the sister's departure, no woman has been represented as an owner, though the Hernández' mother visits the sewing room, and a younger sister works as a cutter. The image of gender complementarity has disappeared and the brothers have appointed a male overseer to supervise the sewing room as well as the loom room.

By late 1985 the workshop had fifteen motor looms and despite problems of credit and investment financing, the brothers decided to acquire a Carrousel in November, 1985, but kept seven of the motor looms in production. By early 1986, the Hernández were producing the largest number of garments of all Santiago workshops (around 100 dozen per day) and employed the largest labour force: nine men and twenty-seven women.

The Hernández owned two trucks which were on the road most of the time. The brothers shared the burden of travelling and seeking out new clients while a brother-in-law was employed as a full-time transporter to bring thread and deliver garments. The workshop bought thread in bulk direct from the factories and sold the excess to small and medium-sized producers locally. The bulk of the garments (sweaters, sports shirts, jogging suits) were taken for sale in northern Mexico, and a substantial proportion entered the US. In addition to selling their own output, the brothers also bought up good quality garments from other producers in Santiago. Thus profits in this workshop were derived from deals made with other producers with respect to thread and product as well as from the workshop's own production and exchange relations.

The Hernández workshop had earned a poor reputation with regards to labour relations. The workshop constantly strove to lower production costs by paying low wages. This policy was criticised as exploitative not only by workers but also by owners of other large workshops who saw the brothers as trying to undercut them.

A Large Established Workshop

As a member of the Espinoza clan, José has spent the whole of his adult life in the sweater-making business. At present, his is probably the most securely established workshop in town. Through preference he has stuck to sweaters, and has refused to diversify production; owing to the seasonality of demand the workshop is closed for four months every year.

In the past, José used to acquire thread through a special agreement with the factory at Aguascalientes, but this came to an end with the withdrawal of credit facilities by the factory and a decline in thread quality. When younger, José travelled throughout the country exploring market potential, and sold much of the output in Chihuahua, Monterrey and in the border towns. He came to know in detail what styles, colours, sizing and decoration would sell best in the different markets. With advancing years, he stopped travelling so extensively and changed his selling policy. He began producing higher quality goods for outlets closer to home in Mexico City, Moroleón and Guadalajara.

José was the first to begin a process of capitalisation of production when he purchased a Carrousel in 1978. The time for investment was propitious. He found no difficulty in raising the purchase price through the bank. Indeed, he claimed that a Zamora branch had first approached him with the offer of a loan to make the purchase, while his own bank in Jacona was unable to come up with such favourable terms. With hindsight, José rationalised his decision to invest in a Carrousel with reference to his desire to improve quality and end the workshop's reliance on domestic out-work. He stopped hand embroidery and concentrated on new weaves and colour mixes. At the same time, labour protest was beginning to grow; he foresaw that by substituting capital for labour, the more discontented male workers could be laid off.

The next stage in the strategy to improve quality was José's decision in 1980 to alter the basis of remuneration from paying piece-rates to paying a fixed weekly wage. Under the piece-rate system, he had observed, workers were prone to work as fast as possible with little attention to detail. Only when workers were assured of a weekly wage did José find he could insist on improvement. Threats of labour action in the early 1980s forced José to review his employment policy and in 1983 he turned 'legal' to the extent of reimbursing all workers with wages pegged to the official minimum wage. The strategy brought benefits; with a higher wage policy, José could take his pick from among the most skilled sewers in town and did not have to lose money through training. He bought a second Carrousel in 1983, partly in order to avoid night shift work. In early 1986 all women workers regardless of job in the workshop were receiving the official minimum wage, while the men were receiving between 13 000 and 15 000 pesos depending on their experience.

By the summer of 1986, José was preoccupied by the workshop's future. The rising price of thread and the continued decline in its quality posed major problems. He had already negotiated his autumn season's orders with his main customers in May; and was taken by surprise by the new price rise in July. He feared he would be unable to recoup enough through the sales to buy the next season's thread. Furthermore, he could already mark that customers were reducing their orders: some who had formerly bought van loads were now ordering only a few dozen. A year later, his only option had been to reduce output and work shorter hours.

Though concerned with the short-run problems, José remained optimistic about the future of the garment industry of Santiago. With regards to his own workshop the prospects looked bright. Although he had hoped to settle his children in the professions, one of his sons had long wanted to learn the sweater trade. After an apprenticeship in the workshop, this son took a technical course in loom knitting and business management in Guadalajara and returned to operate his father's Carrousels. José foresaw retiring in the near future so that his son would be more free to expand the business along new lines.

RELATIONS AMONG WORKSHOPS

Formally, those who own looms and overlocks, manage workshops and employ wage labour belong to the same capitalist class in local society and their common interests should come to the fore both with respect to other property-owning classes (the old agrarian elite) and to labour. But class positions in present-day Santiago are not yet so clear cut. This is partly because there is some overlapping in both directions: on the one side a chosen family strategy may be to own both workshops and cattle with the result that industrial and agrarian interests are 'mixed' and, on the other, as some male workers are given the opportunity to later become workshop owners the distinction between owners of capital and sellers of labour can be blurred. More importantly, the idea that workshop owners constitute a class of itself is undermined by the perpetuation of differences among workshops. Though many prosperous owners may now dwell on their past poverty and tell dramatic 'rags to riches' stories, these owners have come from more privileged families and have never believed that they share a social identity or have material interests in common with poor small-scale producers of low quality garments.

The workshop differentiation in Santiago suggests that not only are opportunities for advancement out of the small size category now relatively limited, but that strategies of accumulation may include the exploitation of the weaker concerns by the stronger. One example of this tendency has been the decision by larger businesses to buy thread cheaply in bulk for sale at higher per unit prices to smaller workshops. However, one must be careful not to overemphasise the extent of the linkages of dependence. Quality differentials have tended to put a break on the formation of sub-contracting agreements across size categories; many owners of small workshops point more to the absence of links rather than to the exploitation they suffer. Indirectly, the small workshops may be more prejudiced by the larger. Owners of larger workshops can reinforce their dominant position in several ways: they can capture the bulk of the credit available through official channels; they are better able to 'buy' off government inspectors and lawyers; they can exert greatest political clout.

In the past, perhaps the most visible interest which workshop owners shared was to keep labour 'in its place'. Labour unrest and protest in one workshop was a threat to all; no owner wanted official attention turned in the direction of labour conditions in Santiago. But that was before any division in employment policy had occurred. After some workshops began to pay minimum wages and conceded some workers' benefits then a rift appeared within the same stratum of workshops between those which were more or less 'legal' and those which remained illegal and had most to fear from cases being brought before the state authorities.

Apart from collaboration to ensure the black-listing of 'difficult' workers, there appears to have been no common strategy pursued by owners, even within the same stratum. Unlike in Moroleón, workshop owners have been reluctant to act collectively so as to secure workers' training facilities in the town (in spite of the offers made by the secondary school to develop programmes of technical training).[6] Nor have the majority of owners supported the schemes suggested by government bodies encharged with fomenting small-

scale industry (such as to open a joint sales outlet in the town).
Inter-workshop relations tend to be more intense between owners belonging to the same family or who share a similar social status (which may then be translated into the idiom of kin through *compadrazgo*). These social ties usually mean that workshops of similar type and size are linked, but the relationships are likely to be both highly personalised and ambivalent. Within workshop groupings, owners will sometimes help each other out; such as by collaborating when rushed orders must be completed, or by lending money and maybe workers with particular skills. But since owners are well aware that they are competing in the same markets then there are limits to the extent of trust and collaboration.

Notes

1. The first 'official' list of enterprises was compiled by a reforming Municipal President. On the basis of local knowledge he pressed workshop owners to contribute in cash or goods to public works for the social good.
2. The changing dollar-peso exchange rate is given in Appendix II. In early 1986 men's basic wages were US$25–30 per week; while Carrousel workers could earn US$30–50.
3. Trainee women received some US$10 per week; menial workers, US$15–17; overlock workers, US$17–20; experienced overlock workers, US$25 per week.
4. Industrial home-workers received from US$0.60–0.90 to US$1.20 per dozen garments in early 1986.
5. The dollar value of thread has stayed roughly the same at US$5 per kilo.
6. The headmaster of the secondary school in Santiago thought that workshop owners could do much more to help train workers and secure a better future for the industry. He had tried to interest owners of the larger enterprises in training schemes run from the school but had received no support.

5 Labour Relations and Workers' Strategies

LABOUR RELATIONS IN THE WORKSHOPS

This chapter will discuss the social relations of production in the knitwear workshops from the perspective of labour in terms of a double relationship. It will first explore how *pre-existing relations of gender and class moulded the form taken by labour relations in the workshops*. Second, it will suggest how an *industrialisation process of some twenty-seven years' duration has conditioned and reformulated the relations of gender and class expressed inside the workshops*. To do this, the discussion will try to sketch out the character of a *'household model'* adopted in the early phase and surviving in some workshops to the present day, summarise the pressures leading to its partial overthrow and discuss the institution of an alternative labour–capital relation.

The early phase of labour relations in Santiago is impossible to reconstruct with any accuracy, and will not be attempted here. Relevant for this chapter is the question of how the older model of workshop relations appears at the present day. The discussion will begin by focusing on two categories of women workers who still most commonly portray themselves as 'helpers' rather than as waged employees and then examine the constituents of labour relations in a selection of medium and large workshops that can still be said to be underpinned by a model of household relations. Conditions in these more traditionally organised workshops will be contrasted with those of 'improved' workshops where a different labour policy has been instated. Within this analysis instances of labour protest in Santiago will be explored in order to illustrate the issues and abuses workers have confronted and show how workers have tried to renegotiate the terms of their relations with capital.

Workshop workers in Santiago belong to four main categories: inside the workshops are male loom operators, skilled and unskilled female sewing room workers; outside the workshop are female industrial home-workers. Not only have the workshops' demand for the different categories of labour altered over time, each type of worker has had a different relationship with the workshop. The analysis will begin with the two groups of workers which to the present day most commonly portray themselves as 'helpers': the home-workers and the most highly skilled 'artisan' overlock sewers. Workshop relations in general will then be explored

Labour Relations and Home-workers

From 1960 until the early 1980s most married women took in outwork from the workshops at one time or another, and their daughters might begin to embroider independently from when they were eight years old. The workshops had initially called on owners' relatives and neighbours, and on women's networks to supply home-workers: word would be passed around that a particular owning wife needed 'help' and new home-workers would be given personal recommendations by friends. After this introduction, a home-worker might secure regular work. But the majority of poor women who most needed out-work were not presented through friends; instead they had to come to the workshops on a daily basis queuing up outside the doors from the early morning in the hope of getting a few garments to sew.

Former home-workers usually speak of there having been obligations on both sides. Home-workers were prepared to help *comadres*, neighbours, or the señoras who had previously employed them for domestic labour but it was also customary for 'help' to be returned in the form of cash loans. According to Ramiro, his regular home-workers had all wanted a substantial cash sum before they started, which both parties acknowledged would never be repaid. It represented a form of 'contracting' by the out-worker of the owner which Ramiro and the others had to accept. Indeed, his brother Manuel later offered all women seeking out-work an initial cash 'loan' as a matter of course. Home-workers expected owners to continue to advance them money in emergencies while they were linked to the workshop: these later loans were generally repaid. A 'good' owner in out-workers' eyes was one who was prepared to lend large sums, and would tear up the note of the loan before full repayment had been made. Access to cash loans was as important a part of the relationship as the amount paid per sweater embroidered.

For the women taking in out-work, the returns to their labour have been remembered most clearly in terms of the goods that could be bought with the proceeds of one garment embroidered or sewn. They say that for the last twenty years the exchange value of the remuneration has stayed roughly the same. But what does not generally enter into their calculation is the length of time required. Some women entered domestic out-work in order to provide their children with additional food that was only available through purchase; other women became 'target' workers taking in out-work until they had saved enough to buy one expensive household item. (One women worked seven years to buy a television set.) Sometimes they asked workshop owners to withhold payment until the savings were sufficient.

The distribution of cash from workshops to home-worker in this fashion through gifts, loans and payments bore a connection with a vision of household relations. Entering a workshop could be marked by a gift, and thereafter the owner (usually the owning husband as 'head of household') would express concern by giving help at times of need. Payments converted into access to food goods and household items reflected a more benevolent and redistributive aspect of household relations. But the way garment distribution and collection was organised was more consistent with authority and hierarchy. While owning husbands tended to take charge of loans, the owning wife was mainly responsible for organising the out-work itself.

A book was kept at each workshop to note down names of home-workers and numbers of garments taken; the owning wife gave strict instructions as to design and colour and gave out skeins of thread, but never needles. On return the embroidered garments were thoroughly checked for faults and a great fuss ensued if a garment was missing. Old home-workers still recall the relief they felt that they had lost none, for there were heavy penalties imposed. Were an out-worker to 'lose' a garment, then she would be called a thief and black-listed. Dirtiness was also a difficult problem to avoid especially for those from the central slum area. Workshops rarely directed penalised workers for bringing back dirty garments but they would not be rewarded with more regular 'contracts'. A workshop's regular home-workers had reached a relationship of greater trust with their employers and for them the counting, and checking of workmanship and dirtiness were more a formality.

The impression had been given by owners that home-workers were made redundant because of technological change, the re-organisation of workshop production and changing consumer taste. This was undoubtedly true, but only up to a point. The home-workers' version of events stressed that domestic out-work declined because women in Santiago were no longer willing to do it. This was partly a matter of generation and the domestic cycle. When daughters were old enough to enter the workshops as sewers then mothers could thankfully 'retire'. Not only has out-work been badly remunerated compared to work inside the workshops, it has been seen as seriously damaging health, especially the eyesight of many women as they struggled to sew by candle-light. Neither owners nor workers could find a way of 'modernising' the relations of adornment home-work.

Santiago workshops continuing to put work out tend to be those where owning wives are still active in the enterprise, or where a substitute female 'agent' could be found. After Jesús and Manuel Espinoza transferred their workshops to Zamora in 1984 they continued to rely on home-workers in Santiago and appointed elderly home-workers as their agents to take care of the sweater distribution and collection, recruitment and payment. The woman who has received greatest benefit from out-work in Santiago is Marta, who works for Jesús Espinoza. She combines sweater distribution and embroidering with running a small shop selling vegetables, sweets and potato crisps. Marta, now in her sixties, has been a home-worker since the industry began. Each week Jesús brings at least thirty dozen sweaters to her shop and stops for a chat. She usually keeps some five dozen to embroider herself and distributes the rest among twenty regular home-workers. In return for her supervisory role Marta receives an annual 'tip'. At first her earnings went towards consumer durables such as a television set, but as her elderly husband finds it more difficult to work his *ecuaro*, most of her income now goes on food. She spends the 'tip' on taking her family to Acapulco for a weekend at a hotel. Marta is the only home-worker in a strong enough position to challenge or negotiate with a workshop; this she does now and again. She has tried to stop the deterioration in the home-workers' 'terms of trade'. She argues for rises in payment in a tough, no-nonsense manner when she sees that the sum paid for embroidering a sweater has fallen below the price of a food item she believes an appropriate equivalent. She also checks that her employer is not demanding designs that are more complicated and therefore more time consuming than 'normal'; she is not going to let Jesús exploit women's labour more than he has already done.

The present home-workers have certain shared characteristics and constitute a specific labour group. They belong to poor social strata.

Most have been married for at least ten years, have many young children and, prior to marriage, did not work in the workshops. The majority are married to agricultural labourers who find only intermittent employment, most of the others have husbands in the US who send money home infrequently.

Home-workers agreed that one could not survive on the earnings of out-work alone. Though some periodically have had to fully support themselves and their children by working very long hours, for the most part out-work can only contribute a part of the household income. Thus most of the women who were regular home-workers have access to other sources of household income. The following biographical notes illustrate the situation of many women who still take on domestic out-work.

> Lupe has worked for over sixteen years as an embroiderer and has taken work from most of the putting-out workshops. Each day she rises early (at around 4.30 am) so as to start embroidering before her children are awake and she aims to sew some four dozen sweaters per day. She shares the domestic work with her daughter, who although old enough to enter a workshop has not been given permission to do so by her father. The family is very poor, living in Lupe's mother's house in the central slum. They have not managed to acquire any consumer durables, and still cook on a wood-burning hearth. Lupe's husband is an agricultural labourer who often spends his earnings on drink; they have two unmarried sons in Mexico City who occasionally send money back and two children still at school. Until her husband relents about the daughter's employment, Lupe must continue embroidering. She considers that the conditions of out-work have deteriorated; and workshops have stopped the former practice of giving workers garments occasionally as presents.
>
> María has worked for Lola ever since she married eleven years ago. They had been introduced by her brother-in-law. She embroiders sweaters, babies' shawls and clothes, being paid 600 pesos per dozen (in early 1986). She is able to sew unusual stitches and is the only regular out-worker kept on by that workshop. María sews some six or eight dozen garments per week working two to three hours in the afternoons. She thinks Lola has been generous, giving her sweaters and shawls for her children and lending her money. Her husband usually carries the bags of sweaters on his way to and from work. When the

embroidery is required urgently, the workshop sends them round to her house. María is married to a loom operator at Mario's workshop who brings home some 16 000 pesos per week after working a twelve hour day. They have four small children, but the two eldest daughters are badly handicapped. Her husband does not have 'vices' and hands over most of his wages to her. She spends her own earnings on clothes, and household needs, but there has never been enough income to seek medical help for the handicapped daughters.

For the last three years Hilda has taken in out-work from her brother, Francisco (who puts out to four home-workers). She tacks the side seams and sleeves of sweaters, preferring this work as it is less demanding than embroidery and can be done more easily at night. The quantity available fluctuates but there are always some garments to sew. She can sew eighteen dozen per day, working four to five hours in the afternoons and evenings. She was paid thirty-nine pesos per dozen (in early 1986) and considered that her brother had been ungenerous. She has asked to be paid every three months in order to save up to buy clothes for the children and meet medicine and doctors' bills. At first Hilda used to go to the workshop in order to get the sweaters, but having many small children, this was difficult; now her brother brings them to her house. Hilda has nine children ranging from two to nineteen years; five are still at school. Her husband has no fixed job and seeks occasional employment as a brick layer, or agricultural labourer; sometimes he has gone to the US as an illegal immigrant. Up to three years ago he used to provide some of the family's maize and beans by sowing an *ecuaro*. His refusal to provide food precipitated Hilda's decision to take in out-work. Sometimes he gives Hilda a share of his wages, but he often spends all his money on drink. She is the poorest member of her family and lives in the central slum. Some of her brothers in the US send money back to her. They have wanted her to bring the children to live in California, but she has refused to leave her husband. Her eldest daughter works independently as a homeworker. She embroiders so as to pay her way while taking a course in business administration in Jacona.

Skilled Sewers as 'Helpers'

Though the number of skilled sewers who can be classed as 'artisans' has always been very small, nevertheless their presence in the labouring community has been of considerable importance. Despite the restructuring and re-organisation of workshop activity, their skills continue to be in demand. They are therefore more free to set some of the terms of their working conditions. By having a choice as to which workshop to enter, what system of remuneration to demand and what conditions to accept, the artisans provide an indication of aspects of the 'household model' of labour relations that women have seen as important. Artisans tend to be older than the average workshop workers, and are generally unmarried; they have reached phenomenal rates of output while at the same time being highly proficient in understanding and repairing their machines.

Artisan sewers may work their whole lives for one workshop or they may prefer to help a number of owners out of temporary production problems, often choosing workshops belonging to relatives. Characteristically, artisan sewers ask to be paid according to piece-rates – as virtually all workers were in the 1960s and 1970s. Given the common assumption that piece-rates are a more exploitative form of labour remuneration, it is interesting to understand this preference. Working at high speeds clearly means that sewers can earn more through piece-rates than through fixed weekly wages. But as important if not more so is the fact that piece-rates allow workers greater control over their labour time.

They have a greater right to come and go from the workshop without interference. Where highly skilled overlock sewers have not been able to negotiate piece-rates, most try to make a special arrangement to work different working hours from the other sewers.

Contests over control of labour time has generally led to highly conflict-ridden relationships between artisan sewers and owning wives. This can be rooted at various levels. Wives in charge of managing and disciplining 'ordinary' workshop workers see the artisan as setting a harmful example to the others. A wife, furthermore, may resent that an artisan usurps her symbolic position alongside her husband on the loom. Many artisan sewers who 'help out' and insist on rights to some personal freedom do not feel any deep social difference between themselves and their employers.

> Teresa, working her brother Toribio's overlock in 1986, had previously 'helped out' in many workshops, including spending two months at the Ecuadureo workshop (owned by Ramiro's brother-in-law). She is twenty-nine years old, unmarried and lives

at home with her parents (who formerly possessed land and cattle and had been dealers in agricultural goods). Teresa enjoys her professionalism, and the sense of being valued as a sewer; she was not unduly upset by the criticisms of 'irresponsiblity' as to her hours of work coming from many owning wives, including her sister-in-law, Rosa. But as she did not want to spend the rest of her life in the workshops, nor was tempted to start her own, she enrolled in a beauty-care and hairdressing course in Zamora (while working part-time for her brother). Finishing the course, she opened a 'salon' in the front room of her parents' house. After leaving her brother's workshop (because of the change of product which slowed down her output), she received many offers of sewing work. She still sews a few dozen sports shirts each week for a local dentist with a couple of looms to keep 'her hand in' and the rest of the time she works in her hair salon.

Many artisan sewers have come from wealthier strata in town and consider themselves closer to owners than to young ordinary workshop workers. So although they have struggled for better working conditions for themselves as individuals, there is no evidence to suggest that artisan sewers are interested in contributing to more collective struggles. Many consider that the opening of the workshops brought enormous benefits to the women of Santiago.

María Rosa had worked for Manuel Espinoza since 1962; she never married. As an old school friend of Manuel's wife, she had a 'tu' relationship with the family (i.e. used the familiar form of address). At first she took in homework while continuing to run a private primary school, two years later she entered the workshop. She became very proficient at overlock sewing and proud that her needles lasted a year, while other sewers might break several in one day. Manuel often took her to Moroleón when buying machinery for the sewing room. Manuel paid María Rosa wages a little higher than the other sewers, and latterly gave her social security. She occasionally asked for a wage increase when she thought it justifiable. Working in a room by herself, she was allowed to work a 9 am to 6 pm day instead of the 8 am to 5 pm day worked by the rest of the labour force. She could also leave the workshop for short spells in the daytime, but often stayed on late to play with the owners' children.

After fifteen years on the overlock, Manuel insisted she 'rest' and have a change of scene; he put her in the main sewing room as supervisor and checker of goods – a job previously done by his wife. When the workshop moved to Zamora in 1984, María Rosa retired because she could not leave her old sick mother for so long a day. Manuel kept up her social security payments until she reached the official retirement age and gave her a cash sum. This 'nest egg' was soon used up on paying private doctors fees for attending to her mother; though privileged by social security, María Rosa had wanted 'only the best' treatment for her. She is now nearly destitute and runs a small sweet shop from the front room of her house.

The 'Household Model' Surviving in the Workshops

The majority of workshops in Santiago demonstrate the survival of facets of the 'household model' of labour relations; but, as there are important differences in the way the household model underpins social relations of production in the medium and large workshops, three contrasting workshops have been selected for analysis from which a more general discussion will be developed.

(1) Raul's workshop is in a two-storied brick building adjoining his house, some distance from the town centre. He produces sports shirts for sale in a nearby circuit of towns: Uruapan, Sahuayo and Guadalajara. On the ground floor are the looms (twelve motor looms in 1986) and on the first floor, reached by an outside staircase, is the sewing room. The workshop has few windows, low ceilings and is insufficiently ventilated. To keep the workshop 'out of sight' the ground floor windows are often closed although the clank of machinery makes detection easy. All the workers come from the same *barrio*: Raul has recruited them by first approaching their parents with an offer of jobs for their children. The three men working the looms are in their late twenties and married. They are conscientious workers but see their employment as temporary before they go north to the US.

The eight women employed in the sewing room are divided into two groups: machine sewers and other workers. None are married and they range from seventeen to twenty-four years of age. The machine sewers have been employed the longest, two sisters from the day the workshop opened in 1982. This group is rewarded with higher wages and other favours but each sewer is paid at a different rate, from between 7000 and 9500 pesos per week. Wage differentials do not only reflect length of time in the workshop or type of machine worked. In the case of the two sisters, the older sister has sewn necks and button holes and receives the top workshop wage of 9500 pesos, the young sister has sewn buttons and checks the finished garments receiving 8500 pesos. They had not been allowed to change jobs. The sisters could not explain why their wages differed but they saw it as 'natural'. In their opinion, not only was it right that the elder of the two sisters should be paid more on account of her position in the family, the younger sister's job 'depended' on the elder's, i.e. it came later in the labour process and was on those grounds deemed of lesser worth.

The other group of workers are younger and were paid wages of 6000 pesos or under, even though some have been employed by the workshop for more than two years. These workers are resentful of their lower status and earnings, and do not normally mix with the higher paid group of sewers. Soledad, an ironer aged twenty-three years, had never wanted to go into a workshop, hoping instead to work in a strawberry packing plant in Jacona. But her parents sent her to work for Raul whose workshop lay just around the corner. Working the heavy steam press in an unventilated room is unpleasant work, especially in the hot season and it was only reimbursed with a wage of 6000 pesos. Raul has refused to increase the wage levels of this group claiming that he cannot afford it. When Soledad is particularly fed up she takes days off and Raul has to come to her house in search of his 'muchachita' – the young women laugh at him behind his back for calling them 'little girls'. She is fairly certain Raul will never sack her as nobody else would accept such a low wage.

In the workshop Raul is not a strict taskmaster nor does he enforce a harsh work discipline. His wife comes in now and again though has not played a major role in management or production. The women are allowed to talk and sing and play radios or tape recorders while at work. Raul and his wife organise excursions for the women twice a year, taking them to Guadalajara, Guanajuato or down to the sea at Manzanillo; for most, this has been the only opportunity to leave Santiago. Raul pays full medical expenses of the machine sewers and transports them to Zamora for treatment if necessary; but he pays only half the expenses of the other group. None of the workers believe it would be in their interests to press for social security. The workers get a bonus of an extra two weeks' pay at Christmas time and two weeks' paid holiday per year. The workshop rarely closes, so the workers can earn all year round. The wages rise every six months, in January and July, at the same time as the Government legislation on wages and prices. All of the women, however, receive wages below the official minimum level.

(2) Lola and Juan have taken over her father's workshop which opened in 1978. In 1986 they were employing one man and five women to make some twenty dozen sweaters per day for the higher priced market. Many more workers were formerly employed before the workshop reorganised production and tried to improve quality. A two-storied workshop has been constructed at the back of their large house; there is no sign of it from the street. On the ground floor is the sewing room while the upper floor serves as a store for the finished sweaters and for thread bought in bulk. A Carrousel loom (operated by Juan or his son) and two remaining motor looms occupy a different part of the house.

The labour division in the sewing room is as follows: one cutting, one sewing on an overlock, two sewing necks and one pressing garments. In addition Lola has expected that younger workers help her in the kitchen. All workers are unmarried and aged from sixteen to twenty-four years. Each receives a different level of pay negotiated individually with the owners; they did not know how much their companions were receiving. The wages are increased twice a year; workers received two weeks extra pay at Christmas and an additional week's pay at Easter. But they are laid off for about one and half months in January/February when Lola and Juan take a holiday. The owners pay medical costs and maintain that providing the workers with social security would bring the workshop too many 'problems'. In summer they organise trips to Irapuato or the coast, and occasionally the women are given presents of sweaters.

This workshop, like Raul's, also employs sisters in the sewing room; once again the discrepancy in their wages coincides with their seniority. The elder sister, Guadalupe, had worked previously for eight years in other workshops and now operates the specialised neckband sewing machine receiving a weekly wage of 8000 pesos while her younger sister, Emilia, is on the overlock and paid 6800 pesos. The elder sister felt hurt by her low wage, but she was bashful at demanding a rise, nor did she feel justified in seeking better-paying work elsewhere with the excuse that 'they are all the same, anyway'. Lola always lets it be known how many young women come to her door asking for work: now many girls who have completed secondary education are turning up. The sisters are concerned lest the better educated young women take jobs away from workers who like themselves had been forced to leave school before completing primary level.

The younger sister has suffered bad health for a long time and always feels tired. She has pains in her legs and has fainted frequently; sitting down all day at her overlock is very difficult. Though the owners pay medical costs, she is frightened to complain too much about her bad health in case they do not call her back after the seasonal closure. She expected they would soon criticise her for lack of output.

The sisters felt they worked in a highly respectable workshop which pleased Beatríz, their mother. This emanated principally from Lola. She is very Catholic, taking her children to Mass each day, lining the walls of the workshop with pictures of the Virgin of Guadalupe, asking the workers to pray for the success of the workshop and for more orders to come in, and persuading workers to organise prayer meetings. This demonstration of religiousness was criticised by the workshop workers. Lola was called a 'hypocrite' by many, largely because her apparent piety contradicted her behaviour as a sewing room manager. Both Lola and her husband demand extreme workshop discipline. Workers are not allowed to talk during the working day, and an owner is present all the time to enforce the rules. Workers are constantly attacked for shoddy workmanship, both owners often losing their tempers.

(3) In the Hernández brothers' workshop at the start of 1986 some twenty-six women and nine men were employed. Of the women employed, twenty-four were unmarried and aged between fourteen and twenty-four years; two were married and in their thirties. A twelve-year old had been employed in late 1985 with a wage of 2500 pesos per week but was sacked for lack of discipline. In terms of the wages paid them, two groups could again be discerned: the fourteen machine sewers received wages of 7000 to 7800 pesos and the nine performed other sewing room work for wages between 4000 and 6000 pesos. The wage hierarchy is shown in Table 5.1. There were three workers who never divulged their wages to the others and were suspected by their companions of receiving more. The wages were handed out in sealed envelopes on Saturday morning. Of the nine men employed, two were more highly paid: the overseer and driver. Wages of the other men ranged from 12 000 pesos in the motor loom to 15 000 pesos on the Carrousel.

Table 5.1 Wages for women workers in the Hernández workshop, early 1986

Job	Age	Years in workshop	Weekly wage
Sewing	18	4	7800
	20	4	7800
	22	4	7500
	16	1	7200
	18	4	7200
	22	4	7200
	30	1	7000
	17	1	7000
	20	4	7000
	18	1	7000
	20	4	7000
	21	0.5	7000
	22	1	7000
	17	1.5	6500
Pressing	17	2	6500
	17	1	6000
Finishing	15	1	5000
Tacking	16	1	4500
Labelling	17	1.5	4000
Finishing	15	1	4000
Absent from list:			
Cutting	34	4	
	22	1	
Sewing	21	3	

About a third of the women employed had previous wage work experience: in other workshops, strawberry packing plants or domestic work, the rest came straight from school. The majority (fourteen) had left school after finishing seven years at the primary level; some (six) had left school earlier while three had gone on to complete three years additional secondary education. Educational level attained had no bearing as to what wages or prospects women could expect in the workshop.

Though reimbursement in the sewing room still differentiated the two main categories (machine sewers and others) the Hernández brothers have followed a highly personalistic policy whereby the precise level of wages and other payments is open to negotiation on an individual basis. This being known, workers tend to compete with each other and try to find favour in their employers' eyes. For example, when one of the two ironers said she was leaving as she was tired of the hot heavy work that brought her a wage of only 5500 pesos, the owners offered her first a 500 pesos weekly increment and then 1000 pesos. She accepted and stayed on but her companion remained with the old wage. Other sums are also open to negotiation. Every worker leaving employment is legally entitled to a separation pay linked to the length of time spent with that employer. When two overlock sewers left to marry in late 1985 after the same number of years in the workshop, one received 14 000 pesos, the other 30 000 pesos. The latter worker, Lupita, had first been given a cheque of 15 000 pesos; this she refused to accept on the grounds that it was a humiliating amount after the millions of garments she had sewn for them. The brothers responded by doubling their offer so as to have 'no more problem'.

It has become well known among the women workers that the brothers give special attention to their favourites. These women are rewarded with better wage deals, less criticism about their work and bouquets of flowers on their birthdays. (There has been no allegation, however, that their attentions have been in any way improper.) The Hernández brothers' apparently arbitrary wage policy has been extremely manipulative of the workers. They have used this policy to reward 'good', non-complaining women as well as sometimes buy-off the more critical, outspoken, 'awkward' women. In addition, the policy has been successful in keeping the women suspicious of each other and unwilling to risk collective action.

This policy has gone hand in hand with a contradictory attempt to instil unity and solidarity. The owners take workers on outings in the summer and a discotheque is organised at the end of each season for all members of the workshop where lavish gifts and prizes are given out, and photographs taken and distributed to all. The owners have also instituted a '*tanda*' partly to persuade workers to stay for longer periods. Each week workers put a share of their wage into a common fund and one stands to 'win' each time. But this is not a game of chance as each will win, only the order remains in doubt.

The physical conditions in the Hernández' workshop are particularly bad. In converting an old family house, interior walls have been torn out and windows boarded up. There is no natural light; workers work by fluorescent strip the whole time. There is little ventilation and the whole workshop stinks with the fumes from the motorised looms still occupying one half of the building. Acrylic dust hangs in the air and in the hot months, the workshop heats up like an oven. The workers are shut up in the workshop from 6 am to 3 pm with only a half hour break around midday to buy a drink or fruit.

The workers are frightened about the health risks they run and are angry that the owners do nothing to improve the working environment, and refuse to pay any of the workers' medical costs. No worker has social security. Nobody is allowed to leave their work during the day – not even to buy an aspirin; there is no first aid box kept on the premises. In the hot months especially, many workers faint and must go home to rest. The owners deduct the time lost from the workers' wages. When one woman became seriously ill working the steam ironing press in the heat, she was dismissed. The owners' lack of concern over the physical well-being of the workers is considered very unjust. It is also seen to contradict the 'religious' atmosphere that the mother of the Hernández brothers tries to bring to the workshop, by setting up pictures of the Virgin of Guadalupe and suggesting the workers pray for business success.

An owner or the overseer is usually walking about in the workshop and many workers recorded how they hated to have them 'breathing down their necks'. The men have adopted different personal styles of management. The younger owner is apparently 'sweet' and 'considerate', though also flirtatious. He is generally liked. The older owner is considered 'grosero' or rude, swearing and speaking harshly to the workers. He is disliked as is the overseer. The overseer is seen as a 'false' authority figure and many jokes are made about him behind his back. It was claimed that his chief function was to stop women spending too long a time in the lavatory.

The expression of labour control most deeply resented by the workers was the verbal abuse they received from the older owner and overseer. According to Lupita, they sought to humiliate and ridicule the young women, screaming at them or treating them with icy disdain. Their use of the formal 'Vd' term of address took on a sarcastic tone. Many workers said wistfully how they longed for just a few words of praise. Some of the workers have never accepted that the owners had a right to be rude to them. Lupita, for example, recalled saying once to the older owner: 'Why are you shouting at us? You have no right to. You are not my father. You should not treat us this way. I am a worker, and I demand that you treat me with respect as a worker.' The owners responded by referring to her and the small group of more out-spoken women as 'niñas malcriadas' – 'naughty little girls'.

Characteristics of the 'Household Model' Surviving at the Present

The transference of household relations based on gender and generation to workshops and their recomposition as a way of organising production has had many facets. It has governed systems of job and worker hierarchies; it has links with the payment of differential wages; it has influenced the perception of rights assumed by workers as well as employers; and it has found expression in models of labour management.

First, the highly personalised relations owners adopt with workers giving rise to both threats and favours deter women in poorly paid jobs from protesting or looking for better paid work elsewhere. Many workers fear that if they make a fuss or move between workshops their reputation will suffer for being 'disloyal' and 'irresponsible'. Pressures are put on the women to remain loyal to a workshop, as though it were their family.

Second, an underlying logic in the older, more traditional workshops is that wage differentials are broadly related to a job ranking that stems from the sequence followed in the labour process. In the workshops, a view has been fostered that the sequence of jobs indicates their relative worth. As knitting the cloth is the first stage carried out, male loom work is seen to 'naturally' carry greater value; differentiated machine sewing tasks follow and finally the menial tasks. Such a sequential estimation of worth remains in place for so long as the labour process itself is unchanging. Though occasionally when sisters are employed the labour process sequence comes into conflict with the 'real' seniority of workers outside the workshop. In such a case, older sisters are always reimbursed at a higher rate than younger sisters irrespective of the task performed.

The significance of the underlying logic of the old pattern of wage differentials was brought out clearly by sewing room workers who themselves had experienced the change from an 'unimproved' to an 'improved' labour situation. One of José's sewers commented how formerly owners had easily made workers believe that the separate phases in the production of sweaters carried intrinsically different values. Young worker's began at the bottom in the phases of lowest prestige at the end of the labour process and over the years they worked up the ladder to the top position of overlock sewer, the stage that was next in line to the men's work on the looms. This worker thought people must have been 'crazy' to have accepted this hierarchy, for logically all parts of the labour process were equally valuable as everybody was contributing to the manufacture of a sweater.

No clear interpretation of the meanings attached to labour process sequence can be given here. But it does suggest that one might explore other types of labour process within households in greater detail to find out whether there is a parallel association between position in the labour process and inferred value on the one hand and gender and generation of those undertaking the work on the other. One can perhaps see a similarity in the 'traditional' allocation of jobs within local households in connection with the provision of food. Men (husbands) grew and stored maize; older women (wives) transformed maize into flour and *tortillas*; younger women (older daughters) made the fire for cooking; girls (younger daughters) cleaned up and washed dishes after cooking and eating. As women went through life, so they advanced from low value, unskilled, cleaning work to high value, skilled, *tortilla*-making.

However, a rejection of the way labour hierarchies have been transferred to and recomposed in the workshop can also be seen as connected with a vision of household relations stressing communality and collectivity. Household membership in itself gives identity, status and value whatever way members contribute to it.

Third, the management models pursued in the more traditional workshops can be described as being patriarchal or matriarchal. With regards to owning husbands (patriarchal heads of household), there are two versions. The benevolent father appears to care for his workers (their health) and gives them treats (annual outings); the wrathful father complains and criticises very directly and familiarly. By and large, where workshop owners produce cheap low quality goods the benevolent father version prevails as there is less necessity for an owner to press workers into better work. Where workshops struggle to increase the rate of profit and aim to supply higher priced markets then greater stress is put on the wrathful father version. The Hernández' workshop suggests that there are possibilities of combining both versions where two male owners can adopt contrasting management styles.

With respect to owning wives (matriarchal heads of household), they embody the closer link with a household model of labour relations. Owning wives take on a typically multi-faceted identity.

By virtue of generational difference, they are entitled to instruct, command and safeguard the honour and respectability of young workers. They usually bring in a particularly suppressive form of Catholicism to the workshop. But at the same time owning wives may also emphasise communality among women by helping workers at time of need and protecting them from the threat of sexual harassment from owning husbands and male employees.

From the point of view of workshop owners, the 'household model' is not always in line with their interests. The model is not conducive to labour dismissal. Strategies other than outright dismissal have been sought whereby less suitable workers (and the workshops never encountered a completely docile labour force) are weeded out. In the examples given above, both sides know in Raul's workshop that absenteeism is not punishable by dismissal, instead the owner is forced to try to cajole the offending worker back to her place. Furthermore, in a society which puts heavy emphasis on religion, the use of religious symbols within workshops is difficult to separate from the right workers claim to attend church functions and celebrations even though this means leaving the workshop during the working day. As in a household, workers demand the right to some control over their time and to meet duties and obligations which society considers worthy and important. These questions of dismissal and labour time will be explored in greater detail in the next section focusing on the history of labour protest.

The discussion of the Hernández workshop has attempted to show that there are important points of difference between it and other workshops. One difference is that despite the job ranking in the sewing room, owners have opened up greater possibilities for individual negotiation with workers and have used this as a specific tactic for labour control. This more overt manipulation means that the workshop has already departed from one underlying premise of the household model. Another point of difference is revealed in the owners' callousness about workers' health. Even when sickness can be directly related to conditions in the workshop, the owners make workers entirely responsible for their own health; this also represents a departure from assumptions implicit within the household model. The Hernández workshop represents one way that labour relations have developed from out of the household model, where workers see themselves in an even more exploitative situation than before.

WORKERS' STRUGGLES

From the earliest days, workshop owners made use of certain strategies of labour control to nip resistance in the bud. Manuel Espinoza, for example, had two methods of dealing with troublesome workers (those who were lazy, or complained too much or were suspected of stealing). One was to pay them lower wages than any other worker, ignore their complaints until finally they left of their own accord. The other was to shut the workshop for a month and only call back selected workers. As María Rosa, his chief sewer commented: 'There was always a very mixed group of women who looked for jobs in his workshop', in other words the workshops retained only the more 'suitable'. This policy worked well for the workshop owners until the late 1970s, but in 1978 there occurred a number of protest 'outbreaks' in the larger enterprises.

The Early Protest Phase: the Late 1970s

The stimulus to labour organisation and protest was coming from both outside and inside the town. The Mexican labour unions were becoming interested in the 'industrial town', and supported the male loom operators' determination to fight for higher wages. As a result from 1978 to 1980 a major attempt was made by the male loom operators to organise a labour union; the initiative coming from workers in Mario's workshop. Several meetings were held. Since the workers had won support outside the town from labour unions belonging to the governing party, owners had to treat the threat of labour organisation carefully. Mario at that time was a member of the municipal council, and his position was supported by the municipal President, a wealthy cattle owner. The President warned workers not to get involved with 'all that shit' and the leaders were dismissed. The struggle was given up to organise a union.

In 1978 came the first official complaint made by women workers in the town. This indicated the beginning of more open confrontation between women workers and workshop owners. Workers had considered they had the right to leave the workshop now and again during the day. As all were paid piece-rates, it was not the owners who had to pay for the absence. Increasingly, owners were trying to force women into a greater commitment to the workshops so that they came every day and stayed at their sewing machines.

This led in 1978 to the dismissal of the Sanchez sisters from José's workshop. The four sisters had been employed for between four and eight years; they had no previous problems with their employer. On the occasion of their brother's wedding, they had requested and thought José had consented to their taking four days off unpaid in order to prepare for the celebration. When they returned to work José locked the doors against them, told them not to return and handed them a joint separation pay of 20 000 pesos. They sought legal advice in Zamora at the office of the Council for Labour Conciliation and Arbitration, and secured a lawyer willing to take up their case against wrongful dismissal. He later refused to bring their case. The sisters assumed he had been bought off by José, and considered it hopeless to continue their stand. They were now unemployable in the workshops, blacklisted for being troublemakers. But as their family had some property and cash, they were able to establish an independent enterprise, as dress-makers employed largely by the young workshop workers.

During the same year, 1978, the frustrations felt by workers at the workshop of Lola and Juan erupted into an attempted strike. At that time Teresa was employed at the workshop with her sister (she later became an artisan overlock sewer) and they tried to rally the ten women then employed in the sewing room to fight for higher wages. They collectively went to the owners to demand a pay rise. The owners said little in front of the group, but that evening visited workers at home to intimidate the weaker, younger women and offer separate wage deals to the leaders. Teresa and her sister refused to be bought off and declared they would not return to work unless their demands were met. They received a promise and work was resumed. But once the workers had returned, the owners went back on the promise. The workers were unable to carry through another strike action.

The following year, 1979, Teresa once again tried to persuade the workers to demand an improvement in working conditions. This time the focus of the protest was the right to have national holidays free from work. The chosen date was May Day. The women were initially keen to demand this workers' right and planned to stay away from work. Lola and Juan heard about the plans and the evening before went round the workers' houses. In front of their parents, the owners accused them of disloyalty and dishonesty, demanding to know who had put them up to the 'nonsense' and whether they were really going to let them down. Workers were worried by the threats of dismissal and also by their parents' reactions. All except Teresa and her sister appeared for work on May Day.

The men's attempt to form a union and the women's expressions of dissatisfaction in the late 1970s can be related to the changes that the larger workshops were trying to institute at the time.

The expansion of production during the 1970s had meant that many more loom operators were employed; they no longer came predominantly from the same social class as the owners and not all could hope to separate and form their own independent enterprises. Employed men were seeing themselves increasingly as workers, rather than as aspiring workshop owners. Thus, before the first Carrousel was introduced in Santiago, the climate surrounding labour's relationship with capital had been slowly changing; no longer could a model of household relationships obscure the nature of capitalist production.

By the late 1970s, owners of the largest workshops were being pressed into increasing output and improving the quality of their product so as to reach higher priced markets through the greater capitalisation of production. The capitalisation of knitted cloth production spelled redundancy for many men and the gathering momentum of the men's protest was partly a response to the threat of dismissal. It was plain that when owners bought Carrousel looms many men would lose their jobs. But at the same time, the attempted unionisation itself provoked more owners into thinking of substituting male labour with capital.

In line with the owners' attempts to improve quality, greater demands were being placed on the female sewing-room workers. The pressure on women was two-fold. First, in the formation of a more disciplined labour force, the concept of 'work' was being changed so that control over labour time was increasingly prominent. Owners demanded rights over worker's full labour time in the course of the working day. The ideology whereby women came to 'help out' and could come and go from a workshop was now bankrupt, and this was being replaced with the assumption that women sold their time as well as their skills. Such a confrontation over an owner's rights to worker's labour time had led to the dismissal of the Sanchez sisters.

The second pressure women faced was that they should work more carefully, with greater attention to quality and detail. But this was difficult for owners to enforce under the system of remuneration according to piece-rates. They could not compel sewers into better quality work just through more stern ('wrathful') labour management. They had to also consider the payment of a fixed weekly wage for only when assured of a regular income would workers improve quality. From 1980 the majority of enterprises went over to the payment of weekly wages to workshop sewers; but the form of payment to other workers varied. Some loom operators were paid weekly wages, others still produced for piece-rates; all industrial home-workers continued as piece-rate workers; and the artisan sewers fought to avoid the weekly wage.

Women's open confrontation in the late 1970s was only the 'tip of the iceberg'. In the case of the sewers, it was not only in the workshops of José and Lola and Juan that women had become dissatisfied. Several workers of that period recalled their determination to find time during the day to stop sewing, relax and chat, which was still possible especially when the owner was frequently travelling and when they worked in several small rooms of the owners' house that could not be supervised. It had been a fairly conscious strategy of 'go slow' to demonstrate that they were people and not just workers, and to thwart the mounting demands that owners were making on them to improve quality.

Labour Protest and Changes in Employment Conditions

After more concerted efforts by workers to give voice to grievances and demands in the late 1970s, the early 1980s was a period when individuals confronted their employers. The remaining male loom operators who took up issues such as low wages, other payments (such as holiday pay), or worker benefits (money to meet medical costs) were usually dismissed. Some tried to lodge protest petitions at the local Council of Labour Conciliation and Arbitration about wrongful dismissal, but they were then black-listed in the town. The form of protest women tended to adopt was to leave the workshop. It was becoming more common for sewers with some experience to look for excuses to leave unsatisfactory employers in order to take work in a rival workshop. Fewer women felt as chained as they had in the past to an individual workshop or owning wife. Since changing labour relations were meaning that women were being treated more like contracted workers and less like surrogate daughters, this gave the workers more 'right' to vote with their feet.

Individualised forms of protest could be more harmful to owners than had been the case earlier. Once workshops were stressing quality rather than quantity, and expecting workers to handle more complex, expensive machinery then a policy leading to dismissals and resignations was likely to rebound on workshops through a drop in labour productivity and by the need to constantly train new recruits. While motor loom operators were expendable, men trained to work Carrousel looms were not; and while the loss of one experienced sewer at marriage brought few problems, a walkout by several at the same time could be serious especially when they took their skills to a rival workshop. The pressures forcing owners to improve employment conditions were coming from just such examples of more individualised protest; no longer did workers need to come out on strike in order to get owners to respond to their demands. One example of an individual labour protest that expressed major changes in labour's contract with capital took place in José's workshop when a sick Carrousel operator made the first successful protest to the authorities in Morelia.

After José had bought his Carrousel loom in 1978, it was kept running for twenty-four hours a day by three shifts of workers. Pedro, a young loom operator, had been given the chance to learn to operate the new machine and he was put on the night shift, from 10 pm to 5 am, though paid at the same rate as those on the day shift. Sometimes he was obliged to work two shifts running, a total of sixteen hours. Pedro worked the night shift for four and a half years until his health seriously deteriorated. He suffered increasing problems with his eyes and began spitting blood. José refused to take Pedro off the night shift but gave him 5000 pesos to consult a specialist. Pedro was advised to take a month's rest, work fewer hours and give up night work for good. But José was adamant: if Pedro was not back on the night shift by the end of the week, then he was dismissed. José did offer, however, to give Pedro social security. He was not fit enough to return to work, so was sacked receiving a small sum by way of separation money.

Pedro decided to fight the case of his wrongful dismissal and talked first with the Office of the Council for Labour Conciliation and Arbitration in Zamora, but they were not willing to intervene. He was then counselled by friends in Santiago to get in touch with a PSUM lawyer in Morelia.[1] This lawyer agreed there was a case to answer and drafted a petition of protest which described the workshop's illegality. José was summoned by the Council to appear before a session in Morelia.

After receiving the summons, José called on Pedro at home

offering him 40 000 pesos to drop the labour petition, but he refused. At the hearing, the Council took note of the employment conditions and ordered José to pay 80 000 pesos in compensation to Pedro. For Pedro, the loss of his job at José's workshop was not so damaging. As a competent Carrousel operator, he did not suffer the same fate as loom operators who worked the motorised looms. His skills were in demand and despite his membership of PSUM he soon found work with Ramiro and Alicia's son in Zamora.

The success of Pedro's demand forced José to take two decisions in the workshop. First, he began to pay all his workers wages at or above the legal minimum. Now that his workshop was known as 'illegal' to the Morelia authorities, he could expect much greater harrassment by inspectors in future. José recognised that the workers had 'put a noose around his neck'. The other decision he took was to purchase a second Carrousel so as to avoid night work.

In 1982 José joined Ramiro by offering wages at or above the official minimum level to his entire workforce. Soon a few other owners followed suit (including Mario). The policy these owners followed was to pay all women workers, whatever their specific job in the labour process the same wage. The sewers welcomed this improvement in their employment conditions, and in their eyes the benefits went beyond just the increased pay. The women workers in José's workshop remarked that one implication of the new policy was that there was much less jealousy in the sewing room; no longer were wages secretly negotiated with the owners and handed out in sealed envelopes. Workers could be more open with each other as nobody now got preferential treatment.

In Mario's workshop, the repercussions of the new wage policy went further. Equal pay in the sewing room led to the breaking down of the pre-existing hierarchies based on age and to greater job flexibility. The restructuring of labour relations has meant that women can now switch between different jobs: they can alternate between machine work and the less stressful tasks of sorting, packing and running errands in the town. One worker who had experienced the changes recorded that she thought there was less 'slavery' in the workshop now. Not only was the working day less monotonous, there was more possibility of coming into contact with fellow workers as in some jobs there was time to talk.

Despite the advantages that workers saw in the new wage policy, labour struggles in the workshops were far from over. In José's workshop workers still had no security of employment nor had they been given social security. José continued to close his workshop for at least four months of the year and he recalled to work only the workers he wanted. Those who were not recalled had no possibility for redress; and José was relieved from paying separation pay or from fighting cases of wrongful dismissal. Worker dissatisfaction surfaced in the autumn of 1985 in both workshops when a new attempt was made in the town to found a labour union, this time the initiative was taken by members of the radical Partido Socialista Unificadora de Mexico, PSUM. Once again loom operators from Mario's workshops were among the leaders, and they were later dismissed.

The main unresolved issue in José's workshop in 1986 and 1987 related to health. Only three or four favoured workers had been given social security, though several others were promised it. For those without social security, José refused to pay medical costs and there was no first aid box in the workshop. As one worker bitterly commented: 'He does not care whether you live or die.' There were commonly cases of women fainting due to pressure of work, yet the owner would never 'help'. Although José paid minimum wages, he did not see himself as bound by any other obligation towards his labour force.

Once José began paying minimum wages, he had hoped his workshop would be free from further labour protest. Many skilled workers sought employment and he could select the best workers. But the question of responsibility for health costs had not been solved, as this case of individual labour protest shows.

Blanca, twenty-one years old, had worked for José for some three years as a cutter. Her job was dangerous for it involved using unguarded electrically powered shears. But only once had she cut her fingers badly; without social security she had paid for her own treatment. In late 1986, Blanca developed a painful cyst on her eye which she thought had been caused by the dust in the workshop. Treatment involved a minor operation in Zamora. Despite previous promises to her, José had never given her social security and once again refused responsibility for the expenses. Blanca paid her own bills, but was incensed to find her wages deducted for the days she had been absent. She demanded that José either pay the bills or give her full wages. When he refused, she told him he could look for another cutter for the following season. She was not going to work for him when she 'only got problems'. José accepted her resignation, saying it was only with her that he had trouble. Once the workshop had closed, instead of working in the strawberry packing plants as she had done for several seasons, Blanca took a job in the Hernández workshop as an overlock sewer. At first, their wage offer was lower than the minimum wage she had received with José, but she negotiated a deal whereby they paid her minimum wages and promised her social security after the slack season. She then left so as to accompany her mother going 'under the wire' to Los Angeles, where she thought she might remain with her sister if she got a job in a US garment workshop.

Cutters willing to work with electric shears are rare in Santiago; usually only an owner has been willing to accept the risks that this form of mechanisation has involved. At the start of the new season José put one of the sewers on the cutting work, but she was slow; he tried another, but the result was the same. He therefore tried to get Blanca back, calling on her sisters and writing to her in the US offering her social security with her job. After her return he left very 'polite' messages with, Concha, her mother, repeating his offer. Blanca therefore found herself with two work offers, and in both cases, owners had been forced to accede to the demand for social security. To strengthen his request, José sent a delegation of workers round to Blanca's to persuade her to return.

Blanca weighed up the alternatives: for her own self-respect she did not want to go to José's. However, were she to go back as a machinist to the Hernández workshop, she would have to sit down for the whole of the working day. The advantage of cutting was that she could stand and walk around the cutting table. In the end she considered the greater physical freedom of the cutting job outweighed the risks of injury from the shears, and was also preferable to the bodily strain of sitting over a sewing machine. As the only wage earner of her family, access to social security (that automatically covers near family) had been extremely important.

Though Blanca's negotiations with employers have been individualistic she set an important precedent and other workers can follow her example. Increasingly the 'modernising' workshops are being forced to include social security payment in their offer to experienced workers.

Labour Protest and the Fight for Respect

Departure from the 'household model' of labour relations has been associated with the owners' fight for greater worker discipline and for greater control over the workers' person: workers cannot leave the workshop during working hours; machinists are not allowed to get up from their machines. They may be prohibited from talking or even singing while at work, and are checked for the time spent in the lavatory. Workers have strongly contested the narrowing definition that has been given by owners to what is the worker's 'person'.

Although the improved wage policy limits the extent to which owners can manipulate workers, it has been given a mixed reception by workers. Though proud of the higher earnings, at the same time workers feel they have lost individuality; they are treated as 'machines' rather than 'people'. In this context, issues other than wages take on major importance. Owners no longer demonstrate any 'benevolence' when it comes to workers' health; or they 'off-load' their responsibility to an organ of the state, the social security. Owners consider themselves more free to dismiss workers. The depersonalisation has gone hand in hand with changes of management form.

In response to these changes, workers have appealed to local society for what they consider are affronts to 'natural justice'. The workers' feelings of moral justification have been extremely important; and local society has not been entirely indifferent to their complaints. One particularly clear element present in women's confrontations has been the demand for 'respect'. The encroachment into what women consider are their legitimate rights has been countered by the demand for greater respect. The use of a simple cash wage as a measure of worth, the arbitrary dismissals, the callousness as to workers' health have been seen as evidence of owners' lack of respect.

The fight for respect on the part of the young workshop workers mirrors to some extent their mothers' fight for respect from husbands and male society in general (as discussed in Chapter 2). The representation of this struggle contains elements that are gender specific. At heart it reflects women's reaction to forces serving to erode women's social and economic position and devalue their work and their selves. But the fight for respect has been double-edged. Ideally it seeks to express reciprocity and mutuality: the giving and receiving of respect. But differences of generation and social status easily intervene to connect respect with dominant-subordinate relationships. A young worker's parents may collude with a workshop owner (of the same generation) in believing that the worker owes respect of a deferential kind, that is not reciprocal but expressive of hierarchy. Workers demand greater respect from employers for their personal rights, but workshop owners frequently claim that young workers are lacking in 'respect' by protesting. The result is deeply confusing; for there are limits as to how much support young women can find in their pleas for 'natural justice'.

While an egalitarian interpretation of 'respect' is in contradiction with the ruling ideology and working practice of dominant-subordinate relations of gender and generation, then workers' struggles will remain fragmentary and inconclusive. Nevertheless workers who are convinced of their right to respect can sometimes achieve victories through labour protest and force some reconsideration of their position. The chapter will conclude by recording one such protest brought by two young workers from the largest, most exploitative workshop in town.

Lupita and Silvia had been employed at the Hernández workshop since it opened in 1982. Lupita (Amalia's daughter of twenty-two years) had the reputation of being 'clever' and able to work all the machines. Silvia, (Josefina's daughter of nineteen years), sewed in trouser zips. They had contested the verbal abuse of the owner and overseer and been labelled 'niñas malcriadas'. On various occasions they discussed their complaints with other workers in the sewing room but the first concerted effort to struggle for a specific demand came in March 1985. The workers' action centred on their right to have national holidays free from work and they demanded Mother's Day, 8 March. Their choice was dictated partly because of their own close relationships with their mothers. But it was also an astute choice for the prevailing ideology behind Mother's Day fitted well with the Church support of 'marianism'. A sewing room 'spy' kept the owners informed of the discussions and they threatened to dismiss any worker who stayed away. Only four stayed away; Lupita and Silvia being publically reprimanded at a chance encounter in the central square. They lost their day's pay but not their jobs.

Lupita left the workshop in November 1985 when she married but Silvia decided to try again to channel the women's growing sense of grievance into demanding the right to hold national public holidays free from work. This time the date was 5 February 1986, Constitution Day. The workers pressed for their legal right: a day off or double pay. Once again a spy kept the owners informed. On 4 February, the owners confronted Silvia at her sewing machine and in front of her 'compañeras' threatened her with dismissal. She spoke up bravely, but looking round for support, found herself now alone in the workshop for the other women had fled. Only Silvia stayed away from work the following day.

The older Hernández brother summoned Silvia to his office on 1 March – a Saturday – to complain about her slow pace of work; she was sewing zips into 700 pairs of trousers per day, her rate had not diminished. He also complained she was a trouble-maker, a 'niña malcriada', and at the end of a torrent of abuse, shouted that if she did not like the conditions of work, she could 'get the Hell out'. Silvia replied that she knew the conditions in the workshop to be bad and illegal. Since she did not accept them, she considered herself dismissed. She was handed her week's wages and in an already prepared envelope 20 000 pesos 'separation' money. The latter amount Silvia refused, being far too little in comparison with the number of years of employment. Silvia intimated that the Hernández would hear from her again to which the brother replied: 'You can ask the help of whatever lawyer you like, but you'll never get one centavo more from us.'

On 12 April the younger Hernández brother came to Silvia's house and offered her back her job and a sum of money to buy 'a new dress' by way of compensation. By this time the Hernández knew that Silvia had taken advice from her brother-in-law (a school teacher and well-known political activist) who was looking for a suitable lawyer in Morelia. On 15 April the lawyer came to Santiago to gather details about her case. Together they prepared a 'demanda' or petition listing the many ways in which the workshop transgressed the law and claiming larger compensation for loss of job. The 'demanda' specified the following points: the workshop did not pay minimum wages, nor give social security provision; workers did not receive the statutory two paid weeks vacation nor did they receive national holidays; the women workers had to work extra hours to clean up the workshop each day; only one lavatory was provided for both men and women and the owners abused the labour force as in the case of Silvia's dismissal.

By coincidence, the candidate from the ruling PRI party campaigning for the post of state Governor visited Santiago on 11 May. At a rally in the plaza, a young doctor stood up to inform Martinez Villacaña of the abuses in the town. Here, the workshops employed minors of twelve years, did not pay minimum wages or social security; there were no paid holidays nor distribution of profits. The candidate was seen to take notes.

The petition arrived at the Hernández workshop on 13 May summoning the owners to attend a hearing of the Council for Labour Conciliation and Arbitration in Morelia on 22 May. The brothers were furious, and telephoned the news around other workshop owners. But both owners came to Silvia's house on 18 May to try and charm her out of the fight. They offered her 70 000 pesos and her job back if she would give up 'the joke'. They also told her that the worry of the pending case had made their mother ill. Silvia replied that she was not in such desperate need of money and that for her, the case was no 'joke'.

On 22 May, Silvia, her mother and brother-in-law went to Morelia to the hearing of the Council of Labour Conciliation and Arbitration. In a closed session (Silvia's family sitting outside the court) the owners claimed that Silvia had said a week before 1 March that her mother wanted her to stop working; there had been no dispute like the one she claimed. They were prepared to offer Silvia her job back with the same conditions of work. She refused on account of their misrepresentation of her dismissal and because working conditions were so bad. The owners then offered her 100 000 pesos by way of compensation, to which Silvia replied that the money did not interest her. She did not want them to go on making a fool of her; she was prepared to go on with the fight. A document was prepared by the Council summarising the proceedings and noting that the hearing would continue on 12, 13 and 16 June. To this meeting, Silvia would need to bring witnesses in support of her claims of illegality while the owners were charged with finding documentary proof to show they complied with the law. Silvia told the court she would bring Lupita and another worker (who had resigned in June 1985) as witnesses. The owners said their witnesses would be the overseer and two current workers.

On returning to Santiago the owners spread word around the town that Silvia had behaved so badly that even her own lawyer had been forced to reprimand her. Her mother, Josefina, they claimed had spent the time weeping outside. Her mother was incensed by the allegations, especially that she had ordered Silvia to quit her job. As she put it: 'As her mother I am responsible for safe-guarding her honour, her health and her person, but as she is now nearly twenty years old, her work is her own affair.'

By chance on 30 May the younger brother met Lupita in the plaza. He said how surprised he had been that she had been taken in by Silvia's lies; did she not realise that she would perjure herself if she testified about the dismissal? That was why he himself could not be a witness. If she went on with her silliness, she risked being sent to gaol. Didn't she realise she would get a sentence of at least two years for perjury? Silvia was only out for herself, that was why she was claiming the ridiculous sum of 1 000 000 pesos from them. Neither of Silvia's friends were in any position to act as witnesses for neither had been employed in the workshop at the time of Silvia's leaving. She had not been sacked so why was she complaining?

Lupita broke in constantly to challenge these remarks. What about their own witnesses she asked. They had not been present at the dismissal either. They were not ordinary workers like she and Silvia, everybody knew they were better paid because they informed against their fellow workers. She knew she too would have been sacked sooner or later, and that it was just accidental she had left before this happened. She was just as fed up as Silvia with the rudeness, coming especially from his brother. If she did go to gaol, it would be his job (as a lawyer) to get her out; would he really like the town to know he had put away a pregnant woman? (Lupita was by then three months pregnant.) The owners were not going to make a fool out of her either.

The owners circulated a letter around the workers on 31 May, asking them to sign it. The letter stated that workers received regular wage increases, extra payment at Christmas-time and paid holidays. The owners explained to some workers that Silvia was holding them to ransom; but to her friends they said nothing. The latter did not realise the letter was connected with the pending case. All the workers signed.

Lupita was then threatened by her uncle, also a workshop owner who depended on the Hernández for access to thread and markets. He visited her and her mother at home. He repeated what the younger brother had said and added the following points: the owners had already bribed Silvia's lawyer; the younger owner still had good connections in the legal field and was determined to win the case. If there was more trouble in the town, owners like himself would close their workshops since they could easily live off their investments in the bank. But the workers would lose everything; Lupita's mother, Amalia, became extremely nervous.

These allegations appeared to carry weight when Silvia's lawyer did not appear at a meeting arranged on 5 June to talk the case over with the witnesses. Nothing was heard from him. There was much speculation as to whether he might really have been bought off by the owners; Silvia and Lupita felt worried and less decisive. They talked over the possibility of organising a second letter and collecting signatures from former workers who were more prepared to speak out about the illegal conditions, and they asked Silvia's brother-in-law to draft one. But he was busy. By 10 June, nothing had been heard from the lawyer. Silvia's brother-in-law set out to look for him, taking a day off from school teaching. The lawyer was found on 11 June in Los Reyes where he had been trying to get peasant clients out of gaol. He was furious about the story that he had been bought off, but he was no longer in a position to represent Silvia the following day. He rang a colleague to take Silvia's case and it was agreed that they would meet in the Morelia bus station at 9 am.

They left Santiago long before sunrise. But at the appointed time there was no sign of the lawyer in the bus station. He finally arrived five minutes before the hearing was due to start. He briefly explained to Silvia what the Council would wish to ask her about the working conditions. By the time they arrived at the Council's offices the Hernández brothers and their lawyer were already waiting. Immediately they offered her a new settlement; this time 250 000 pesos (of which 50 000 pesos would go on her lawyers' fees). There followed some confused negotiations with the lawyers running back and forth to their clients. After some minutes' hesitation Silvia decided to drop the petition and accept the settlement. So with a certain air of festivity the two sides entered the Council offices and signed an agreement; and Silvia was congratulated on her 'victory'.

For Silvia the victory felt hollow. Many reasons could be given in retrospect as to why it had been a good decision to settle. Clearly the case would have gone on for months and have posed heavy financial and emotional costs for her and her family. The cost of getting to Morelia by bus for a day had been heavy for a family where nobody had a regular income. Silvia felt constrained by her mother's request the night before that she settle if offered a decent amount. Furthermore, Lupita might well not have been in a position to act as witness and supporter in later stages of pregnancy. For Silvia, the part she relished most was not the money, but the few moments in which the workshop owners had had to wait for her to decide. The compensation amount was the largest settlement yet awarded to a worker from Santiago.

Two days after the meeting in Morelia the owners announced they would raise wages in the workshop. This was partly due to the petition from Silvia. But it was also because so many of the machine sewers were leaving the workshop. A few days after the settlement, Silvia and her mother met Jesús Espinoza in the street. He had heard of the case and congratulated Silvia warmly on her courage and determination, saying how the owners of the 'legal' enterprises were fed up with 'pirates'. They could cut production costs to a minimum and undersell reputable, responsible owners like himself. He did not, however, offer Silvia a job.

Though some workers in the town had known about Silvia's struggle with the Hernández workshop, she received no support from the loom operators who only a short time before (in the autumn of 1985) had tried to start a labour union. The struggle for a union was waged by men; the language and symbolism that came 'naturally' were heavily masculine. Neither the radical PSUM party nor the loom operators had considered re-interpreting their images and arguments to fit better with Santiago's women workers. Women workers have been expected to attend meetings, but only to support what men say. They have felt uninvolved in action.

Only through personal/family connections have the men of the political parties assisted individual women workers in their protests and difficulties. There has been no organisational move that would help channel even minimal support to individual workers so as to help them with their fight (such as to cover the basic costs of a labour protest, and the transport and food costs that visits to Morelia entail). While the images of the 'proletarian' and 'class struggle' remain so divorced from the reality of the young female workers and their struggle for respect, then concerted labour organisation and action seem doomed to fail.

THE PLACE OF LABOUR STRUGGLE IN WORKSHOP TRANSFORMATION

Workers in Santiago, especially the younger women, have been heavily disciplined all of their lives. They are used to taking orders from seniors, working long and hard, being beaten by fathers and brothers, not complaining. Parents' 'natural' authority over children and men's domination of women have been transferred from society to the place of work; there, relations of generation and gender have been reconstituted. At first sight, social relations in the workshops have meshed closely with relationships which elsewhere are seen as 'right and proper'. Yet even when imprisoned in the highly conservative small town society, not all workers have accepted the legitimacy of the transference nor have workshop owners been able to cow workers into submission.

A minority of workers have stood out courageously against the pressures of oppression. They have done so, not under the premises of any European-styled workers' or youth 'rebellion' but because their experiences in the workshops conflict with a very deep sense of morality whose tenets they know are acknowledged, if not shared, by the society in which they live. This sense of morality has been described above as a fight for respect. Furthermore, workers with a more articulate moral consciousness are also those who have refused to be 'fooled' by the attempts to replicate some of the aspects of the 'household model' in the workshops. This refusal was summed up beautifully in Lupita's comment of outrage quoted above: 'Why are you shouting at us? You have no right to. You are not my father. You should not treat us this way. I am a worker and I demand that you treat me with respect as a worker.'

The young workers who have staunchly defended their rights have found little support from fellow workers, but they may have found support from home. The idea of protest may be handed down from one generation to the next. Support can be both direct and indirect. Another group of more forthright workers are those who for a long time have been economically responsible for parents and siblings.

The courage which young women need to make a labour protest should not be underestimated. Not only can confrontation in the workshop (and in the town) be hurtful and humiliating, taking a case before the authorities in Morelia demands that a young woman goes to a distant place and into a world of men where the lawyers and public officials share gender, class and age characteristics with workshop owners. She therefore becomes the 'outsider' breaking many social conventions.

Labour protest has become more open and generalised at particular junctures in the town's industrial history. The owners' efforts to capitalise production and change working relations went hand in hand with labour's attempts to defend and maintain their 'human' rights in the face of threat. They have fought against unacceptable new demands and encroachments into what workers consider lies outside the workshops' right of control. The workers' protests have also turned from defensive to offensive lines: the demand for medical help, or for a just separation pay or for the right to hold national holidays – all of which are recognised within Mexico's official labour legislation.

Despite the labour protests only limited improvements have yet been made to working conditions, and the two brief attempts to unionise the male workers were quickly suppressed. But in the last few years, the situation facing workers has greatly worsened. Economic recession began to have serious implications for the workshops in 1986 and was weakening labour's bargaining position still further. By 1987, workshops had begun to close, shut down for longer periods of 'rest', cut back labour forces. Workers are feeling much more vulnerable. At the same time their financial contribution to their families has become even more essential. Coming back to Santiago in the summer of 1987 I was struck by a loss of hope and a spirit of resignation among many workers. They saw little point in continuing the struggle until the recession was past.

Note

1. The Partido Socialista Unificadora de Mexico (PSUM) united various left-wing tendencies and in Santiago was the most concerned to fight for workshop workers' rights.

6 Relations of Gender and Class Outside the Workshops

CHANGING CONTEXTS

The growth of industry in Santiago has affected the local economy and society in many ways. The implications can be explored in a number of dimensions. Of primary interest in this chapter is an exploration of the way in which workshop-based industry has interacted with gender and class relations. During the last twenty-five years, not only have the workshops drawn upon and reconstituted prevailing social relations, but processes of workshop differentiation and proletarianisation have played a part in altering gender and class relations in the local society. Though one can point to the importance of industrialisation in changing local society it is not easy at this level of analysis to specify precise mechanisms and relationships. There are two fundamental problems preventing one from drawing clear-cut conclusions about the wider effects of the industrial development.

The first analytical problem lies in the difficulties of isolating the effects of workshop-based industrial growth from other, possibly more transcending, pressures and tendencies. Conditions of life generally in the Mexican countryside have been altering in response to a number of influences. In Santiago the most visible signs of other fundamental changes underway have been the following:

Changing Patterns of Migration

Whereas formerly in western central Mexico men usually migrated without their families and women stayed at home, in recent years increasing numbers of women have migrated, especially to the US, to earn an income. Many more women now have experienced Hispanic society and culture than in the past. Given economic changes in the southern US, more migrants (men and women) are taking jobs in the urban service sector than find seasonal work in agriculture.

The Greater Reach of the Mass Media

New images of Mexican (and US) life are being communicated to the regions by cinema and television. The media's message has incorporated a highly materialistic, consumption oriented vision of Mexican culture.

Political Renovation and Social Improvement

Popular pressures and actions originating from various points have led to initiatives to 'clean up' local politics, improve social facilities and make greater investments in public infrastructure in many small towns. This has partly resulted from higher levels of education in the countryside and the expanding numbers of 'professionals' in the population.

These broader influences interact in specific localities with the dynamics of industrial (or agricultural) production and with changes in social relations of production.

A second set of analytical problems lies in the *meaning of historical comparisons*. The comparison of class and gender relations over time demands that appropriate phenomena are selected to act as bench marks. But such a comparison only becomes valid when certain elements of continuity are known to be present. For example, if the institution of marriage has in fact entailed a significantly different type of 'contract' for the grandmothers, mothers and daughters then their marriages may be hard to compare if (as is usually the case) the underlying differences in meaning cannot be clearly pinpointed. Given the sweeping drastic changes overtaking rural Mexico throughout this century, little continuity can be assumed at the outset. Detailed inter-generational comparisons are therefore hazardous. The contexts of women's lives in the past are elusive and women's recollections may be difficult to interpret. In this analysis, a 'second best' strategy has been adopted. While not presuming to draw hard and fast conclusions, the same aspects of gender relations are described as far as possible for three generations of women in Santiago. Life histories of the grandmothers' and mothers' generations have been recorded in their contexts in Chapter 3 and these serve as reference points for the discussion of the daughter's generation in this chapter.

The focus of this chapter is on the lives of present workers and young former workers outside of the workshops. The introductory sections explore what changes have taken place in the workers' class background and in the rise of a new domestic knitting industry undertaken by married women. The principal discussion centres on the young women's family and gender relationships, singling out those areas which have apparently been most open to negotiation and reassessment. This discussion will be organised under the same headings as were employed in the latter part of Chapter 3 when recording the life experiences of the mother's generation. Some cautious points of similarity and contrast are presented by way of conclusion.

SOCIAL ORIGINS OF WORKSHOP WORKERS

Comprehensive material on class background was collected from all workers only in the case of the largest workshop (that of the Hernández). No single indicator of social position was considered sufficient in itself, so information was gathered on three aspects: father's work or employment; type and standard of parent's house; and number of years workers had attended school.

Very few of the workers' fathers were at the time migrants in the US (only three out of twenty-six) and this points to a generational change. The families of migrant men are no longer among the most impoverished in the town or most in need of daughters' earnings as had been the case earlier. In contrast, a third of the workers were daughters of men who tried to eke out a living locally combining occasional wage labouring in agriculture and construction with subsistence farming. More than half of the fathers from this group were periodically unable to work because of drinking. In addition, two workers' fathers were unable to work at all. At the other extreme the fathers of four workers were loom operators in Santiago and two fathers belonged to the privileged stratum of cattle owners.

According to the type of house in which workers lived, a third came from the central urban slum, La Colonia, of two-roomed shacks whose inhabitants share collective lavatories. These are houses belonging to the old urban poor. A third lived in poor adobe houses, located on the outskirts of town, being the houses of a more recent group of urban poor. The remaining third were better off and lived in modern brick houses that their parents had managed to construct usually from incomes earned in the US.

Over half the workers (fourteen) had completed the seven years of primary school education before being sent out to work. Eight workers had been forced to leave school earlier without completing the primary level, often so as to allow brothers to go on with their studies or because of a family tragedy. In contrast, four workers had completed secondary education before entering the workshop. Despite their better education, these women had been prevented from looking for 'better' work in the nearby towns of Zamora and Jacona on account of parental opposition.

Lacking information as to the precise social origins of earlier generations of workshop workers, it is difficult to draw comparisons as to changes over time. But it seems clear that the most pressing need for daughters' earnings is found among a class of urban poor who do not migrate for work in the US. Unlike in earlier years there is now also a group of workers who are better educated and come from wealthier households. These workers usually have greater power to dispose over their own earnings and may save much of it for when they marry.

There is still a sizeable group of young women who combine workshop work with seasonal employment in the strawberry packing plants of the Zamora valley. The two occupations dovetail well with each other: the peak strawberry season coinciding with the summer slack time in the workshops. The most dexterous strawberry sorters and checkers can earn through piece work at least double their workshop weekly wage. The packing plants give workers social security as a matter of course and most send buses to transport them. But the harvest season is short and earnings vary directly with the size of the harvest. In a poor year many women feel it is not worth the effort of going. But this is no longer the only option open to workshop workers in the slack period. There is now a growing number who accompany mothers or brothers on visits to the US; some of them even find temporary employment in sweater workshops north of the border. This trend may be indicative of the incipient formation of an 'international' workshop labour force.

Though workshop employment has always been most strongly associated with young unmarried women between the ages of fourteen and twenty-two years there has always been a minority of older women who take on workshop work. A few have never married. Older married women who enter workshops have pressing financial needs, but to work they must also win the support of their husbands. The husband's agreement is still a decisive factor. A great many wives have tried to persuade their husbands to let them work, without success, and a few have tried to 'work on the quiet' when husbands are away in the US. When asking the present unmarried workers if they want to continue in workshops after marriage, they invariably answer that it would depend on the husband's wishes. Some clearly 'hid' behind this rationale in that they had little desire to continue working after marriage, but a few were prepared to battle with their husbands for the right to work.

Apart from the husband's permission, married women have encountered several obstacles preventing them from taking workshop work. First, there is the problem of how to hand over the duties of household management to another; only when a mother can 'help out' or daughters are old enough to undertake the heaviest domestic labours can a wife be 'free' enough to take on the long hours demanded in the workshops. Second, there is the problem of machine sewing and health, especially during pregnancy. The older women who sit at a sewing machine for eight to ten hours each day complain of various ailments that they attribute to the working conditions. Some working wives had faced considerable difficulties in giving birth and they believe that the foetus had not 'sat well' in the womb due to the long hours crouched over the sewing machine.

As far as could be judged, the married women who were employed in the workshops faced no social recrimination; rather they were admired for their physical strength, at least by other women, because they took on the double load of workshop and domestic work. But it was the heavy expenditure of physical strength which primarily put full-time workshop employment beyond the reach of the poorest and least well nourished group of older women.

For poor married women there is still the option of undertaking out-work. As in the past, the densest concentration of embroidering home-workers is in the central urban slum. There are now few home-workers from the better-off groups in society partly because former workshop workers who might have taken in out-work have been able to develop their own domestic industry independent of the workshops.

DOMESTIC INDUSTRY: WOMEN'S INDUSTRY

In the early 1970s a different type of shawl began to appear in the weekly markets of Michoacán ousting the shawls made of silk or cotton (that had previously been adorned by out-workers in Santiago before the rise of the workshops). The new shawls of acrylan were produced by women working at home on small manually operated knitting machines. The shawls soon became very popular; they were warm, washed well, and came in a wide variety of colours. They were cheaper than silk shawls, and though they cost more than cotton ones, they were considered more fashionable. Women in Santiago decided to enter production. The new type of knitwear industry which spread to Santiago on many counts has become the counterpoint to workshop production.

Within the prevailing gender division of labour, knitting machines have been equated with sewing machines, even though like looms they knit thread into cloth. Knitting machines are women's machines. They own and operate them and so far have retained control over the new domestically based branch of the knitwear industry. The size of the sector is difficult to assess but probably more than 200 households in Santiago possess a machine and produce goods for sale, most women own one or two machines, a few have three or four and the largest domestic enterprise has five. Women usually employ helpers: young girls come in daily, while hand sewing is often put out to women in the neighbourhood.

The first hand knitting machines were brought to Santiago in 1973 by married women previously trained as workshop sewers who came from better-off families. New machines could be bought through hire purchase from agents in Zamora who offered favourable credit deals, and there were also second-hand machines available especially in Sahuayo. Machine ownership appears to have expanded fast in the early 1980s and spread among women who were less well-off. This outward spread resulted from three main opportunities for saving. A Church-sponsored 'Caja de Ahorros' (a savings and loan scheme lending money with minimal interest charges), set up in 1982, was drawn upon by many women who could not contemplate bank loans. With the goal of buying a knitting machine women without resources went to find work in the US. And young machine sewers in the workshops tried to save enough by the time they married so as to 'retire' into independent domestic production.

Though all the knitwear producers come under the heading of

domestic enterprises, there are variations amongst them. At the lower end are poor women who with great sacrifices have invested in a machine and learnt to operate it but who now, given shrinking markets and increasing costs, find it impossible to keep in production. At the other end are relatively prosperous small domestic businesses which can now constitute the main income earning activity of the household. A selection of domestic enterprises will be discussed in order to show the possibilities and limitations of a domestic industry run by women.

An Enterprise that Failed

Veronica, employed in Yolanda's workshop as cutter and overlock sewer, has worked in the workshops for eighteen years. Though she earns high wages she has been desperate to leave. She is solely responsible for her sickly child and very old mother. In 1985 she was awarded a sizeable sum in compensation for wrongful dismissal from a workshop in Zamora and this she saved. In early 1986 she put down the initial payment for a small knitting machine her cousin was selling and paid the rest through monthly instalments. This was the first knitting machine to come into La Colonia, the central slum. While Yolanda's workshop was closed following the flood, Veronica learnt to operate the knitting machine, but discovered she was not as dexterous as on the overlock. She spent two months in training, taking lessons from a *comadre*.

At first she was delighted to have found an escape from the future-less life of the workshops. She made clothes to order mainly for neighbours and friends, but she did not find any reliable outlets through traders. As the price of thread rose, so the knitted clothing was put out of reach of many of her clients. Orders dwindled. When Yolanda re-opened her workshop in 1987 and beseeched Veronica to return she had little choice but to go back. Now her knitting machine stands idle in a corner until she can afford to buy thread. She now despairs of ever finding 'a way out'.

A Small Successful Business

Carmen worked ten years for Jesús Espinoza as an overlock sewer before marrying late at the age of 26 years. Her husband owns a funfair ride which he takes around the region. With her workshop savings she bought a new knitting machine in 1983 and discovered great talent as a knitter, learning quickly. Many recognise that she is the best knitter in town.

Carmen works every afternoon after preparing and cooking the household's food. To give herself this space she employs a young girl to wash the household's clothes and look after her five children. She has sometimes trained girls on the machine but has never regularly employed a machine worker, being aware that her skills have given her reliable, but discriminating, clients. On average she completes one knitted suit each day.

The bulk of her output is paid for in advance and is taken to the US for sale. Most of her clients are women from the larger towns who take charge of this trade. She uses only the best quality thread and therefore charges high prices. Her suits sold for between 6000 and 7000 pesos in May, 1986 and she reckoned to earn some 2000 pesos per suit after the cost of the thread had been deducted. Despite the rising price of thread, Carmen has never lacked customers. She is a nervous woman and often becomes very agitated for fear that she cannot complete the orders. At these times, her husband helps out. She allows him to do the simpler machining work while she sews and presses.

An Extended Family Enterprise

María belongs to an extended family where five member households own knitting machines and produce knitwear. María's mother was the first to acquire machines which she and her unmarried daughters worked. María bought her two machines in 1984 and was followed by two of her brothers and a sister. With the increase in the family's output, María's mother decided to stop machine work and take charge of selling in the local circuit of weekly markets. She visits four markets each week, taking the garments by bus.

María and her husband run a small shop selling dry goods and beer. Though the turnover is small, they saved regularly with the Caja de Ahorros and in time could afford the down-payments for new knitting machines. María was taught by her sisters but did not like the work, seeing herself as far too impatient a person to knit. She decided to employ two young women as trainees; with a steady income from the shop they could afford the initial high expenditures and low returns during the training period. One of the young workers stayed a year before marrying and acquiring her own machine; the other has continued working for four years – a very unusual situation, earning some 7000 pesos per week and her food. The only part of the production process María personally undertakes is the finishing and pressing.

After the first trained worker left, María decided not to employ another worker and instead her husband began to take turns on the machine. He was much better at operating the machine than her and began to experiment with new styles and colour combinations. With this new division of labour in the household, María spends more time minding the shop while her husband works the machine. They are able to produce on average fifteen women's suits per week.

A Large Domestic Enterprise

The domestic industry run by Silvia and Jesús verges on being a 'workshop'. At the back of their house is a work 'room' for the three workers and five machines. The output of this, the largest enterprise, is some six dozen sweaters per week (very small compared to the output of the smallest size group of sweater workshops making five dozen garments per day). Though the enterprise makes a range of goods, they have specialised in sweaters.

Silvia left school early, being the oldest of fourteen children from a poor family and made clothes by hand for sale before and after marriage. Jesús, from a wealthier cattle-owning family went seasonally to the US as an agricultural labourer from 1973 to 1983. Savings from this work were used to buy Silvia her first knitting machine in 1975. In 1982 they bought new machines and started to expand the business. Jesús stopped going to California when his father died in order to tend the twenty cows he inherited, and he has occasionally taken wage work locally. From 1983 the household has run the two joint enterprises, the knitting enterprise being the most profitable.

Though Silvia is represented as owner and manager, Jesús has assisted in many ways. Having some earlier training in accountancy, Jesús deals with the financial side, working out in detail the costs of production. He buys thread direct from the factory in San Miguel del Alto and takes charge of machine repairs. In addition, he has experimented with new designs and colours so that the product is quite distinctive. But Jesús always points out that the enterprise's success is due to Silvia's skills as a finisher and presser. The bulk of the knitwear is sold through local traders but there have also been important export channels to Los Angeles arranged through a sister living in Guadalajara. Export orders are irregular but pay well. The enterprise has been able to steadily increase the selling price; by mid-1987, though there were difficulties, there was no threat of closure.

The Constraints of Domestic Industry

Women in Santiago have been able to generate and keep control over a new form of domestic production and many 'informal' channels of exchange. This demonstrates that women's traditional command over domestic production is not just a historical phenomenon. A successful domestic knitwear business has given households greater financial security and has lessened the pressures placed on men to search for wage work in the US. For many in Santiago avoidance of migration, family division, and settlement in the US (even in wholly Hispanic communities) carries great value. Thus the rise of the domestic industry can be seen in a positive light. The limitations of the industry become clearer when one looks at the restrictions hindering expansion of enterprise, the respective obligations placed on women and men and the industry's volatility.

Obstacles to growth mentioned by Silvia and Jesús with respect to the largest enterprise are illuminating. While Jesús emphasised the high cost of the machines and the problems with repairs, Silvia considered that further growth would be unacceptable to her workers. She suggested that the knitwear produced was not fully the property of those owning machines. Therefore she did not label a garment as this would denote her ownership and its separation from the person producing it. Owners of the larger enterprises are aware of the need to uphold an ideology of 'collective' as opposed to 'workshop' relations of production. This is interpreted as ensuring that not too great a social distance is allowed to develop between employers and workers. The practice of employers eating with workers has important symbolic value.

Paradoxically the 'cost' of this collective form of labour relations from the workers perspective is the low level of reimbursement. Since returns to labour are so low, few women are willing to work for any length of time. Instead, workers aspire to own machines themselves. The domestic knitwear producers have been unable to alter the form of production; they have not been able to accumulate sufficient capital to transform social relations of production, nor can they enter into direct competition with the workshops for more permanent workers. The industry women control seems doomed to remain small in size and limited in profitability. While providing a useful addition to household earnings it is of no direct threat to either workshop-based production or to men's activities in general.

In recent years, there is evidence to suggest that men have begun to take a more active part in the domestic knitwear industry. To a limited extent, men have been involved from the start. Contrary to assumptions about 'machista' society, some husbands have had no hesitation in portraying themselves as 'helping out' their wives. But the situation may be changing now. As male unemployment grows, there are increasing numbers of men who are working daily on the knitting machines and are now beginning to threaten women's control of the industry. The increasing stagnation of the Mexican economy may mean that men see their best prospects as lying in domestic industry. The pressures on the former gender division of labour have not gone unnoticed. As one machine owner commented: 'It seemed odd at first to see men on the women's machines and people raised their eyebrows, but it is more common-place now.'

FAMILY AND GENDER RELATIONS OF WORKSHOP WORKERS

Family Responsibilities of Unmarried Daughters

Young, unmarried women enter workshop employment in order to lessen the financial burdens that fall on their families. Sending daughters out to work is in most cases vital for the household's reproduction but the long hours of workshop employment mean that these cash earners cannot contribute much labour time to the other forms of household work necessary. Mothers and younger daughters therefore must fulfill all these other tasks. Parents normally press older daughters to take income-paying work; mothers decide the specific allocation of young women's labour power as between income earning, domestic and subsistence producing work but it is the father who gives a daughter permission to go out to work. When families face acute need, daughters are taken out of school and sent to work as young as ten or eleven years.

Thus the fact that a young woman enters workshop employment, does not imply a decision made by her nor does it have any immediate connotation of emancipation or separation from household control. Instead, young women are expected to respond to a sense of duty to help out their parents.

Genoveva scolded her eldest son harshly for not forcing his oldest daughters to take regular income earning work. She told him that he was a fool to let them lounge about; he had worked himself nearly to death to provide for his ten children while they were small. He had been a responsible father and had always given them enough to eat. Now it was the daughters' turn to repay their parents by providing for them. She was furious with her son for having lost authority over his children and with her daughter-in-law for failing to force them either into a workshop or into undertaking the major household tasks, such as making the daily ration of *tortillas*.

Most of the workers interviewed demonstrated a profound sense of responsibility with regard to their mothers and siblings. Usually workers hand over a half of their earnings for daily household expenses to their mothers (in no case did this money go to a father); while a substantial minority gave all their pay.

Blanca was taken out of her first year at secondary school when her father died in order to provide for her mother, Concha, and sister who still lived at home. She has been determined that her younger sister should not be forced to quit her education, and will not let her take on out-work as this would diminish her concentration at school. While she is the only income earner in the household she feels she cannot marry.

The two sisters paid top sewing wages in Raul's workshop have to support a household of fourteen people. Their father suffered a nervous disorder for years which has prevented him from working; he can only manage to supervise a small corner shop (with virtually no turnover, which the sisters keep stocked for him). They have nine siblings still at school, and their mother is trying to give the boys a secondary education.

Rita's mother died when she was ten years old and she had to take charge of her six siblings. Her father had been extremely irresponsible and rarely gave them enough money to live on. She and her younger sister took in embroidery out-work and when Rita could hand over the domestic work to her sister, she became a workshop sewer, the only regular income earner in the family.

Julia, was deeply affected by her father's death from blood poisoning when she was eighteen years old. She worked as an overlock sewer in the workshop of Lola and Juan, but she suffered a breakdown and had to give up work just at the time when the family needed her earnings most, there being nine younger children still at home. Her mother borrowed heavily so as to buy medicines for Julia; she recovered and her uncle, Jorge, suggested that he install an overlock sewing machine in her house so she could work for him while avoiding the stress of coming to the workshop. To help the family out, Jorge agreed to pay her a wage that was above the official minimum.

The workers earnings directed to household consumption go to various types of expenditures. Mothers use most of the cash for daily necessities but they may put a little aside to pay for medicines and doctors' bills. The working daughters take charge of other kinds of household expenses often paying for the family's shoes. They may save up to invest in large consumer durables; the most common purchase being a washing machine, as this can relieve the women of washing by hand. This kind of expenditure is only possible in households that possess various sources of income and where men do not drink. Daughters of alcoholics generally find that cash cannot greatly improve the lives of their mothers, as fathers try to take away and sell whatever goods are brought into the house. One very young worker in the Hernández workshop had for a long time saved up to buy a bed for herself and her siblings to share (all the family had previously slept on the floor), but her father immediately sold it to buy alcohol.

When questioned about the advantages they found in working, women replied immediately and unhesitatingly that these derived from access to cash that wage work gave them. They no longer had to ask anybody for money, and since the wages were paid out directly to them, they had some power to decide on the precise proportion going into the household fund and the destination and timing of the other money allocated to family members. Although pressed to contribute, this does not detract from the pride they feel in being the providers of cash. Unmarried sons who receive an income are also expected to contribute to household expenses, but not the same demands for regular payments are placed on them as on unmarried daughters; sons have more freedom to spend the money they earn as they wish.

The money workers retain for their own use can be spent on only a relatively limited array of expenditures. First and foremost, they buy clothes, shoes, make-up and jewellery. Most buy cloth to sew themselves or pay local dressmakers to sew up garments of their choice; or they buy ready-made clothing at the weekly market or from shops in Zamora. Traditionally, women acquire new clothes to celebrate the patron saint's day in July and for the Christmas pilgrimages; these are still the most important occasions for 'dressing up' but young women also like to show off new clothes on the Sunday parade around the central square. Apart from clothing, personal expenses are limited. Unlike the spatial freedom allowed unmarried men, unmarried women have little possibility of travelling (unless they go to the US with their family), neither can they use cash on entertainment, tobacco or drink. A few young women are able to save, some wishing to have enough money to buy a knitting machine to work on after they marry.

The Renegotiation of Relations with Parents

At first sight, the right won by unmarried working women to spend money they earn on clothing seems unremarkable. Yet behind this lies a victory of gender struggle and some transformation of women's identity. When workers' mothers were young, they were forced to dress extremely discretely. Most women had abandoned Indian dress when they moved into the mestizo-dominated town from the *ranchos*, where women still used long dark skirts and embroidered blouses. In town, women wore tightly bound bodices so as to conceal their breasts; they did not show their arms in public and they wore shawls when outside their houses to cover their heads and upper part of their bodies. Young town girls generally possessed two or three shapeless dresses (some women referring to them as 'bags') which were altered and patched so as to last the longest time. The ideology towards the seclusion of women coupled with women's need for defence against the violence and brutality of male society at the time found expression in the prohibitions placed on women's dress.

Even after women began earning in the workshops, they did not have the right to dress as they pleased. The clothes women wore were the subject of comment and discussion among fathers and brothers: men in the family considered themselves entitled to compel women to dress in a way that they considered appropriate and beat young women if they failed to obey. The first change in clothing to permeate Santiago society was the adoption of new types of manmade cloth: acrylan was replacing wool in the case of knitted garments (including the traditional shawl) and various types of nylon cloth was substituted for cotton cloth but still there had been little alteration in the style of women's dress.

The fight waged by young women for greater freedom of dress began in the early 1970s. Traders were bringing new types of garments to the weekly markets of small towns such as Santiago and an even greater range could be seen in Zamora. Furthermore, increasing numbers of men were coming back to Santiago with televisions especially after periods of work in the US and more people were becoming accustomed to the way the 'bourgeois' women dressed and behaved on the endless soap operas transmitted. New visual expressions of womanhood were being paraded in front of the rural societies of the Mexican interior; this was both highly alarming and alluring for the young. The first open conflict over young women's dress came with their demand that they leave off the tightly bound bodice and wear a new item of clothing available in the country markets: the brassiere.

> Not long after Teresa had started work in Lola and Juan's workshop in 1976 she began to want to alter her dress; she had always made her own clothing. But the first time she dared to wear a brassiere bought at the market, her father and brothers became furious. In an excessively crude way they reprimanded her for drawing attention to her body, an experience she found deeply humiliating. Although her mother had been equally shocked at the idea of a daughter 'exhibiting' her breasts, so harsh and embarrassing were the men that she found herself coming to Teresa's support. She might not approve of the new clothing, nevertheless there was no justification for the coarseness of the men's response. Slowly and under constant comment and criticism, Teresa maintained her right to wear short-sleeved blouses, skirts that came to just below the knee and a brassiere. But not for many more years was she able to put on a pair of trousers.

> When one looks at the young women parading around the central square of Santiago on a Sunday evening nowadays, then one can observe how total has been the victory of the young women's struggle to dress as they consider appropriate. Most wear high-heeled shoes, the clothes they choose are tight in order to reveal

their bodies. Bare arms are acceptable, none will wear a shawl until after marriage, and many sport blue jeans. In light of the models coming from television and cinema, the vast majority of the young women are extremely presentable, but to the horror of most of their mothers they spend heavily on clothes. The young workers from the more privileged social strata tend to distinguish themselves from their poorer work companions by buying better quality, more fashionable, more expensive clothing for Sunday wear. Women's clothing has become an indicator of a family's social position – even though the women themselves belong to the same working class.

As a phenomenon the change in young women's dressing is open to various interpretations. Without prior knowledge of the struggles that this involved, one might be tempted to see the change as indicating a move toward making young women into 'sex objects', or into passive consumers of an American dream. Such interpretations would probably be a mistake. Women's clothing has become provocative but not in the sense of indicating sexual availability. On the contrary when used by collectivities of women parading en masse, arm-in-arm, this seems to confront and challenge 'machismo'.

Unmarried women's financial contribution has been extremely important to their parents' household and this has helped shape the way family relationships are being reassessed, in particular that between mother and daughter. The 'good' daughter may be the main provider for a household, her earnings filling the gap left by an irresponsible, sick or dead husband. This earning power and position as 'bread-winner' has served to give young women workers a more adult status, especially as they approach twenty years old. Mothers must accept that their daughters can take decisions over more realms of life that they could when young. But the provocation for a reassessment of inter-generational relations among women does not only come from workshop employment. It has also stemmed from broad, pervasive influences on rural society, such as the extension of primary and secondary education, the incursion of the mass media and the greater experience women of all ages now have of US/Hispanic society. Young working women are fighting to have the lines controlling their behaviour shifted outward, while their mothers are prepared (albeit reluctantly) to give in to the legitimacy of certain demands but not others.

Beatríz could never object to her daughters going out to work as the household needed money (her husband being particularly 'mean' about handing over a regular amount). But she disliked the new habits they acquired from working (even in the most restrictive Catholic workshop belonging to Lola and Juan). She did not like their provocative clothes, high-heeled shoes or make-up but could not stop them from 'dressing up' whenever they went out. Neither did she approve of their leaving the house without her permission. But after several years of workshop work (the elder working daughter now being twenty-four years old) this has been very difficult to enforce. Her daughters have claimed the right to leave the house to visit or shop in Santiago during the day. But they still may not go out on their own at night nor travel outside Santiago without a chaperone. The latter restrictions the daughters accept, commenting on how people would otherwise gossip that they were off with their boyfriends if they were seen out alone. They recognise that despite the relaxation of many of the older rules, their lives are still much more restricted than if they lived in the US. They laugh at their mother's and local society's strictures but are not prepared to fight against them. (Their attitude had been partly conditioned by the fate of their eldest sister who 'came to grief', bore an illegitimate child and was later murdered by her husband.)

It is now many years since Teresa and her sister were obliged to seek their parents' permission about leaving the house (both are in their late twenties). Their father is now old and weak and cannot rule them as he once did. Teresa sees that as a workshop worker she has won much greater freedom especially with regard to mobility than women of her mother's generation, who whether as daughters or wives had been confined to the house. Indicative of this freedom was Teresa's decision to take a course in hairdressing in Zamora even though this entailed travelling alone by bus. Furthermore, she and her sisters have insisted on joining holiday parties organised in Santiago, where buses are chartered and accommodation rented on the coast. In earlier years their mother had demanded that she give permission when the sisters wished to change employment from one workshop to another. The last time they asked permission was several years ago when requested by their father's cousins to 'help out' in the workshop at Ecuandureo for a couple of months as this entailed living away from home.

Working women's greater freedom with respect to dress and mobility and their stronger position within the family is also connected with their changing relationship with men. Courtship and marriage continue to be of overwhelming importance for young women. And relations with men can still be the site of much conflict between the generations. Many mothers sincerely hope that their daughters will find greater happiness in marriage than they have done themselves but how this can be achieved is highly contested.

Courtship and Marriage

Young women have long demanded to have closer contact with their suitors in Santiago. The movement towards less restrictive courtship practice is hard to date, but seems to have been occurring at the same time that women were demanding the right to dress more as they pleased. By this time the Sunday parade around the central square after Mass had become the preserve of the young. Unmarried women dressed in their best clothes would walk several times around the square; sisters might accompany each other, but more commonly work companions from a particular workshop would parade arm-in-arm while the older generation looked on. The eligible unmarried men joined in by walking around the square in the opposite direction eyeing the women as they passed. For the last ten to fifteen years, the Sunday parade has become the most important place of first encounter for the young. No longer does collecting water have a place in courtship conventions; though the religious pilgrimages and festivals continue to be linked to courtship especially in the light of the secularisation processes that have taken place.

Though the Sunday parade and religious festivals are open to the whole community, in both these public arenas there is considerable differentiation in the way people participate on account of access to wealth. The poor are usually reduced to being bystanders as the 'costumes' needed for both types of parade need money. In addition to these more public events, there have also grown up 'new' traditions in recent years which are the particular preserve of the emerging bourgeoisie. Wealthier families, typified by the workshop owners, arrange large parties to celebrate the fifteenth birthday of daughters which marks their eligibility for marriage but only within a restricted social circle. These same families have also begun to sponsor annual 'beauty' contests for their eligible daughters which demand heavy outlays of cash not only for the expensive clothes but also for the organisation of a dance and other festivities. Though 'beautiful' young women from a relatively wide social spectrum may be invited to compete, poorer families cannot meet the costs of their daughters' entry. Thus the last decades have witnessed the development of more class specific courtship conventions through which young women and men from similar social backgrounds are brought together. Thus the loosening grip of the general restrictions as to contact between young women and men has been accompanied by moves aimed at containing courtship within social class.

Young women have won the right to speak to and accompany the young men who interest them and the practice has developed whereby couples are allowed to talk outside the woman's house. But present social convention demands that they do not touch even though promised in marriage. Brothers and older sisters keep watch on the couples and report any misdemeanour back to parents. More recently, 'novios' or engaged couples have demanded the right to go to local dances on Sunday evenings. And to the great consternation of many mothers, a discotheque was opened in the central square. In the case of older daughters with long-standing boyfriends, mothers have sometimes turned a blind eye to the couple sneaking off for a walk or a visit to the cinema. Publically, they should not condone this rule-breaking, but privately many believe that only with some privacy can their daughters get to know a prospective husband.

Thus, one of the demands young women and men have consistently made to the older generation in recent years is that they have a youth; a time in their lives when they are permitted by society to possibly change partners several times before being impelled to marry.

Though conventions and practices concerning courtship have changed there is less apparent sign of changes surrounding the institution of marriage. No unmarried woman in Santiago can openly declare that she wishes not to marry. Nor do the religious orders now provide the socially acceptable way out for women who reject a fate of wifedom and motherhood (as they had done for past generations of Mexican women). Young women speak of the 'sadness' and 'loneliness' of remaining single 'on the shelf'. Remaining unmarried means that 'you have nobody's respect'; that there is 'no place for you'. 'Life gets very sad and boring if you don't marry and raise your own family.' However risky the prospect of marriage still is, it is seen as preferable to alternatives.

Although open declarations of young workshop workers go along these lines, there is a small group amongst the most skilled, better paid workshop workers who find good arguments for delaying marriage. These arguments usually stress the obligation of continuing to support their parents' households. Some of these women are now so old (approaching thirty years) that the chance of their marrying is seen by others as very slim. Yet from hard-won freedoms concerning dress, greater mobility and the opportunities for further education or training, they defy society to label them as 'pitiable creatures'. Though few in number, they represent an extremely important potential 'alternative' model for women now growing up in Santiago.

For the time being, however, marriage is the fate and prospect that all young women must plan towards. While older men have always been able to find young women to marry, mothers and daughters are conscious that time is far more limited for women if they want to 'marry for love' or 'marry well'. Women who delay marriage too long find that their choice narrows quickly once they reach twenty-three or twenty-four years of age. But the young women of Santiago are now faced with highly contradictory pressures channelled to them both through their mothers and through society. They are caught in the crossfire of messages, some of which stress the wisdom of delay and a more profound knowledge of the man they intend marrying, while other messages stress urgency if a women wants to maintain the illusion of choosing to marry for love.

Images of romantic love and the right to individual choice are constantly communicated and indoctrinated by cinema, television and 'love story' picture books. The individualism the mass media portrays conflicts with the traditional social mores that see choice of marriage partner as primarily an arrangement between families. As the Santiago priest commented: children used to obey their parents, but not any more. As the young have greater command over money, they now believe they can make all the decisions with respect to marriage. Some ten years back engaged couples generally waited from six months to a year before marrying, now couples marry younger and they want the space between engagement and marriage reduced to the shortest possible time, around a month.

Differential responses to the contradictory messages surrounding marriage appear to have led to the re-establishment of a bi-modal pattern of age of women's marriage within the population as a whole. Analysis of the civil registers in Santiago for the period after 1960 showed that the overall average age of marriage for women has gone up once again, to a level comparable to that prior to the period of the 'robberies'. Average age of marriage for women in Santiago town rose from 18.3 years in 1960 to 19.8 years in 1970 and to 20.8 years in 1980. In the *ranchos* women tended to marry a little earlier than in the town though age was also showing some tendency to rise: from 17.9 in 1960, to 19.2 in 1970 and to 19.0 in 1980. Men's average age at marriage remained at around twenty-two years in the town and between twenty and twenty-one years in the *ranchos* from 1960 onwards. With respect to the range of marriage ages, data from the registers revealed much confusion in the early 1960s but by 1968 the beginnings of a return of a bi-modal distribution could be noticed, with women tending to marry at eighteen years or at twenty years. During the 1970s and 1980s, the bi-modality has become more marked, marriages concentrated at around seventeen years and at twenty-one years.

Women who have lived through the experience of a mother's 'bad' marriage and who are important wage earners for the parent's household are more likely to marry late. These young women know that they must continue earning until another sibling is old enough to take on the responsibility.

Lupita, brought up by Olivia, her grandmother, had been treated especially harshly if caught talking to a boyfriend. When she first got to know her future husband, Olivia used to pull her inside the house by her hair or slap her hard in public. This Lupita found mortifying; but at the same time understandable as she knew her grandmother still felt guilt about her mother, Amalia's, robbery and abandonment. Her mother's traumatic married life and defenselessness as well as the household's dependence on her wage meant that Lupita did not want to rush into marriage. Furthermore, she was at the time the only regular income earner of the family, her mother having given up domestic work in Zamora, once Olivia could no longer manage the household. Lupita was courted by her boyfriend for six years before finally agreeing to marry him. At twenty-two years, she was getting near the upper age limit for marriage, and her boyfriend was pressing her to live with him in Guadalajara. At the same time, her financial responsibilities towards her mother, brother and grandmother were easing as a brother in the US had begun to send dollars home regularly. This meant that Lupita felt a little freer from her obligations. Lupita found her wedding a sad affair; her husband's parents were already dead, Amalia refused to attend because of all the terrible memories marriage evoked, her father refused to come back from the US and Olivia was by then bed-ridden.

Young women marry early when they are desperate to experience some romance in their lives, or when they are unable to accept the heavy burdens put on them by their parents. In some cases, parents agree to an early marriage; but for many others the best way to realise the romantic dream is through elopement. The tradition of abduction has been carried on, though no longer does it entail 'robbery' for the young women are willing participants.

The outcome remains the same as in the past; the young couple must be married, as quickly and discretely as possible. Many mothers and responsible working daughters lament the foolishness of the fourteen and fifteen year old girls and are greatly upset by the permanency of the elopement tradition.

Particularly in the case of working women who marry later and have become accustomed to responsibility as income earners in their parent's household, considerable negotiation about money and goods may now take place with the 'novio' prior to marriage. Couples from the younger generation generally organise the distribution of cash in the household in terms of a husband's payment of a weekly and monthly 'diario', a fixed monetary sum for the family's food (weekly) and clothing (monthly). Workshop workers, like Lupita, are concerned that the amount of the 'diario' should not fall below the wages which they had received before marriage. The women's wage packet therefore can act as a benchmark in the negotiation of the financial terms of marriage. Women who have not worked prior to marriage are in a weaker position to fight for their 'rights' from husbands.

The negotiations before marriage do not stop with money; many young women have already decided on the kind of houses and consumer durables which they want to acquire and may press husbands to go north to work in the US after marriage in order to get them. The experience of wage work has allowed women to struggle for financial rights in marriage in a way that their mother's generation could never have done. Not all, of course, are successful in altering the conditions of their married life, and there remain many other areas of gender relations which have been far less open to negotiation.

When discussing marriage with groups of workshop workers and their older married sisters, there was general agreement that virginity for women remained of paramount importance. Though attitudes are changing, men still consider they are entitled to return wives to their parents' house if found not to be virgins on the wedding night. This is though not uncommon in the Santiago *ranchos*. The social rules governing the sexual behaviour of men and women are vastly different. Women who remain at home know that their 'novios' and husbands have affairs with other women in the US. Infidelity is still part of being a man, though many young women are highly critical now of this aspect of male identity. In contrast, in Santiago the lives of married and unmarried women are still heavily restricted and gossip is still a powerful constraining force. The families of absent husbands and 'novios' take upon themselves the task of making sure the women's reputations remain spotless.

The Struggle Against Patrilocality

The vast majority of the mother's generation felt they had suffered greatly as young wives incarcerated in the houses of their mothers-in-law. This shared experience has meant that many older women have tried to take a strong stand on the matter of patrilocality.

Beatríz refused to allow any of her sons to bring wives back to her house after marriage, telling them to save up for their own place before marrying. She remembered the terrible nine years with her husband's parents and vowed not to make another woman suffer in the same way. But despite the protection and warnings she has given to her daughters, two of them eloped with their boyfriends while still very young (fourteen and sixteen years) and as they were without savings they have been forced to live with their mothers-in-law.

Genoveva and Jaime have insisted that their family remain united. The eight sons have been pressed to live close by their parents. Genoveva saved all the money she could from Jaime's migrant work in the US and this allowed them to buy land on which to build a house in the early 1970s. The remaining land was divided into small plots and allocated to the sons. The daughters-in-law live in close proximity to Genoveva but they have been allowed to form their own separate households. Genoveva, like Beatríz, talks of her desire not to cause her daughters-in-law suffering and claims not to meddle in their affairs. This view is not always shared by her daughters-in-law; they remember painful occasions when husbands went back home to their mother after quarrels, and times when Genoveva 'forgot' to offer them food. Nevertheless, Genoveva considers herself very fortunate to have 'good' daughters-in-law who help her as though they were her own daughters. Though the households are all considered separate, there are differences between the generations as to attitudes towards 'privacy'. The door of the parents house is always open and family members come and go constantly; but the daughters-in-law demand the right to close their front doors even when this leads to strong criticism from Jaime.

Some young wives, especially when husbands are in the north, find that they must still live in their parents-in-law's house. But this generally lasts for a shorter period than in the past. Though the price of urban land and construction materials have been rising fast, young men and women struggle hard to earn and save in order to acquire an independent home. Workshop workers have often been able to put away savings for use after marriage; and in some workshops, savings schemes are enforced so that workers receive the earnings withheld as a large lump sum when they leave to marry. Wage work for women means they have a better chance of 'buying' their independence from the husband's family after marriage.

But the tradition of patrilocality has been undermined in another way. There is now a growing number of couples who make their first home with the wife's parents rather than with the husband's. For the women, this is seen as an extremely important advance, especially when they are with small children and/or abandoned by migrating husbands. Many women, however, find themselves caught up in agonising divisions of loyalty. Lupita and Silvia, the two workers involved in the labour protest in the Hernández workshop (explored in the last chapter) have both confronted difficult decisions with regard to residence after marriage.

After marrying her boyfriend of many years standing, Lupita continued to live at home in the central slum with Amalia and Olivia even though her husband has a permanent, relatively well paid job as an insurance salesman in Guadalajara. He wanted them to move into his sister and brother-in-law's flat in a lower middle class *barrio* of Guadalajara. But even after two years of marriage and the birth of a son, Lupita refused to abandon her own family; her husband must support her household and spend most of his remaining earnings commuting each weekend to Santiago. After the years of taking full responsibility for her family, Lupita cannot bring herself to abandon them, especially now that they are older and weaker. But at the same time she dreams of a time when she can leave the squalid unhealthy slum where her son is constantly ill. If she continues to prevaricate, she knows that her husband will eventually leave her. But this she will face when it comes.

Silvia married a couple of months after her protest came up in the Morelia court. She and her husband had been 'novios' for several years, but their courtship had been severely constrained due to her mother's watchfulness over her daughters. After the marriage, they lived together in her mother-in-law's house for a month before her husband, a mechanic, went to the US. Silvia then returned to her parent's house where she had her first child. The problems arose after her husband returned home when the child was a couple of weeks old and insisted she move back to his mother's house. She did so but under duress, especially as her mother-in-law was 'old fashioned' and would not let Silvia out of the house unless accompanied by a member of her new family. Silvia found the abrupt changes in her life confusing; she felt like a widow when her husband had left her so soon after the marriage. But on his return when she was trying to adjust to motherhood and in the house of his mother, it was difficult to find the basis of a relationship with him. She was pressing that they go back to live with her parents, while he was urging her to go north with him to Los Angeles.

The Distribution of Cash and Goods within Households

In comparison with the confusion over rights to cash that characterised the mother's generation, young couples in Santiago today generally follow the custom of a weekly allowance or 'diario'. Husbands undertake to pay a fixed sum to wives to cover housekeeping and the family's clothes. But still the amount that husbands hand over varies greatly. Some give wives virtually all the cash they receive; others, especially alcoholics, give virtually nothing. In late 1986, wives who received over 10 000 pesos per week for food thought themselves well off; many had to make do with around

5000 pesos. Even where some negotiation about the 'diario' had taken place prior to marriage, after some years very few wives felt they could openly or objectively talk about money with their husbands. Very few men have suggested that their wives ask for or take additional money should they find themselves short. Money from husbands is still seen principally as the means to acquire food – husbands are the providers of food whether handed over in kind or in the form of cash.

The basic food necessities of the households remain maize/*tortillas* and beans, the official price for *tortillas* being critical in determining poor families' nutritional situation. No longer are the majority of households in dire poverty as in the 1940s and 1950s, most can acquire the staple foodstuffs if not through the market, then through their own subsistence production or as 'loans' from family members. For households that must buy all their needs, the basic basket of goods for a family of two adults and four children came to around 5000 pesos per week in late 1986. Nutritional status is still primarily expressed in whether households can afford milk and meat. A better-off family with, say, four young children spent 3000 pesos per week in late 1986 for milk, and would buy a small quantity of meat once or twice a week. Women who had lived for any length of time in the US often came back with altered preferences for food, generally adding 'hamburgers' as a festive dish.

Household expenditures other than food may be met also by husbands, but they are more likely to come from other sources: from children's or the wife's own earnings.

Lucía is a former workshop sewer who continues to machine sew as an out-worker as well as make snacks for sale in the evening. Her husband, a loom operator working for her father who owns a small sweater workshop, hands over most of his earnings (12 000 pesos in late 1986) to her for the household food. Her husband is fortunate in having social security which covers the health costs of the whole family; this has been important as she has needed hospital attention for her recent confinements. They have five children between twelve and two years and she was pregnant again. As they produced about two-thirds of the maize requirement only occasionally did Lucía buy *tortillas*. She reckoned to spend 2500 pesos per week on beans and 2000 pesos on milk. They ate meat twice a week. A portion of her husband's wage was spent on buying construction materials for the house they are slowly building on land given them by her father. They had not acquired titles to the land, as the legal costs are more than they can afford, though they are worried that family wrangles may dispossess them if they do not soon put the legal transfer in order. Lucía has relied on her family to give her old clothing for her children. Her own earnings from out-work and food sales are spent on shoes, the down-payment and monthly instalments on large consumer durables such as a television and capacious fridge. She has also raised pigs so as to meet occasional unexpected expenditures.

Households face many problems when children are small and when parents have problems in finding work. This becomes acute when they need money for urban land, construction materials, furniture and consumer durables. These pressures have prompted more young couples to go north so that both can work and earn an income. Even when they have young children, it still makes economic sense to go to the US taking a young girl with them for childcare. Though husbands and wives share the task of earning and saving, gendered divisions between different kinds of goods remain. By and large, wives are recognised as owning furniture and consumer durables, even though men's wages may have bought them. Once children are old enough to be released for work, the acute pressures facing families mostly ease. But this is only a temporary phase. It is generally accepted that after marriage neither sons nor daughters will contribute regularly to their parents' household. Old age therefore can be a time of great penury; and many elderly people's savings are swallowed up by exorbitant medical bills.

Relations of Gender in Marriage and Parenting

Women in the mothers' generation bore large numbers of children. Statistical evidence concerning changes in family size in Santiago is difficult to find. The only data that give any impression of the order of magnitude of temporal shifts come from the 1980 population census. The census records the number of live births according to age of mother and this allows some comparison to be made of completed family size of women at the end of their child-bearing years.

One indication of fertility change can be found in the different percentages of women who bear very large numbers of children: more than thirteen live births (Table 6.1).

Table 6.1 Changes in the number of very large families: 1950s to 1980

Age of women, 1980	% women with more than 13 live births
55 years +	13.2
50 to 54 years	10.0
45 to 49 years	15.0
40 to 44 years	13.8
35 to 39 years	2.1

A second indication can be seen in the change from relatively large to relatively small families – from seven to twelve live births to one to six live births, as shown by Table 6.2.

These data suggest the following points. First, fertility was highest for the cohort of women aged between forty-five and forty-nine years in 1980, i.e. women whose main child-bearing years were in the 1950s. Their higher fertility was probably accompanied by a greater likelihood of child survival so that family size was growing. Second, there seems to have been a rapid increase in the general fertility level among women in this cohort compared with older women; whereas some 45 per cent of the women in their early fifties were recorded as having seven to twelve live births, this figure leaps to 54 per cent for women between forty-five and forty-nine years. Interestingly, the sharp increase does not show up in the case of the most fertile group of women in the different cohorts who bore thirteen or more children. The behaviour of this group varied in a different way. Third, fertility levels appear to have been falling again from the 1960s onwards. Though the thirty-five to thirty-nine

Table 6.2 Changes in family size: 1950s to 1980

Age of women, 1980	1–6 live births (%)	7–12 live births (%)
55 years +	37.3	41.2
50 to 54 years	38.1	45.2
45 to 49 years	26.4	54.0
40 to 44 years	30.5	51.8
35 to 39 years	43.8	48.6

year old women have not reached the end of their reproductive life, this cohort has been included in the tables primarily because they show the sudden end of the era of very large families: while 13.8 per cent of women in the forty to forty-four cohort had thirteen or more live births, the proportion had diminished to only 2.1 per cent among the thirty-five to thirty-nine year olds. Thus, one can say that some parents of the present generation of workshop workers had already altered their fertility behaviour. Undoubtedly they are influencing the attitudes and positions taken by their daughters when they come to marry.

The mother of a young worker in the Hernández workshop thought it a sin to limit family size if there was sufficient food in the house. She had eight children between fourteen years and six months. Prior to her last birth, she had taken contraceptive pills as she considered seven children was as many as she could support. She worked long hours taking in washing, while her husband was a day labourer in agriculture. She had not told her husband of her decision to 'look after herself' as he was 'dead against' the pill. But she had suffered worsening health problems which she attributed to the contraceptive so had abandoned it. After her eighth child, she was trying a different brand of pill hoping it would suit her better; she was not yet thirty-five years old. Though she considered the pills were extremely dangerous she would support her daughters' decision to 'look after themselves' once they had borne four or five children.

Maria whose daughters worked for Yolanda did not want them to put their trust in contraceptives when they married. She did not really see birth control as making women's lives any happier; instead it was far more important that they came to know their 'novios' before they married. María had 'bad luck' as to her choice of husband and she hoped her daughters would not make the same mistake as her. Contraceptives did not help women much for two reasons. There were great health risks once women went on the pill and furthermore women did not see the money that was saved if pregnancies were avoided; all it meant was that men kept more of the money to spend on their vices rather than hand it over for the family. María thought that paradoxically women might be better off having more children as this gave them a better claim on the money their husbands earned. Her daughters needed to work out the financial aspect of marriage first, only after that were contraceptives useful.

When asked about the number of children young workshop workers wished to have after marriage, many looked to the 'American family' of two or three as being ideal. But their older married sisters have not been able to reduce their pregnancies to that level, and after five or six children are anxious to avoid more. Obviously questions about fertility cannot be viewed only from women's perspective, nor from the perspective of the availability or safety of contraceptives on the market.

The majority of young couples still rush into child-bearing immediately on marriage; as yet this practice seems to go unchallenged. Births are not being delayed or spaced, instead there is a wish to stop reproduction after a number of children have been born in quick succession. The arrival of a first child nine or ten months after marriage seems to be particularly important from both women's and men's point of view. Among brothers or male friends who marry at the same time much joking surrounds the question of who will impregnate their wives first; potency, virility and masculinity are very intimately intertwined. At the present time, women would not seem to stand much chance of getting a husband's agreement to the decision to delay the birth of a first child.

After the birth of the first two or three children, wives may indeed start to consider the possibility of 'protection' but they hesitate. This is partly because of the reputed bad side effects of the contraceptives available in rural Mexico; partly because of their husband's stated desire for more children; and partly because of their own indecision and confusion as to how many children they themselves want. The issue of fertility is a live one; many younger married women wanted to talk about it and compare experiences with women elsewhere. Everybody knew of women who 'solve the problem' through sterilisation, and some considered this as an inevitable step if they wanted to live a more comfortable and less suffering life than their mothers.

Some young wives staunchly defend their right to work outside the home after marriage, with the argument that if their husbands could not provide an income, then it was up to them to ensure there was food on the table. Others hid behind a certain submissiveness to a husband's will.

The young wives determined to work after marriage generally shared a conception of marriage as a partnership. They saw that both partners should be responsible for the well-being of a household. However, most young men in Santiago continue to give their support to the age-old customs and practices that keep women in their place and at home. Men leave the house frequently, and only on rare occasions are there social events which include the participation of men and women in the same activity; at most public and private functions women remain separate from the men. In no case have wives been able to insist on a more equitable division of domestic labour in the household; a limited amount of child-minding is all that even the most enlightened husbands have been willing to provide. For women who work, either at a home industry or in outside employment, the domestic tasks are off-loaded onto young girls employed for a pittance to 'help out'.

Direction of Change in Gender and Family Relationships

From the discussion so far, what changes can be seen in the lives of the present generation of young women which make their experiences radically different from those of their mothers and grandmothers?

One implication of workshop employment has been that a proportion of the working women delay marriage until they reach their early twenties, marrying generally later than the mother's generation. As a result, young women can live through a longer period of youth in their parents' house. But although this appears as a major change when compared to the mother's generation, it also partly reflects a return to social patterns more characteristic of the grandmothers' generation when women married after a longer period of 'helping' in their parents' households. But in contrast to their grandmothers, as wage earners women in workshop employment now have some rights over the disposal of their incomes and possibly a superior position as the principal earners in the parental household. Not only have women a longer period of youth, they may have a different status in both household and society as consumers and providers. Women's changed status through wage employment has become particularly visible because of the men's limited opportunities locally for employment.

Workshop wages have allowed young women to become a specific consuming group in the small town society (for clothes and shoes, cosmetics and jewellery) and the money they hand over for general household expenditure has helped boost the demand for consumer durables (refrigerators, washing machines, televisions, furniture). But what has women's earning power meant with regards to their marriage prospects? Much joking now surrounds the young women who can 'buy' themselves good husbands; women's savings are seen as attracting marriage partners. Furthermore, the money saved can be put to good practical use to speed up a young couple's more independent and better standard of living through acquisition of goods considered necessary in the home. In the latter sense, a certain continuity can be discerned with the grandmothers' generation. Whereas young women in the past were expected to delay marriage until after they had acquired the material goods for a new home (within the parents-in-law's household), now workers' savings fulfil a parallel function allowing the purchase of households goods in the market.

Savings in cash may have either advantages or disadvantages over 'savings' in kind. In the first place, there is a greater flexibility and choice with respect to expenditure; for example, some women choose to invest their savings in a business that can be run from the home so as to continue earning after marriage (one important example of this is the domestic knitting industry). But in the second place, savings in cash are easily 'stolen' and spent by unscrupulous husbands, or wives can be persuaded to direct the money for the benefit of men rather than themselves.

The workers' savings together with support from the mothers' generation have contributed to a loosening of the bonds of patrilocality in the small town. Though the break with this tradition has not been total, women have negotiated rights to a living space that is more independent of husband's families than in the past. This has been achieved largely through a consensus among women across generations; in other words, women have come together to fight a practice they consider wrong and unjust when transposed from an agrarian to an urban setting. Of all the changes taking place in the last twenty-five years, this may be judged as being of the most far-reaching importance for the conditions of women's lives. The pursuit of a more independent living space can also be seen as one aspect of the changing hopes and desires that women now have with regard to marriage. They demand the right to experience romantic love and possibly long for a greater sense of partnership with husbands; their attitudes are changing as to desired fertility; and they demand greater material comfort than their mothers.

Women as workers have won some greater freedom with regards to certain areas of their lives. They are no longer so tied to the house, they can take decisions as to how to spend a proportion of the money they earn. They have also won the right to associate with other young women at a later age, in the period after leaving school. The meaning and importance of the companionship of the workplace is difficult to assess and evaluate. But in some cases, friendships are maintained after marriage. This can be seen for example in the choice of *comadres*; some women now extend kin links to wider networks of women who can be expected to offer material and emotional support.

A comparison of the extent of domestic violence is virtually impossible to make. Wives are still beaten by husbands (a middle-aged women was murdered by her husband during the fieldwork period). Yet confronting society's hesitation to 'interfere' in the private realm of the households is the determination expressed by many young women to stop husbands from beating or maltreating them; unlike their mothers, they are going to defend themselves and they will call on their families and friends to help them. Slowly, it appears that social attitudes towards male violence are changing; violent men are more likely to find open disapproval. The fathers and brothers of beaten wives sometimes threaten the husbands. New models of behaviour are being inculcated partly by the schools and partly by a general desire for social improvement and modernisation and the realisation of a more cultured, civilised life in the rural small towns. To some extent, this has been associated with the spread of industrialisation and the generation of greater material wealth. People want to turn their back on the poverty and brutality of the past.

Confronting these instances of change attributed in part to women's wage work, there are obvious constants which continue to structure and direct women's lives. Marriage remains of primary importance; very few women decide not to marry. Furthermore, divorce is no more acceptable socially now than in the past. Women are married for life, and still their conduct is watched over by their own and their husbands' families. After marriage the majority of women believe that husbands possess the right to control a wife's activities, such as the decision to take wage work outside of the house. After marriage women may dress more soberly, covering themselves with a shawl when leaving the house. And there has been no apparent change in the gender division of labour in the domestic work in the houschold.

The limited employment possibilities locally still force many men to migrate for work; married life may be constantly disrupted by men's migration in search of wage work, especially in the US. Though a new tendency has emerged whereby wives no longer necessarily remain at home, for those women who do stay in Santiago, like their mothers before them, they must fight to keep their husbands concern and affections, and they suffer the social and emotional deprivations of their abandonment. The reality of these deprivations still appear to outweigh feelings of having greater control over their lives. Wives managing alone tend to feel vulnerable, and they may try to involve their distant husbands even in trivial household and family decisions. Under these conditions, wives may prefer to travel north with their husbands.

Drawing conclusions from material discussed in this chapter is difficult. Changes in women's lives associated with the development of the workshops can be interpreted in several ways. The predominating impressions given me have been the *ability and readiness shown by women to use the opportunities presented by the industrial growth to struggle for a more valued and dignified position in the household and society*. This can be shown both with respect to the marriage contract women try to negotiate as well as the search for greater relative autonomy after marriage through the fostering of a new domestic manufacture which in itself builds upon and extends their skills and experiences in workshop employment. This positive general finding is more a comment about women's sense of identity and purpose than about any progresive tendencies 'automatically' stemming from workshop-based industry. Industrialisation (like any other wide-reaching change) has shaken old ways of doing things and opened up new spaces for thought and action. Thus the changes set in motion by industrial growth have permitted women the chance of trying to fight for and recapture a comparable position in society to that held by earlier generations of women. But to what extent they have mapped out new perspectives for themselves in relation to their gender and class positions remains unclear.

7 A Tentative Model of Workshop-based Production

Analysis of the field material when put together with more theoretical discussions led to certain generalisations as to (i) the origins and conditions of industrial growth; (ii) the dynamics and mode of appropriation specific to capitalised workshop production; and (iii) the implications of gendered production. These constituted a framework through which I might abstract from the immediate specificity of Santiago and of western-central region of Mexico. I wish to present these generalisations as a preliminary model which, although derived primarily from a single field enquiry, is capable of being explored further, tested and refined in the light of evidence about 'informalisation', capitalised workshops and gendered production coming from other localities.

ORIGINS OF CAPITALISED WORKSHOP PRODUCTION

Gender and Clandestinity/Illegality

Capitalised workshop production inhabits a social world where workers sell their labour power but where enterprises are often officially illegal due to non-compliance with labour and tax legislation. Where informal industry has flourished, it has been widely accepted that the letter of the law does not apply to certain types of worker and therefore to certain types of activity. Typically, the labour of women, children and ethnic 'minorities' (in a social sense but not necessarily numerical sense) has been seen as 'outside' the realm of organised labour, and therefore the work they do has been seen as falling 'outside' the orbit of 'formal' industry where labour legislation is considered rightly applicable.

Thus, where such deviation from legally established norms and standards is widely tolerated, or considered legitimate for reasons that contradict the rhetoric of democratic rights, then paradoxically, 'clandestinity' has only limited social meaning. The disenfranchisement taking place with informalisation does not affect the working population equally: some types of workers are considered by the dominant classes (and others) as less suitable or worthy for protection through the law enforced by the state and more amenable to private forms of protection and control.

At the same time localities with a strong sense of history and regional distinction are none too keen on the state's presence or interference: a reaction that may unite people across social divisions. There is often a tension between a locality's quest for autonomy and the practice of political organisation demanding the co-optation and active support of local leaders in return for political favours. The interpretation of 'illegality' and 'clandestinity' in such localities is ambiguous. The more privileged social strata view workshops as 'legitimate' activities that ought to be outside the arm of the law, the state having no right to intervene. Workers consider workshops as 'illegal' but see the state as too corrupt, weak or uninterested to intervene on their behalf.

Violence, Male Migration and Semi-Proletarianisation

The origins of an industrial capitalist class and an industrial labouring class lie in a history of violence and displacement. This can be viewed from both a rural and urban perspective. Prolonged warfare and social unrest in the countryside together with the violent destruction of traditional agrarian systems have been prevalent in twentieth century history. Following on the heels of agrarian destruction has come the greater intervention of capital in agriculture in which command over scarce resources in increasingly vested in few hands while many face relative and absolute impoverishment and dispossession. In some societies impoverishment has heightened the mobility of men who leave the locality in search of cash incomes and become semi-proletarians. In the face of sweeping rural impoverishment and lack of local wage employment, female mobility (women migrating without men) tends to be more restricted.

From a rural perspective, the industrialists have sprung from more privileged social or ethnic backgrounds who had first left the countryside to avoid social violence and/or were excluded from access to more productive agricultural resources and therefore unable to tap the higher profits emanating from capitalist agriculture. These migrating men usually had several years' schooling and kept some limited property back home. The majority took wage employment in cities and were being sucked into the burgeoning urban working class, especially at times of economic growth and industrial expansion. But access to wage work did not bring high monetary rewards nor social status in the cities. Some resisted permanent incorporation into the urban proletariat. Such resistance could only be effective under certain conditions; only at certain periods could a more autonomous, independent way of securing a livelihood be found.

The poor peasantry has borne the brunt of the damaging effects of agrarian change. Robbed of rights to land or unable to find the capital necessary to keep land in production, peasants have been forced to combine occasional wage work with reduced subsistence production on marginal land beyond the areas of capitalist agriculture. In some cases, families move from region to region seeking work; in others, women and children remain behind in the countryside while men migrate in search of work or take labour contracts offered by large estates or agri-business.

Under these conditions, there is considerable variation as to the nature of women's labours back home. In some places women may be pressed into making an increased contribution to agriculture: maintaining output from land already held, producing a proportion of the staple foodstuffs required for household consumption (possibly on marginal land rented on an annual basis) or working as day labourers in agriculture. Elsewhere, especially where agrarian transformation is accompanied by a re-settlement of population from scattered localities into small towns, women's labours may be less bound up with the processing of goods produced by households for direct consumption and directed more to exchanges of domestic manufactures and services with other households, some of which transactions are reimbursed with cash.

Migration, Semi-Proletarianisation and Tensions in the Household

Prolonged male migration and semi-proletarianisation generate many tensions at the household level. Already impoverished, the household as an economic and social unit is under threat. The life experiences of those leaving diverge increasingly from those who stay, meaning that the worlds of men and women become more insulated, contained and unknown to the other. New conditions are being created for social divisions rooted in gender relations, facilitating the resurgence of more forceful expressions of gender dominance/subordination while at the same time traditional gender identities are being undermined and altered.

Reactions to the dislocation of social and cultural life are also gendered. Alcoholism, physical violence and 'irresponsibility' – a term often used to describe men who fail to provide adequately for their families – have become closely associated with an aggressive expression of masculinity that counteracts the humiliating employment conditions suffered. In contrast, especially in areas of strong religious faith, the glorification of the suffering woman may suppress and confuse women's responses to changes taking place, for a time.

The threats posed to household relations have served over time to highlight particular areas of gender struggle. Women at home struggle to survive on a daily basis while remittances from men arrive irregularly or not at all. Women must fight for rights to cash earned by men, this being particularly prominent where no clear norms had emerged earlier as to household members' rights or intra-household distribution. A second area of gender struggle centres on the exercise of men's rights of control over younger women. With the absence of husbands, the control/protection of young married women passes into the hands of the older generation. Especially where patrilocality remains customary (in spite of the passing of the old agrarian system) young wives may suffer greater oppression than in the past, incarcerated in the house of their parents-in-law. Though these women may have little option to alter the course of their own lives, they may actively struggle to ensure that their daughters' lives are less harsh and more rewarding.

In the face of widening divisions based on gender and the dislocation of social and cultural life, the centrifugal tendencies in themselves tend to provoke a contrasting reaction at the level of ideology. The disruption is met and contained by an active emergence or reinforcement of pervasive ideologies stressing family loyalty, duty and solidarity. Such ideologies may arise at first in connection with religious teachings and be interpreted as part of a society's cultural base. They find particular resonance among societies suffering destruction, in which people try to cling to fragments of former gender and generational relationships.

Capital's Invasion and Colonisation of Gender Relations

The early development of industrial production along capitalist lines demands the immediate extraction of surplus value from labour and some form of consensus that permits (or at least does not prevent) this. Characteristically, a suitable labour force is one in need of cash but whose labour is under-valorised. This means that such a labour force has limited actual employment possibilities (at home or at the end of a migration channel); is considered a 'bearer' of lower value labour; can be recruited, disciplined and rewarded through means and mechanisms not primarily located in market relations. While the overall dispossession of resources lies behind cash need, a suitable labour force is one that has no clear socially recognised access to incomes earned by others nor previous direct experience of incorporation into the more formally constituted capitalist economy. Such a labour force is therefore largely drawn from among social groups attributed subordinate positions in relations of gender, ethnicity and generation (and often reflects an overlapping of all these identities as in the case of young 'Indian' women). In situations of endemic male migration and semi-proletarianisation, migrant men may not be a sufficiently needy labour force to draw upon for the development of local industrial production; but their wives and daughters may well be.

In the initial phase of industrialisation, capital invades and colonises relations of gender domination/subordination already prominent in local society (though by no means 'traditional') which have only indirect connection with capitalist labour relations. As a prelude to this colonisation, other dimensions of social differentiation rooted in class or social status have been temporarily rendered insignificant. Shared migration and wage work experiences serve to unite men across local class divisions, prompting them to give less weight to underlying class differences. By the same token, women share an identity and experience as migrants' families relegated to the home-based domestic and subsistence sector. By constructing networks of inter-dependencies, gender identity rather than class or status differences is emphasised.

Industrialisation and Social Reproduction

The struggle for physical and cultural survival waged by women under conditions of impoverishment and male migration has led to the development of strategies of social reproduction significantly different from those characterising agrarian systems. Women must themselves find the cash they require for the most vital of necessities (directly from their own cash earning work, or negotiated from their menfolk); arrange for the domestic production and processing of goods needed for subsistence; engage in relations of reciprocity to ensure collective help at times of emergency. The demands of household reproduction may only be met through the exercise of highly authoritarian relations among women: as between mother and unmarried daughters, or mothers-in-law and daughters-in-law. Older women control and discipline younger women. This gives rise to particular sets of social relations among women that may find most elaborate expression within the household but are not confined to it.

The resilient strategies for household reproduction developed by women following the collapse of traditional agrarian systems and male migration may be amenable to further adaptation so as to allow certain categories of women the possibility of undertaking cash earning work while the bulk of the other necessary subsistence/-domestic duties are undertaken by others. In small rural towns often the only cash-earning work previously open to women had been occasional, extremely low paying domestic manufacturing (selling processed foodstuffs, embroidery, garment sewing) or domestic servicing (washing work and child care). To allow time for the further adaptation of strategies for social reproduction, the early phase of workshop industry may well be marked by a fragmentation of the labour process so that work can be put out to home-workers who dovetail work for cash with other home-based occupations. This is a way of incorporating workers who also face social barriers against undertaking activities outside the domestic sphere.

DYNAMICS AND DIRECTIONS OF CHANGE

Stages in the Diffusion of Capitalised Workshop Production to Rural Areas

At particular historical moments, the available technology permits a fragmentation of industrial production and the spread of production to places that are 'remote', lacking in social and physical infrastructure, and with few direct industrial antecedents. When technology offers no impediment, the social will to develop industry in particular localities can outweigh the disadvantages of infrastructural backwardness. But the converse of this statement will rarely apply: the improvement of physical and social infrastructure will not in

Model of Workshop-based Production

itself be sufficient to stimulate the decentralisation of industry. For decentralisation rests on the existence of a displaced, 'eclipsed' social group willing to pioneer and bear the risks of investing in a new activity; the presence of a 'subordinate' social group whose labour is potentially available; and the emplacement of resilient adaptable strategies for social reproduction at the household level.

Once production has been successfully established in particular rural settings, then new dynamics are unleashed. Industrial producers may be able to press for their interests within the arena of local politics in competition with formerly dominating agrarian interests. In local political struggle, the new industrialists may find support from among other groups of men, such as returned migrants who cherish dreams of a more civilised, modern, industrial home town. They may campaign to re-direct public money into infrastructural improvements to benefit industry rather than into irrigation or public buildings. The improvement in a locality's electricity supply and in communications (surfaced roads, telephones) then opens up possibilities for the greater capitalisation of workshop production. This means investment in technologically more sophisticated machinery, the substitution of capital for labour, and the reinforcement and consolidation of industrial production in existing centres.

The Household Model of Workshop Organisation

Capitalised workshop production is a form of production where 'free' workers are employed but they are already defined as subordinate. Where workshops are built largely upon women's labour, even though capital accumulation has from the start been derived from the employment of wage labour, the model of labour relations followed in the early phase is taken from the image of household production so that gender and generational hierarchies are carried over from the household to organise workshop social relations of production. Symptomatic of this first phase of workshop production is the joint ownership of enterprises by women and men (usually wives and husbands, sometimes sisters and brothers), and the active engagement of both owning women and men in management and production.

But this adaptation of a household model demands that certain continuities are observed so that the organisation of production and choice of product type are seen as broadly 'appropriate' to women's labours. Industrial organisation will bear a strong imprint of the 'domestic', and the product will have strong connotations with women's work in the prevailing gender division of labour. In its initial phase, the household model of workshop production will uphold labour segregation and the non-comparability of different categories of labour. From this it follows that certain production processes and products have a greater likelihood of being taken up by workshop-based production due to social, not technical, reasons.

The Early Phase of Gendered Labour Relations

In situations of family division and male out-migration, a return to 'the household' as a model for the organisation of production has carried appeal. The transference of the household model further suggests that labour relations in the early industrial phase reflect the contradictory nature of household relations. On the one hand, wage workers can be depicted as 'helping out' and contributing, just like household members according to the dominant ideology. But on the other hand, hierarchies based on generation and gender are assumed as 'natural' within workshops as in households.

As in a household, the expectations of the men and women employed differ. To some extent, young men enter the workshops as apprentices or only temporary workers who are expected to struggle for independence. Hope for future assistance from workshop owners helps keep men's wages low. This position of apprentice is primarily open to employed men from a similar social background to the owners. The working out of these relations generally leads to a proliferation of workshop enterprise, with established owners off-loading obsolete machines to former workers. Workshops have tended to proliferate in certain zones in line with kin and neighbourhood networks.

In the early phase, women enter workshops with the identity of 'helpers'; often they or their mothers are already linked to the workshop owning wife through pre-existing networks developed to safeguard social reproduction. 'Clandestinity', reflected in the hiding of workshop enterprises from public view, together with gender segregation, have at the same time perpetuated the image of the workshop as a domestic rather than industrial place. Owning wives assume an identity as surrogate mothers expecting loyalty, discipline, hard work in exchange for protection and 'help' given in the form of wages and occasional loans. Individual wage agreements are negotiated for each worker and are based largely on age and 'loyalty'. Employment in workshops can be fitted into ruling ideologies concerning both family solidarity, and the protection/control of young women. Their workshop employment has a time limit: just as daughters will leave home on marriage (where patrilocality still prevails), so they will also leave the workshops.

Differentiation Among Workshops

In situations where enterprises accumulate not only on the basis of relations of production but also commercial profits, processes of differentiation distinguish different groups of enterprises. Characteristically, a three-fold stratification becomes visible. Although the workshops produce similar product(s), they supply different markets and face differential opportunities for investment and for changing the social relations of production. An integral part of this differentiation process is the development of relations of dominance and dependency between the strata.

Dominant workshops can reach more profitable (usually more distant) markets; gain access to cheaper sources of inputs and credit; capitalise production at a faster rate; and press hardest for changing the 'contract' with labour. Dependent workshops tend to employ both family and wage labour; use more primitive production methods; produce cheap, shoddy goods for sale to local, low priced markets. These workshops depend upon the dominant workshops for access to machinery, inputs and credit. But the poor quality of their output usually means that they cannot hope to produce under contract for the dominant enterprises. In between is a middle group including workshops that have been prevented from further expansion or are fighting their way up into the dominant group. In this most dynamic, unstable section, owners often take the greatest risks and exploit themselves and their labour forces hardest in an effort to reach higher levels of capital accumulation. These enterprises are the most likely to be seriously affected by economic recession.

Crisis in the Household Model of Workshop Production

Workshops face intense competition: the comparative ease of entry into the business means that myriads of similar enterprises struggle to find ways of improving and making more secure their relationships with markets. One aspect of this struggle is the double demand of lowering the per unit costs of production while improving the quality of the product. This double demand usually presses workshops to invest so as to increase workshop output and also cut down on the number of stages in the labour process still depending on labour skill; and at the same time to reformulate the social relations of production. The reformulation can take several forms, but generally it will lead to a departure from the household model underpinning workshop organisation in the early phases and the substitution of a more impersonal model in which workshops 'buy' for a straight cash wage labour time and skill in a wider labour market.

On the other hand, workers have also struggled to overthrow the household model where low cash wages represent only part of the more complex deals made between employers, the workers and their families in which the wage is supplemented by 'help' and 'protection'. Workers have demanded not only higher cash returns but also a more contractual relationship with their employers so as to avoid abuses and exploitation.

Thus increasingly from both capital and labour's point of view, the household model comes under attack. It no longer fits; it has become an anachronism. Particularly at the time when workshops increase their investment, workers are better able to demystify the nature of their relationship with capital, re-interpret it as being essentially distinct from the 'natural' relations of the household and take a more active stand in defence of their interests and rights as workers.

IMPLICATIONS OF GENDERED PRODUCTION

Relations of Class and Gender

When capital first fastens on to social inequalities rooted in relations of gender and generation, then growing consciousness need not be confined to an understanding of relations at the workplace but will come to inform how workers see their position and their future outside the workshop. There are several implications that follow from the superimposition of a class situation on relations structured by gender, generation and also ethnicity.

Class identity does not come to take precedence over gender (or any other) identity. On the one hand, trade unions, political parties and other organisations are still prone to dismiss women (especially young, 'Indian' women) as proletarians; women cannot count on support from the traditional labour movement for their interests or actions. On the other hand, women's own perception of themselves does not conform to the image of the male proletarian worker drawn from nineteenth century Europe but still relayed through the Marxist rhetoric of the labour movement. Women's self-image as workers is still in the process of formation, being constructed often by the more mature who remain as workers after the age of marriage has passed.

Class inequality does not come to take precedence over gender (or other) inequality. Class inequality is characterised by the clear-cut, relatively permanent differences in the ownership and control of the means of production. But workshop activity drawing on women's labour does not lead to contradictions that are perceived as being so clear or permanent. The gradual withdrawal of owning wives from management and production, for example, means that although one characteristic of the household model is in abeyance, the female labour force now faces male managers; relations of gender are reformulated in line with the changing organisation of the workshop, they are not suppressed. Class inequality continues to be intertwined with gender inequality with the result that the most immediate or the prime locus of contradiction remains confused. Furthermore, the possibilities open for workshop diffusion and for investment in domestic enterprises tend to obscure the roots of class division. Class inequality may indeed be entrenched but its origins pre-date the emergence of workshop activity (and the outflow of male migrants). Existing inequalities have led to a stratification of enterprise rather than to a clearly demarcated duality between owners of capital and sellers of labour power.

Class struggle does not come to take precedence over other struggles. The complexities and violence of history together with the emergence of new activities rooted in multiple social inequalities (gender, generation, ethnicity as well as class) means that class consciousness on its own does not possess the power to unleash or inspire widespread social action. The actions of labour against capital tend to remain sporadic and individualised, though not without significance. However, the consciousness of underlying class inequality can be an important contributor to broader based, popular expressions of dissent and protest where overlapping identities are forged into collective representations of 'the people' or 'the oppressed'. The broad popular actions may find unity by pitting their struggles against external forces: against the powers assumed by the state or nationally dominant classes.

Workshop Employment and Social Reproduction

The strong ties among women that have developed in regions of massive male out-migration are enhanced where workshops draw on a largely female labour force. Cash earned through workshop wages remains within women's control with daughters transferring the bulk of their earnings to their mothers in order to maintain the family. Workshop activity therefore allows women to remain more independent of cash or goods brought in by men, even when men no longer migrate for work. The perpetuation of a separate male and female cash nexus is often seen as being of value especially in the short run as women are better able to meet the social reproduction of the household 'single-handed'. But direct gender confrontation and struggle over the distribution of cash within the household is thereby avoided.

Continued division along lines of gender and the relative autonomy of men and women, at the same time serves to further undermine the significance of the household as being the basic cell of society. Under these conditions and where men are 'irresponsible' towards their families, women may have good reason to want many daughters who can be pressed into contributing to the social reproduction of the household. Paradoxically, there are material reasons as to why older women in the most impoverished social strata want to produce larger numbers of children.

Workshop activity and earnings need to be seen within an intergenerational context. Sending daughters into the workshops still rests on the abilities mothers have in forcing younger daughters to assist in the many domestic duties. The bonds of control governing the deployment of women's labour remain strict. Young women may feel great pressures to 'escape' the burdens of work and crippling responsibilities towards their families. The escape may take the physical form of health or mental breakdown or the desperate search for an alternative which usually results in elopement and an unnegotiated marriage. In places where the benefits of women's education are being better appreciated more complex patterns of allocation can be found where some daughters earn incomes, some assist in domestic tasks and the most able are supported through an education in the hope of the future reward of higher paying work.

The close association between workshop work and social reproduction carries implications for the way household activities are commoditised and cash disposed of. Pressure on the labour time of women in the household means that certain forms of domestic activity and manufacture are cut back: some disappear, others are replaced by purchasing from the market. The incomes generated by workshop employment can therefore give rise to a greater demand for a specific range of goods: food (especially industrially produced foodstuffs) and drink, clothing, medicines from the pharmaceutical industry, household goods and consumer durables which ease the work burden of women. Greater reliance on goods available on the market further undermines the significance of the rights and duties of husbands and wives in the 'traditional' marriage contract.

Workshop Experience and the Reformulation of Social Relations

Though young women are pressed into accepting long hours of labour in the workshops, the experience gives them access to cash wages, recognised skills and membership of a workplace community. The experience has given rise to a distinct phase in the women's life cycle during which they achieve greater social and economic visibility and often a more respected position in their parental home. 'Youth' has been given a new meaning as young women have actively forged their own social identity and have helped overturn old stereotypes emphasising their docility, respectfulness and passivity.

The transformation from a passive to an active social identity has had major implications for relations of both generation and gender. The right to retain a part of the wage, the liberty to spend it and the freedom to leave the parents' house may represent first steps in the renegotiation of household relations with the older generation. But one also sees how the young women have often faced ambiguity rather than outright opposition from their mothers. Indeed, one can detect strong solidarity between mothers and daughters in which mothers, in their own terms, seek to help and protect daughters. Around some issues, young women can expect some collusion from the older generation of women; the young women may lead a struggle which is seen as a 'gender interest' of wider perspective. The fight against patrilocality may take this form where there is a general will to transform the customs and behavioural patterns which drove a wedge in the relationship between mothers and daughters.

In the period of their youth, young women can now more actively confront their prospective marriage partners over the question of how to define the rights and obligations contained within marriage.

A proportion of the young women may opt out by eloping and so avoid pre-marital negotiation. But for those intent on not repeating their mothers' mistakes, youth and courtship also entail discussion of a married future. In this respect also, the young women are helped by the pervading ambiguity and dissatisfaction with the traditional norms and values that have governed the marriage 'contract' in the past. The young, in general, want change: they are better educated than their parents' generation, and they want to escape the hardships and humiliations suffered by their parents. Savings derived from workshop employment (for all except the most impoverished) and the monetary value put on unmarried women's labouring skills (their workshop wage) give a more solid base from which women can press for their own interests in their negotiations over marriage, especially their claim on cash earned by husbands.

Though the young may feel a desire to reformulate some aspects of gender relations, the mass media generally only portray the most conservative or idealised images of gender and family life. These images tend to extend rather than open up for question the overall subordination of women to men. Appeals for social justice may help rectify some of the worst abuses suffered by women in a particular society but there is also a need for the setting out of an alternative model of relationships in the basic cells of society through which men as well as women could realise some of their dreams and yearnings.

Appendices

Appendix I: Discussion of the Fieldwork Methodology

Researching clandestine manufacturing industry presents special problems. The activity is generally purposely hidden from view; one can expect owners to oppose and workers to feel threatened by outsiders wandering about and prying. A researcher needs to tread very carefully, especially if she or he is not to put workers in an awkward, if not dangerous, position as a result of insensitive questioning.

Two kinds of research response are possible. In the first, experience allows one to develop tactics so as to make maximum use of 'secondary' information as a way of unearthing the presence of manufacturing activity during a rapid industrial appraisal. Though workshops cannot immediately be seen, one can look for the ubiquitous small vans, notice the tangle of power-wires, listen for the noise of machinery and watch for throngs of young women in the streets at particular hours of the day. A trained eye can take in a surprising amount of detail from a fleeting glance through a workshop door: number, type and age of machinery; number, sex and age of workforce. But furtive spying has limitations.

For the main part of this research I adopted a different research strategy. I chose to settle in a single small manufacturing centre with my family for six months and slowly build up contacts on a regular or daily basis. Due to the small size, the whole of the manufacturing sector could be studied. From Santiago I could make occasional forays to other centres in western-central Mexico. Thanks to the hospitality and friendship of the people of Santiago, the research experience was exceedingly rewarding in every way.

1. RESEARCH ON SANTIAGO, JANUARY–JULY, 1986

The research was built up on the basis of (a) interviews with representative numbers from among the current workshop workers, their mothers and grandmothers, and workshop owners. From these interviews (b) certain key informants emerged to whom I turned for more intense and intimate discussions. The basic interviews were supplemented with (c) information from central figures in local social and political life and (d) some representatives of groups linked but not central to my analysis of the workshops. Finally, (e) I could turn to local sources of statistical information.

(a) Basic Interviews

Current Workshop workers: My aim was to contact working women at home and outside working hours. No strict sampling could be attempted but several criteria lay at the back of the choice of women for interview. I wanted to draw on workers from as wide a range of workshops as possible, who occupied different posts in the labour process and who were drawn from a range of family backgrounds. Some fifty women from around thirty different workshops in Santiago were interviewed: the majority came from relatively impoverished households either in the central slum or from the outskirts of town. I stopped this interviewing when I felt that the information had become repetitive; I was not attempting to draw quantitative conclusions except in the case of the workers in the largest workshop where I interviewed (or got detailed information about) everybody employed.

Through a local guide/field assistant (a young married woman with two young children) I made contact with the workers in the early evening or at weekends. Accompanied by our children, we were paying social calls; we carried no tape recorders or cameras; we did not make use of notes in the interview. We explained what we wanted to enquire about and asked for help. My research assistant and I carried in our heads a list of some twenty-five questions relating to the work done at the workshop and reimbursement; the workshop itself and the worker's own family background. These were interjected in the course of a general conversation which was free to develop in all manner of directions. We usually began by talking to an individual and were then joined by family members and sometimes fellow workers. The survey included older married out-workers or workshop workers as well as younger and older unmarried workshop workers. In addition, a small number of men (five) working on the looms were interviewed.

Mothers and grandmothers: To deepen my understanding of older women's lives and how they saw the changes taking place I returned to talk with the workshop workers' families during the daytime. These interviews (around forty) were largely devoted to re-constructing life histories, the first interviews suggesting the most salient topics to take up.

Workshop owners: In general, owners were more difficult to contact than the workers. Most were busy or travelling; many were frankly suspicious as to what I was doing and clearly did not want to talk to me. My policy was to establish some initial personal link and be on a footing of polite recognition; I avoided presenting myself at a workshop door unknown and unannounced. This took time which for other reasons tended to work against acceptance by the workshop owners (as my friendship and support of workers became more generally known as well as my contacts with the PSUM leaders). As relations with owners were awkward, so sources of information tended to be circumscribed. A few of the older owners of the better established enterprises (women as well as men) became interested in my work and contributed much information. From them I was able to build up a detailed picture of the industrial history and get 'a feel' for how the business stood at the time, though there were areas of questioning which I tended to avoid unless given the go-ahead. Even workshop owners I knew relatively well gave me misleading or wrong information about some very basic indicators: volume of output, number of workers, wages and other benefits paid. On these matters, information from workers appeared much more reliable.

Discussion of the Fieldwork Methodology 209

(b) Key Informants from Interviews

Workshop workers: From out of the many interviews with workers, several friendships developed. They were mostly with unusually articulate, older women (most in their twenties) who also carried heavy family responsibilities. Often these key informants could contribute much on labour action and protest, on relations in the workshop, on employment policy in different types of enterprise. The friendships led to my involvement in a dramatic labour protest brought by a young worker who had been unjustly sacked from the largest workshop. Not only was I a witness to the many fraught stages of the protest, I was requested by her family to accompany and assist her at the confrontation with her former employers at the Council for Labour Conciliation and Arbitration in Morelia.

Mothers and grandmothers: To some ten of the family members I came to know best, I presented a detailed questionnaire concerning the use and distribution of cash and consumption patterns in the household.

Workshop owners: From key informants among the owners I was able to gain some insight into the business of many local families as well as gain an impression of the more concealed aspects of the clandestine industry: rate of profit, credit conditions, illegal exports to the USA, type of subcontracting deals entered.

(c) Information from Central Figures in Local Society

Much corroborative information came through discussions with the President of the *municipio* (whom I visited formally on arrival in Santiago), the priest, headmaster of the secondary school, local historian (and former reforming municipal President), and active leaders of the local PSUM and PRI parties.

(d) Secondary Interview Groups

Owners of domestic knitting enterprises: Some overview was gained of this branch of local manufacturing by accompanying trading women on buying trips in the town. I later returned to talk in more detail to some of these producers. But given the large numbers (an estimated 200 enterprises), my interviews with some ten women did not constitute sufficient coverage from which I could draw major conclusions as to the tendencies within domestic industry.

Migrant workers in the USA: The implication of migration on local political life was the main theme being researched by my husband, Roger Leys, during our stay in Santiago. This investigation included recording the experiences of migrants as *braceros*, illegals and documented workers and a visit to Merced, Santiago's main daughter settlement in California's Central Valley. This material has been an important backdrop for my study of the workshops.

(e) Local Sources of Statistics

The most important local archival source used was the register of civil marriages kept by the municipal offices, beginning in the year 1926. Though the church records would probably have been more complete, there were many omissions of the couple's ages at marriage which meant they could not be used. In order to discover whether changes could be discerned in the marriage patterns, I made an analysis of the civil registers for every second year, recording the couple's ages, place of residence and occupation (if given), and separating the material according to whether the couple belonged to Santiago town, the *ranchos* or elsewhere. Where women and men came from different places, the husbands' place of residence was taken as being the couple's home after marriage, following the patrilocal customs of society. In years of evident transition where patterns became confused, analysis was made of the intervening years as well in the hope of further enlightenment.

In addition, information from Santiago's tax office was examined to give a breakdown of the recorded economic activity in the town.

2. SUPPLEMENTARY RESEARCH ON THE WESTERN CENTRAL REGION

(a) Moroleón

Material on this capital of 'informal' industry was built up from selected interviews with key informants who could be encountered during a visit of a few days. I talked to workshop owners (five) making bedspreads, knitwear and garments; traders (two) from Ciudad Juaréz and Monterrey on buying trips to the town; the secretary of the Chamber of Commerce; administrator of the tax office; and teachers and students of the local technical college training loom work, sewing and cutting. In addition I read the archives of the local weekly newspaper for evidence on labour relations and actions.

(b) Los Altos de Jalisco

Short visits were made to Zapotlanejo, now full of garment making workshops and retailers as well as being a centre for embroidery outwork; Arandas (womenswear) and Jalostotitlán (menswear) where workshop activity is completely hidden.

3. RETURN VISITS TO SANTIAGO, 1987, 1989

During a month's visit in July 1987 I was able to talk to many of my key informants from among the workshop workers, their families and the owners in order to enquire into how the years of recession were then affecting lives and livelihoods. This presented a far more gloomy picture of greater hardship and impoverishment though no major workshops had yet closed down. A further visit in July/August 1989 (not discussed in the text) confirmed that the industry was surviving but gave a very different impression of the town's potentiality for social and political action. Many have now joined the new political party organised around the figure of Cuauhtemoc Cárdenas and they were 'at war' with the Government as a response to the familiar practice of ballot rigging by the ruling PRI party. But discussion of the upwelling of popular dissent in Santiago as elsewhere in Michoacán must be the subject of a future book.

Appendix II: Dollar–Peso Exchange Rate: 1985–88*

Year	Jan.–March	April–June	July–Sept.	Oct.–Dec.
1985	200.6	218.6	274.7	333.6
1986	423.6	522.1	665.7	836.6
1987	1025.7	1241.0	1460.8	1784.6
1988	2249.4	2281.0	2281.0	2281.0

*Period averages.
(Rates taken from International Financial Statistics of the International Monetary Fund.)

Glossary

agrarista: campaigner for land distribution during 1920s and 1930s.
barrio: urban district or quarter.
bracero: contracted labourer sent to the USA during the Bracero Programme: 1940–64.
chili: chile; the basic flavouring for Mexican cooking; varieties ranging from fiery to smooth tasting. Burning dried chile gives off suffocating acrid smoke.
comadre/compadre: title and mode of address used between people sharing the parent-godparent relationship.
compadrazgo: the bonds uniting parents and godparents.
cristero: a member of the 'Army of Christ' which rose in rebellion against the anti-clerical legislation in the 1920s.
ecuaro: a Tarascan word meaning a plot of ground cleared for planting.
ejido: land handed over to farmers when the large estates were broken up at the time of the Agrarian Reform. It is held in common by an ejido community which has the right to use it but not sell it. Members of the community are known as ejidatarios.
ingenio: sugar mill; many powered by water power.
municipio: political subdivision of a state comprising a town and its surrounding hinterland.
nopales: edible leaves of the prickly pear cactus.
peón: farm labourer especially one who worked on the former haciendas.
rancho: a settlement and land division of the rural zone surrounding a township; usually having indigenous ethnic connotations.
tiangui: a Tarascan word for a periodic market.
tortilla: flat maize pancake that is the staple of most Mexican diets.

References

Alarcón Acosta, Rafael, *La migración por grupos sociales a los Estados Unidos: el caso de Chavinda, Michoacán*, Tesis en antropología, UAM, Unidad Iztapalapa, Mexico City, 1984.

Alonso, José A., 'El estado mexicano frente a las zonas urbanas marginadas: el caso de Nezahualcóyotl', in Alonso (ed.), *El Estado Mexicano*, Editorial Nueva Imagen, Mexico, 1982.

Alonso, José A., 'The domestic seamstresses in Nezahualcóyotl and their relationship to dependent capitalism', in June Nash and M. Patricia Fernandez Kelly (eds), *Women, men and the new division of labor*, SUNY Press, New York, 1983.

Alonso, José A., 'La mujer y el trabajo en México', in Pablo González Casanova (ed.), *El obrero mexicano*, Editorial Siglo XXI, Mexico, 1984.

Alonso, José A., 'Crisis, sismos e industria doméstica' in Gabayet *et al.*', 1988.

Arias, Patricia, 'El proceso de industrialización en Guadalajara, Jalisco: siglo XX', *Relaciones*, vol. I, no. 3, El Colegio de Michoacán, Zamora, 1980.

Arias, Patricia, 'La consolidación de una gran empresa en un contexto regional de industrias pequeñas: el caso de Calzado Canada', *Relaciones*, vol. I, no. 3, El Colegio de Michoacán, Zamora, 1980.

Arias, Patricia, (ed.), *Guadalajara, la gran ciudad de la pequeña industria*, El Colegio de Michoacán, Zamora, 1985.

Arias, Patricia, 'Nuevas modalidades de la industria de la ropa en el medio rural: pueblos maquilleros, pequeña industria y trabajo a domicilio en los Altos de Jalisco', 1986. Manuscript El Colegio de Michoacán.

Arias, Patricia, 'La pequeña empresa en el occidente rural', *Estudios Sociológicos*, vol. VI, no. 17, El Colegio de Mexico, May–August, 1988.

Arias, Patricia and Jorge Durand, 'El impacto regional de la crisis', *Relaciones*, vol. VI, no. 22, El Colegio de Michoacán, Zamora, 1985.

Arizpe, Lourdes and Aranda, Josefina, 'The 'comparative advantages' of women's disadvantages: women workers in the strawberry export agribusiness in Mexico', *Signs*, vol. 7, no. 2, 1981.

Benería, Lourdes and Martha Roldán, *The crossroads of class and gender*, University of Chicago Press, 1987.

Bromley, Ray, and Chris Gerry, *Casual work and poverty in Third World cities*, Wiley, 1979.

Calleja, Margarita, 'Dependencia y crecimiento industrial: las unidades domésticas y la producción de calzado en León, Guanajuato', *Relaciones*, vol. V, no. 17, El Colegio de Michoacán, Zamora, 1984.

Castells, Manuel, 'High technology, economic policies and world development', BRIE Working Paper, Berkeley, 1986.

Cockburn, Cynthia, *Brothers*, Pluto Press, 1983.

Creel Galindo, Martha, *Chiconcuac, pueblo de artesanos y capitalistas*, tesis de licenciado en antropología social, Universidad Iberoamericana, 1977.

Elson, Diane, and Pearson, Ruth, 'The subordination of women and the internationalisation of factory production', in Kate Young, Carol Wolkowitz and Roslyn McCullagh, (eds), *Of Marriage and the Market*, CSE books, 1981.

Feder, Ernesto, *El imperialismo fresa: los mecanismos de la dependencia en la agricultura Mexicana*, Mexico, Editorial Campesino, 1977.

Friedmann, Harriet, 'Patriarchal commodity production', *Social Analysis*, Adelaide, no. 20, December 1986.

Gabayet, Luisa, Patricia García, Mercedes González de la Rocha, Silvia Lailson and Agustín Escobar, (eds), *Mujeres y sociedad: salario, hogar y acción social en el occidente de México*, El Colegio de Jalisco and CIESAS del Occidente, 1988.

González, Luis, *Pueblo en vilo: microhistoria de San José de Gracia*, El Colegio de Mexico, 1968.

Gordon, David, 'The global economy: a new edifice or crumbling foundation?', *New Left Review*, March/April, 1988.

Lailson, Silvia, 'Expansión limitada y proliferación horizontal. La industria de la ropa y el tejido de punto', *Relaciones*, vol. I, no. 3, El Colegio de Michoacán, Zamora, 1980.

Lailson, Silvia, 'De mercaderas a industriales', in Arias (ed.), 1985.

Leys, Roger, 'Labour migration and politics in Western Mexico', Working Paper, Institute of Political Studies, University of Copenhagen, 1987.

Lopez Castro, Gustavo, *La casa dividida, un estudio de caso sobre la migración a Estados Unidos en un pueblo michoacano*, El Colegio de Michoacán, 1986.

Luna Jiménez, Pedro, 'Ejidatarios, ganaderos y maestros en la política local', Working Paper in Antropología Politica, El Colegio de Michoacán, Zamora, 1985.

Massey, Douglas, Jorge Durand, Rafael Alarcón, *Return to Azatlán*, University of Pennsylvania Press, 1987.

Meyer, Jean, *La cristiada*, 3 vols., Siglo XXI, Mexico, 1973.

Mingione, Enzo, 'Social reproduction of the surplus labour force: the case of southern Italy', in Redclift and Mingione, 1985.

Padilla Dieste, Cristina, *Marginados o asalariados. El trabajo domiciliar de maquila en una colonia popular de Guadalajara*. Tesis en antropología social, Universidad Iberoamericana, 1978.

Pearson, Ruth, 'Latin American women and the new international division of labour: a reassessment', *Bulletin of Latin American Research*, vol. 5, no. 2, 1986.

Pinnaro, Gabriella, and Pugliese, Enrico, 'Informalization and social resistance: the case of Naples', in Redclift and Mingione, 1985.

Portes, Alejandro, 'The informal sector: definition, controversy and relation to national development', *Review*, vol. VII, no. I, 1983.

Redclift, Nanneke, and Enzo Mingione (eds), *Beyond employment: household, gender and subsistence*, Basil Blackwell, Oxford, 1985.

Roldán, Martha, 'Subordinación genérica y proletarización rural: un estudio de caso en el Noroeste Mexicano', in Magdalene Leon de Leal, (ed.), *Debate sobre la mujer en America Latina y el Caribe*, vol. II, ACEP, Colombia, 1982.

Roldán, Martha, 'Industrial out-working, struggles for the reproduction of working-class families and gender subordination', in Redclift and Mingione, 1985.

Roldán, Martha, *Yet another meeting on the informal sector? Or the politics of designation and economic restructuring in a gendered world*, Paper presented at the conference on the informal sector as an integral part of the national economy, research needs and aid requirements, Copenhagen, 1987.

MacEwen Scott, Alison, 'Who are the self-employed?' in Bromley and Gerry, 1979.

Soto, Hernando de, *El otro sendero: la revolución informal*, Instituto Libertad y Democracia, Lima, Peru, 1986.

Standing, Guy, 'Global feminisation through flexible labour', *World Development*, vol. 17, no. 7, July 1989, pp. 1077–96.

Stolcke, Verena, *Coffee planters, workers and wives: class conflict and gender relations on São Paulo plantations, 1850–1980*, Macmillan, London, 1988.

Steenbeek, Gerdien, 'Gender, work and ideology: Mexican seamstresses in a rural town', Paper to the symposium on Gender and Work, 46th International Congress of Americanists, Amsterdam, July, 1988.

Uribe Salas José, *La industria textil en Michoacán, 1840–1910*, Universidad Michoacána de San Nicolas de Hidalgo, 1983.

Whitehead, Ann, 'Gender and class in petty commodity production: notes'. Paper written for workshop on Gender and class in the Third World, London School of Economics, 1985.

Wilson, Fiona, 'Women and agricultural change in Latin America: some concepts guiding research', *World Development*, vol. 13, no. 9, September, 1985.

World Development, Special Issue, *Beyond survival: Expanding income earning opportunities for women in developing countries*, vol. 17, no. 7, July 1989.

Person Index*

* Sweater workshop owners, workers and their families.

Alicia López (owner), wife of Ramiro Espinoza 45–6, 71, 77–9, 81, 106, 110–12, 145
Amalia (workshop worker's mother), daughter of Olivia, mother of Lupita 60, 61, 63, 69, 72, 149, 152, 177, 180
Angelina (former outworker, workshop worker's mother) 67

Beatríz (workshop worker's mother), mother of Guadalupe and Emilia 62, 65, 67, 69, 72, 133, 172–3, 179
Blanca (workshop worker), daughter of Concha 146–7, 168

Carlos (owner), husband of Virginia 106
Carmen (former workshop worker) 163–4
Concha (former workshop worker), mother of Blanca 58–60, 61, 63, 66, 168

Emilia (workshop worker), daughter of Beatríz, sister of Guadalupe 132–3
Eva (former outworker and workshop worker's mother), mother of Soledad 71

Francisco (owner), brother of Hilda 127

Genoveva (former outworker), wife of Jaime 41, 47–9, 50, 57, 167, 179
Guadalupe (workshop worker), daughter of Beatríz, sister of Emilia 132–3

Hernández brothers (owners) 106, 116–17, 133–7, 138, 139, 147, 149–54, 159, 169, 180, 183
Hilda (outworker), sister of Francisco 127

Jaime González, husband of Genoveva 46–9, 57, 179
Jesús Espinoza (owner), brother of Ramiro and Manuel, cousin of José 46, 77–9, 80–1, 90, 110, 125, 154, 163
Jorge (owner), uncle of Julia 106, 115–16, 168–9
José (owner), cousin of Ramiro, Jesús and Manuel 80–1, 106, 118–19, 137, 140–1, 143, 144–7
Josefina (former outworker), mother of Silvia 149, 151, 154, 181
Juan (owner), husband of Lola 132–3, 141, 143, 168, 171, 172
Julia (former workshop worker, outworker), Jorge's niece, 115, 168–9

Lola (owner), wife of Juan 126, 132–3, 141, 143, 168, 171, 172
Lucía (former workshop worker, outworker) 182–3
Lupe (outworker) 126
Lupita (workshop worker), daughter of Amalia, granddaughter of Olivia 135, 136–7, 149–54, 155, 177, 178, 180–1

Manuel Espinoza (owner), brother of Ramiro and Jesús, cousin of José 80, 90, 110, 115, 123, 125, 129–30, 140
María (outworker) 62–3, 126, 185
María Rosa (workshop worker) 129–30, 140
Mario (owner) 82, 107, 140, 145–6
Marta (outworker, workshop worker's mother and grandmother) 64–5, 125
Miguel (owner) 106

Olivia (workshop worker's grandmother, mother of Amalia, grandmother of Lupita) 35, 37, 64, 72, 177, 180

Pedro (workshop worker) 144–5

Rafael (former workshop worker, owner) 106, 107–8

217

Ramiro Espinoza (owner), husband of Alicia, brother of Jesús and Manuel, cousin of José   35–6, 45–6, 66, 71, 77–9, 80–1, 83, 106, 108, 110–12, 123, 128, 145
Raul (owner)   106, 130–2, 168
Rita (workshop worker)   148
Rosa (owner), wife of Toribio   106, 108–10, 129

Sanchez sisters (former workshop workers)   140–1, 142
Silvia (workshop worker), daughter of Josefina   149–54. 180, 181
Socorro (former outworker, workshop worker's mother)   66
Soledad (workshop worker), daughter of Susanna   131
Susanna (outworker, workshop workers' mother)   66

Teresa (workshop worker), sister of Toribio   109–10, 128–9, 141–2, 171, 173
Toribio (former workshop worker, owner), husband of Rosa, brother of Teresa   106, 108–10, 128

Veronica (workshop worker)   163
Virginia (owner), wife of Carlos   54–5, 106

Yolanda (owner)   106, 112–15, 163, 185

Subject Index

abduction of women ('robbery') 35, 36, 56, 58–62, 63, 176, 177, 178
Acapulco 125
accumulation of capital
  in agriculture 1, 81
  in small scale industry 13, 81, 89, 105–7, 120, 197, 199
agrarian reform 34, 36, 38–40
agraristas 36–7, 45
agriculture
  agri-business/strawberry industry 1, 2, 25, 48, 49, 50, 55, 68, 74, 101, 193
  peasant/subsistence 1, 34, 36, 39, 40–2, 192, 193
  share-cropping 38, 42, 43
  sugar cane 39, 43, 66, 67
Aguascalientes 1, 3, 32, 80, 118
alcoholism 48, 49, 60, 64, 65, 66, 67, 69, 71, 79, 81, 111, 159, 169, 181, 194
Altos de Jalisco 3, 4
Arias, P. 6

banditry 35, 42, 55
basket-making 38, 41, 54
Benería, L. and Roldán, M. 11
bourgeoisie 15, 31, 82, 87, 88, 171, 174

California 45, 46, 71, 81, 100, 101, 110, 115, 165
Cárdenas, Lazaro 37, 38
Castells, M. 10, 13
catholicism/religion 23–4, 36–7, 68, 69–71, 133, 136, 139, 194
cattle-raising 36, 39–40, 43, 91, 159, 165
Chavinda 97
Chiconcuac 32
Chihuahua 100, 118
Cienega 60
Ciudad Juaréz 101
clandestinity
  and the law 6–7, 11, 13, 15, 19, 191–2
  in manufacturing 6, 7, 9, 11, 16, 19, 20
  and physical concealment 6, 7, 11, 13–14, 89–90, 198

class–gender perspectives 15, 16, 21, 73, 88, 122, 157, 158, 200–1
Cockburn, C. 21
Colima 98, 116
compadrazgo 83, 100, 108, 115, 116, 121, 123, 163, 189
co-operatives 28, 98, 105, 108
courtship 56–7, 58, 60, 61, 173, 174–6, 177, 181, 204
credit and loans
  banks 12, 80, 102, 114, 118, 162
  hire-purchase 12, 80, 102, 162
  restrictions 102, 115, 117, 118
  for small scale production 12–13, 17, 33, 80, 102, 120, 162, 164, 199
  and sub-contracting 12–13, 17
cristeros 23, 36, 37, 38, 45
Cuitzeo 28, 31

domestic violence and wife-beating 58, 61, 69–70, 71, 72, 170, 189, 194
dress 22, 169, 170–3, 187
Durango 59, 100

earthquake, 1985 13–14, 32
Ecuardureo 80, 84, 92, 94, 128, 173
ecuaros 25, 42, 49, 64, 67, 125, 127
education 44, 54–5, 62, 82, 83, 111, 127, 132–3, 134, 158, 159–60, 168, 172, 202, 204
ejidos 38–40, 42, 64
  'new' *ejidatarios* 40, 42, 81, 83
ethnicity 16, 23, 192, 195, 200

family
  as institution 50, 71, 194, 199
  size 49, 70–2, 183–5
feuding 44, 61
food
  famine and malnutrition 35, 42
  meat and milk consumption 41, 42, 53, 182
  staple foodstuffs 25, 40–2, 53, 182, 193
  subsistence base 34, 36, 40–2, 125, 127, 182–3, 193
Fresno 47

219

garment production
  domestic/family-based 3, 4, 7, 14, 26, 30–2
  factory-based 3, 4, 7, 12, 13–14, 25–6, 28–9, 77, 85, 88
  'fashion' clothing 3, 4, 5–6, 19, 30–2, 85
  historical precedents 3, 25–7, 28–32, 55
  industrial structure in Mexico 5–7, 13–14, 18–19, 79–80, 87–8
  industrial structure in western central region 3–4, 13, 30–3
  regional specialisations 3–4, 5, 17–18, 19–20
  seasonality 5–6
  sub-contracting 6, 12, 13, 14, 30, 31
  technical training for 29, 31, 119, 120–1
  trade 13, 30–3
  trouser manufacture 3–4, 85
  workshop-based 3, 4, 6, 25–6, 29, 31
gender divisions of labour
  in agriculture 41, 43
  in domestic manufacturing 14, 162–7
  in garment production 4, 14, 85–6, 90
  in the household 181, 183, 186–7, 189, 193, 194–6, 202
  in manufacturing 3, 4, 17, 19, 21, 29, 197–8
  in migration 1–2, 44, 46, 48, 73, 189–90, 193–4, 195
  in sweater manufacture 78–9, 85–7, 89, 90, 93, 137, 154
gender identity 41, 65, 74, 135, 170, 179, 190, 193–4, 195, 200, 203–4
gender relations
  complementarity 85, 87, 88, 111
  housewives 87, 88
  'respect' 68–70, 111, 148–9, 155
  in rural households 51–3
  segregation/seclusion 4, 55–6, 57, 61, 86, 88, 90, 170, 198
  sexuality/virginity 68–9, 139, 172, 178–9, 186
  in society 21, 154–5, 157, 158, 170, 173, 186, 190, 193–4, 195, 203–4
  subordination 16, 17, 21, 195, 197, 204
  in urban households 21, 34, 70, 68–72, 138, 167–90, 193–4, 197–8, 202–4

at work 85–7, 88, 90, 117, 137–8, 154–5, 164, 197–203
gender struggle 170–3, 194–5, 201–2, 203
globalisation of production theories 8
Gordon, D. 8
Guadalajara 3, 4, 12, 13, 23, 72, 79, 98, 100, 107, 108, 111, 112, 114, 117, 118, 119, 130, 131, 165, 177, 180
Guanajuato 1, 28, 29, 32, 34, 131

haciendas 36, 38–40, 41, 42, 51, 60
home-work see industrial outwork/home-work
households
  and consumer goods 66, 169, 171, 178, 182–3, 187–8, 202–3
  daughters' earnings 159, 160, 167–9, 172, 175, 177, 178, 187, 202
  distribution of cash 48–9, 50, 63–8, 73, 126, 127, 178, 180, 181–3, 185, 194, 202–3
  social relations 40, 48, 50, 51–5, 62–3, 64, 138, 161, 163, 167–90, 193, 194, 195–6, 197–200, 202–4
  social reproduction 17–18, 167, 193, 195–6, 197, 202–3
impoverishment 1, 2, 14, 40, 42, 46, 50, 51, 159, 192, 195, 202, 204
Indian labour 28, 195, 200
industrial growth 2–3, 8–9, 18–19, 26, 77
industrial outwork/home work 11, 14, 16, 49, 55, 67, 74, 79, 94, 96–7, 111, 113, 118, 122, 123–7, 161, 168, 196
industry
  chemical 12, 80, 87, 102
  flexible production 6, 7, 14, 15, 17
  gendered production 11, 17, 19, 21, 197–8
  Mexican policy towards 8–9, 102, 121
  restructuring 9, 13, 17, 79–80
  specialisation 3–4, 7–9
  sub-contracting hierarchies 11, 80, 102
informalisation processes 7, 9, 10, 14–15, 18–19, 191
  and disenfranchisement 10, 15, 191–2

political significance of 14–15
and women in the labour force 17,
   18, 19, 191
inspectors 6–7, 7–8, 90, 104, 111, 120,
   145
international division of labour
   theories 8, 50
Irapuato 4, 132

Jacona 23, 26, 28, 35–6, 45, 55, 79,
   97, 118, 130, 160
Jalisco 1, 34
Jiquilpan 23, 26, 28

La Barca 60
La Piedad 28
labour action
   demands 125, 128, 139, 140–3, 149
   legal assistance 132, 141, 144–5,
      150–4
   protest 54, 137, 140–54, 155, 156
   strikes 28, 29, 32, 118, 120
labour exploitation 15–16, 20–1, 104,
   105, 117
labour legislation 7, 8, 11, 20, 104,
   190
labour relations in garment
   production 4, 6, 14, 28, 29–32
labour relations in sweater manufacture
   blacklisting 32, 120, 141, 143
   control and discipline 86, 124, 128,
      131, 133–5, 136–48, 154
   dismissal 139, 140–1, 143, 144, 146,
      148, 149, 151, 152, 163
   employment policy 96, 118–19, 120,
      134–5, 137, 140, 145, 147–8
   family labour 78, 79, 81, 93, 105,
      108, 109–10, 112, 115, 117
   gender relations 93, 128, 138–9,
      148–9, 154, 160–1
   'household' model 122, 124, 128,
      130, 137–9, 142, 147, 155
   labour process 89, 90, 91–7, 108,
      109, 111, 124, 131, 132, 137
   recruitment 77, 78, 79, 86, 90, 125,
      130
   redundancy 92, 93, 95, 112, 118,
      124–5, 142
   skill/wage differentials 95–6, 113,
      114, 115, 122–8, 130–1, 132,
      133–5, 137–8, 145
   training 83, 93, 110, 113, 119, 144
Lake Chapala 23, 41
Lake Patzcuaro 41

landed elite 36–7, 38–40, 42, 88, 119
León 3
looms
   apprenticeship and training 77, 78,
      81, 83, 93
   Carrousels 30–1, 92–3, 102, 107,
      114, 117, 118, 119, 132, 133,
      142, 144–5
   manually operated 77, 91, 93
   motorised 91–3, 102, 103, 105, 107,
      108, 109, 111, 113, 115, 117,
      130–2
   repairs and spare parts 33, 77, 91,
      108
Los Angeles 32, 147, 165, 181
Los Reyes 43, 67

machismo 61, 70, 167, 172
Manzanillo 98
marianismo 70, 149
marriage 52, 56–60, 63, 68, 70, 72,
   144, 158, 161, 168, 173, 174,
   175–9, 183, 185–6, 187, 188–90,
   199, 202, 203–4
   age at marriage 51–2, 56, 57–8, 60,
      176–7
   elopement 57, 58, 177–8, 179, 202,
      204
   endogamy 51–2, 56
   'robbery' see abduction of women
mass media 158, 171, 172, 176, 204
Matamoros 101
men's work
   in agriculture 43, 52–3, 55, 64, 138,
      158
   in garment production 4, 28, 29
   in sweater manufacture 78, 79, 81,
      83, 86, 91–4, 137, 138
   in the USA 40, 44, 48, 50, 66, 126,
      157, 165, 166, 178, 181, 183, 189
Merced 101, 115
Mexacali 82
Mexican Revolution 1, 3, 23, 27, 34,
   35, 36
Mexico City 32, 45, 46, 50, 58, 82,
   104
   garment industry 5, 13–14, 32, 77,
      80, 100, 109, 114, 118
   sub-contracting hierarchies 11, 16
Michoacán 1, 3, 19, 25–7, 28, 34, 58,
   161
migrants' wives 48–9, 65, 68–9, 73,
   189–90, 193, 195, 202

migration 1–2, 29, 34
  Bracero Program 40, 46–8, 65
  and gender division 1–2, 44, 48, 50, 157, 172, 189–90, 192, 193, 195
  historical patterns 44–50
  illegality 46, 47
  return 2, 18, 197
Mingione, E. 17–18
Monterrey 32, 47, 101, 116, 118
Morelia 26, 28, 98, 111, 144, 150, 153, 154, 155, 181–7
Moroleón 3, 7
  history of garment production 27, 28–32
  links with sweater industry 27, 32–3, 80, 91, 100, 102, 108, 110, 111, 116, 118, 120, 129
  motherhood and parenting 49, 63, 69, 70–2, 73, 74, 175, 183–7

Nayarit 116
New York 32
Nezahualcóyotl 14
Nogales 101

outwork *see* industrial outwork/homework

parenting *see* motherhood and parenting
patrilocality 51, 62–3, 72, 73, 74, 179–81, 188, 194, 199, 203
petty commodity production theories 16, 20
pilgrimage 24, 57, 169–70, 174
population mobility 34, 42–4, 52
PRI (Partido Revolucionario Institucional) 40, 104, 150
proletariat 16, 31, 44, 82, 154, 193, 200–1
Purépuro 97

ranchos
  household relations 51–3
  in Santiago Tangamandapio 24, 25, 36, 38–9, 40, 42–3, 44, 51, 52, 56, 62, 64, 72, 170, 176–7, 178
recession and debt crisis 3, 9
  austerity programmes 9, 13
  effects on garment production 13–14, 77, 87, 110, 112, 156
  regional concentration of industry 1, 3–4, 17–18, 19–20, 196–7

'robbery' *see* abduction of women
Roldán, M. 16–17

Sahuayo 23, 26, 28, 42, 79, 98, 130, 162
Saltillo 101
San Francisco 114
San Juan Potosí 80, 116
San Miguel de Los Altos 4, 165
Santiago Tangamandapio
  agrarian reform 38–40
  agricultural and livestock production 25, 38–40, 43
  barrios 24, 37, 43, 44, 51, 55, 56, 57, 62, 73, 83, 130
  population 23, 42–4, 183–4
  religious life 23–4
  subsistence 40–2
  as urban centre 25, 78–9, 159, 171, 173
semi-proletarianisation 2, 34, 50, 73, 192, 193, 195
sewing machines 94, 95, 103, 104, 105, 108, 113, 115, 128, 129, 131, 132
  overlock 77, 94, 95, 102, 103, 107, 108, 115, 128–9, 132
  and outwork 14, 31, 94, 115, 168–9
shawl manufacture 30, 55
  historical precedents in western central region 26, 28
  outwork in Santiago Tangamandapio 28, 54, 55, 67–8, 74, 162
  women's domestic industry 161–2
shoe manufacture 3, 4, 11, 12, 19
silk production 25, 55
social class 16, 21, 42, 49–50, 53, 68, 88, 119–21, 142, 154, 159, 171–2, 174–5, 192–3, 195, 200–1
social security
  in Mexico 7, 111, 113, 129, 160
  in sweater manufacture 111, 113, 129, 130, 131, 132, 136, 137–8, 145—6, 147, 148, 150, 182
  in the USA 47, 67
sub-contracting
  in garment production 1, 5–7, 12–13, 14, 28, 30, 31, 80, 81
  hierarchies 11–14
  international links 8, 10, 11
sweater manufacture
  apprenticeship and training 77, 81, 83, 96, 119

Subject Index

'artisan' sewing 94, 109
embroidering 79, 96–7, 111, 113, 118, 123–7, 161
historical precedents 77–9
labour supply 73–4, 117
outwork 79, 94, 96–7, 111, 113, 115, 118, 124–5, 126, 127, 161, 168–9
production process 4, 5–6, 77, 78, 79, 89, 90, 91, 91–4, 94–6, 107–8, 109, 111, 115, 144
quality improvement 83, 97, 118, 132, 142–3, 144
seasonality 5–6, 31, 84–5, 98, 100, 111, 118, 160
sports shirts 84–5, 87, 94–6, 98, 105, 107–8, 130
in western central region 3, 4, 29, 49, 62
sweater trade marketing 76, 77, 79, 89, 97
urban retail 32, 98, 109, 111, 114, 115–16, 118
urban wholesale 32, 98–101, 107
on US–Mexican border 32, 100–1, 107, 115, 117, 118, 165
in weekly markets 32, 97–8, 105, 108, 130, 164
women's circuits 101, 113–14, 164, 166
sweater workers
artisan/skilled sewers 94, 109, 110, 127–30, 143, 175–6
cutters 94, 117, 146–7, 163
loom operators 78, 79, 83, 84, 86, 92–3, 130, 137, 138, 140, 142, 143, 144–6, 154, 159
machinists 78, 79, 86, 94, 113, 130–1, 132–3, 134, 137, 142, 143, 145, 147, 162, 163, 168
married workers 133, 160–1
outworkers 79, 96–7, 115, 123–7, 143, 161, 168–9, 182
steam press workers 131, 135, 136
sweater workshops 62, 49, 74
access to machinery 33, 77, 78, 80, 81, 83, 87, 92, 102, 107, 115
access to thread 83, 102–3, 108–9, 116, 117, 118, 152
capitalisation/technological change 76, 83, 88, 91–3, 95, 97, 102, 118, 124–5, 142, 147
differentiation 79, 80, 88, 89, 92, 102, 105–7, 113, 120–1

diversification 83, 85, 110, 116, 119
employment 117, 130, 132, 133, 142, 160, 167
gender relations 85–7, 88, 90, 111, 112–14, 117
legality 89–90, 110, 111, 118, 120, 144–5, 150, 154
linkages 83, 84, 108, 117, 119–21
links with Moroleón 3, 33, 80, 91, 100, 108, 110, 111, 116, 118, 129
management 85–6, 88, 90, 111, 117, 124, 131, 136, 138–9, 148
output 89, 91–2, 94, 102, 104, 108, 110, 115, 117, 119, 132
ownership 76–88, 112, 121
premises 79, 89–90, 130, 132, 135
pricing and profits 87, 101, 102–5, 116, 117, 119, 138
proliferation and growth 77, 79–84, 87–8, 89, 90, 92, 115
sub-contracting 81, 83, 98–100, 105, 108, 120
taxation 104–5, 104, 110, 111, 115
in the USA 101, 147, 160
workers' savings/cash sums 124, 127, 135, 141, 144, 150, 162, 163, 180, 187–8, 204

Tanguancicuaro 26, 97
tax legislaton 7, 20, 104, 191
Tepíc 98
thread
costs 77, 85, 87, 102–3, 110, 119, 163, 164
supply 77, 79, 80, 102–3, 116, 117, 118, 120, 165
Tijuana 72, 82, 100, 101
Tlaxcala 32
tortillas 25, 35, 41–2, 53, 54, 62, 63, 68, 138, 168, 182
trade unions 11, 14, 28, 29, 31, 77, 140, 142, 146, 154, 156, 200–1
transnational corporations 8, 9, 11, 12
transport 90, 97, 98, 100, 103, 109, 110, 113, 115, 117, 164, 173

Uriangato 28, 31
Uruapan 26, 98, 111, 130
USA
agricultural market 25
garment trade 100–1, 107, 114, 115–16, 117, 147, 164
gender relations in 70, 71, 178, 189–90

USA *cont.*
Mexican border 8, 32, 100-1, 107, 115
migration to 1, 2, 12, 24, 25, 29, 37, 40, 44-50, 58, 60, 65, 66, 67, 82, 83, 88, 114, 115, 126, 130, 157, 159, 160, 161, 162, 165, 166, 170, 171, 172, 178, 180, 181, 182, 183, 189
remittances from 63, 66, 73, 127, 177, 179
settlement in 166, 173

Veracruz 32
violence *see* domestic violence

wages
in garment production 31, 55
legal minimum 7, 31, 93, 95, 96, 109, 111, 113, 114, 118-19, 120, 132, 145, 146, 147, 150, 169
of migrants in USA 44, 47, 48
piece-rates 11, 31, 93, 96, 109, 115, 118, 128, 140, 142, 160
in sweater manufacture 31, 93, 95-6, 97, 109, 111, 113, 115, 117, 119, 123-6, 127, 129, 130-1, 132, 133-5, 140, 143, 144-5, 153, 178
for women's domestic work 53-4, 67, 68, 74, 193
water resources
in the countryside 25, 43, 91
in the town 55
weekly markets 25, 46, 77, 97-8, 164, 171
women's domestic labour 161, 163, 167
acquisition of skills 52
knitting industry 159, 162-7, 170, 188
manufacturing 29, 43, 54, 67, 193, 196
servicing 43, 44, 53, 54, 55-6, 67-8, 177, 193, 196
women's emancipation 21, 167
women's networks 68, 74, 79, 113, 123, 188-9, 195
women's work
in agriculture 41-3, 52-3, 54, 55, 58, 67, 74, 138, 193
in garment production 28, 29, 54, 55, 67-8, 74
in manufacturing 3, 4, 9, 11, 16-18, 54, 55, 67, 68, 74, 194-5, 197-9, 202
in strawberry agri-business 48, 49, 50, 55, 68, 74, 131, 134, 147, 160
in sweater manufacture 78, 79, 85, 87, 88, 89-90, 93-4, 94-7, 137
in the USA 157, 160, 162, 172, 183
workers' benefits and rights 7, 15, 29, 31, 111, 131, 132, 135, 139, 143, 150, 152
workers' health 29, 125, 131, 132-3, 136, 139, 143, 144-7, 148, 161, 182
workshops
capitalised workshop production 20, 76, 191-200
historical precedents, Mexico City 77-9
historical precedents, western central region 4, 13, 19, 25-6, 28-32
illegality and physical concealment 7, 11, 89-90, 191-2

Zacatecas 98, 116
Zamora 23, 26, 28, 39, 44, 46, 48, 49, 55, 59, 67, 68, 69, 74, 78, 79, 90, 97, 100, 109, 110, 112, 115, 117, 118, 125, 129, 130, 131, 145, 146, 160, 162, 163, 169, 171, 177
Zapotlanejo 7
Zinapecuaro 26